WORLDWIDE
FAMILY
HISTORY

WORLDWIDE FAMILY HISTORY

Noel Currer-Briggs

Routledge & Kegan Paul
London, Boston, Melbourne and Henley

First published in 1982
by Routledge & Kegan Paul Ltd
39 Store Street, London WC1E 7DD,
9 Park Street, Boston, Mass. 02108, USA,
296 Beaconsfield Parade, Middle Park,
Melbourne, 3206, Australia and
Broadwdy House, Newtown Road,
Henley-on-Thames, Oxon. RG9 1EN

Set in Linotron Palatino by Input Typesetting Ltd, London
and printed in Great Britain by
Hartnoll Print, Bodmin, Cornwall
© Routledge & Kegan Paul, 1982

Library of Congress Cataloging in Publication Data

Currer-Briggs, Noel.
Worldwide family history.

Bibliography: p.
Includes index.
1. Genealogy.   2. Europe—Emigration and immigration.
I. Title.
CS9.C87   929'.1   82–3636

ISBN 0–7100–0934–8   AACR2

Contents

Contents

Preface
and acknowledgments

The number of books on genealogy is already large and growing all the time. It is therefore necessary to explain why we have ventured to add to their number. For those who trace their ancestry generation by generation and line by line the problem differs from that which faces the searcher who seeks to identify a particular individual who moved from one country to another. His purpose, like that of a detective, is to establish the identity of someone who appears, as it were from nowhere, in the records of his country of adoption, bearing with him only the slenderest indication of whence and when he came.

Those who live in the New World, be they Americans or members of the widespread English-speaking Commonwealth or South Africa are not alone in having to face this problem. There are many thousands of people living in Britain who include among their forebears men and women who came to these islands from overseas. The purpose and justification of this book, then, is to help such people to bridge the oceans of sea and time which separate them from remote (and perhaps not so remote) ancestors who lived in countries with whose language, history and archives they may be unfamiliar.

It is impossible for a single author or editor to be familiar with every aspect of such a complex subject as international genealogy, and for that reason we have been fortunate to assemble contributions from specialists in many different countries and disciplines. I would like, therefore especially to thank the following whose knowledge of the genealogical and political history of their homelands is second to none: Margaret Audin (France); Prof. Dr Hanns Jäger-Sunstenau (Austria); Conte Guelfo Guelfi Camajani (Italy); Franciso de Cadenas, Conde de Gaviria (Spain); Dr Artur Norton, Baron de São Roque (Portugal); M. M. Paszkiewicz and S. K. Kuczynski (Poland); Brian Brooks (Australia); and L. G. Pine (Islam). We are also particularly grateful to Professor Gordon East for his introductory chapter on the structure of Europe and to Peter de V. B. Dewar for his appendix on the uses of heraldry

viii

in genealogical research in Europe. Among the many whom I consulted by letter or through their published works I owe debts of gratitude to the following: Isobel Mordy, Cecil Humphery-Smith, Arthur Fawcett, Anthony Camp, Mildred Surrey, Reuben Ainsztein, Edgar Samuel, Thomas E. Daniels, Janet Teal, Pontus Müller, Nils G. Bartholdy, Dr D. S. Coombs, K. Q. F. Manning, Dr Adam Heymoski, Winston de Ville, Ian C. C. Graham, E. G. Hartman, Richard O'Conner, John S. Lundberg, Ralph J. Jalkanen, Eino Jutikkala, Reino Kero, Tauri Aalto, Jon Wefald, Lucian J. Fosdyck, Marcel Giraud, Charles L. Dufour, J. F. McDermott, John H. Burma, Antonio Mangana, Luciano Iorizzo, Salvatore Mondello, Joseph A. Wytrwal, George J. Prpic, Theodore Saloutos, Edgar McMinnis, D. C. Willows, Stewart Richmond, J. C. Beaglehole, James Cowan, Eric A. Walker, G. M. Theal, Thomas W. Chinn, Toshiyuki Yanase.

I am especially indebted to Rena Beech for typing most of the script and keeping a voluminous correspondence up to date and under control. I have likewise received much help from Timothy O'Sullivan, who, I am sure, will accept both his share of responsibility for persuading some of the contributors to write important chapters as well as my thanks for his advice and forbearance.

The book falls into two parts. The first eighteen chapters describe the history and archives of the countries of Europe and of Islam, China and Japan. The second part deals with migration from Europe to America and the other great English-speaking countries. Because it is designed as background reading, the book omits much detailed information the reader will need once he embarks on research in any foreign country, especially addresses, which are apt to change from time to time. For purely practical considerations of space we have had to omit everything to do with African, Indian, South American, Polynesian and Indonesian genealogy. This is partly because so much of it is based on oral tradition, as Alex Haley found out when he traced his own African ancestry, but also because the records of so many totalitarian countries are inaccessible to the amateur. This especially applies to those vast areas of Europe, Asia and Africa lying in the grip of Marxist regimes whose fear of people discovering the truths of history is positively paranoid.

Noel Currer-Briggs
Les Cluzeaux, Celles, 24600 Riberac, France
January 1981

PART ONE

PART ONE

1

The structure of Europe

For the geographer the phrase 'Structure of Europe' has at least two distinct meanings. The geological structure does not concern us; the human structure, however, is a complex reality which is the product of a long history of population movement and settlement. It is that which concerns us in this book. We shall attempt, by reference to Europe's historical past, to explain and locate its principal national groups who have contributed so much by their fertility in both population and civilization to the world as a whole. More specifically we shall try to light the way for those whose genealogical problems beckon them towards a European country from which their forefathers stemmed.

It can be said of Europe that it has too much history and too much geography. While it is small as a continent – only Australasia is smaller – it presents a remarkably variegated physical geography and it offers numerous 'core areas' for national development. Over long periods, when the horse provided the greatest means of mobility, though only for the favoured few, communities of different tongues, history and material culture developed within specific homelands, separately and largely aloof from their neighbours. This was despite the effects of welcome and unwelcome contacts and interchanges brought about by the efforts of rulers, churches, traders – and armies, for Europe must be held notorious for its addiction to war.

The pattern of languages

Europe is remarkable among the continents for its compressed patterns of language groups, national communities and independent states. It contrasts sharply in these respects with North America, where the English language is virtually everywhere dominant and only two nations and two independent states have emerged, although the latter are themselves federated states uniting many component states. The hu-

Map 1.   General Language Map of Europe (present day).

man complications of Europe's language map, least in the north and west and most marked in its central region, mirror the effect of a prolonged history, which began with successive invasions and settlements in prehistory. 'Languages', wrote Dr Johnson, 'are the pedigree of nations', and languages appear at first sight to characterize nations clearly. However, the same language may be shared by several distinct nations and some nations are not monolingual. To clarify the compli-

4

cations of national identities, it will help to explain broadly how different languages came to exist within particular areas of this continent.

Already within the Bronze Age of prehistory, in the third millennium BC, Europe was overrun by incursors from Asia who brought their Aryan or Indo-Germanic speech. From this common speech developed the three largest European language groups of today, namely those known as Romance, Germanic and Slav. One can visualize how the many distinct languages which these groups comprise slowly emerged over the centuries by a process of linguistic differentiation, regionally controlled. The speech of discrete human communities took on its own special character, foreshadowing the formation of an independent language, distinct from though related to many others. The background to this process can be imagined when one recalls how communities lived bound to the soil by their agricultural economics, within settlement areas suitable to their needs, yet much insulated from one another by wide stretches of woodland, marsh and mountainous terrain, all of which were little settled because of the physical difficulties they presented to penetration and utilization. Indeed, one can contrast, on the one hand, certain small cradle areas where human groups settled and where nations eventually emerged and, on the other, much more extensive hinterlands between them which, as their numbers grew and as they learned the arts of woodland clearing and drainage reclamation, were only slowly and partially brought into use.

The Romance languages derive from the Latin speech which was introduced widely into southern and western Europe during the centuries when the Romans, originally natives of Latium in Central Italy, carried out their remarkable career of military, territorial and political expansion. The European regions which they conquered and organized were largely Celtic-speaking and, despite the later dominance of Latin-derived speech, evidences of this survive on the western margins of the continent – in the Irish, Gaelic, Welsh and Breton languages, use of which is now being actively encouraged. The no-less ancient Basque language, spoken on both sides of the western Pyrenees, still survives from pre-Roman days. At its greatest extent in the second century AD, the Roman Empire included all of southern Europe, southern Britain, Gaul and, beyond the Rhine and Danube, territories of modern Austria, Switzerland, the Federal Republic of Germany, parts of Hungary, Yugoslavia and the whole of Romania. Roman traders penetrated even beyond these limits, as far north as central Sweden and as far east as the Vistula river. So long did the Roman Empire persist – it lasted in the west until the late fifth century and in the east (as the Byzantine Empire so-called) until 1453 – that the provincial Latin speech, despite later invasions by Germans and others, gave rise to the many languages of the Romance group – French, Italian, Spanish, Galician, Catalan, Portuguese and Romanian, as also to Provençal (now no longer spoken), Walloon (in Belgium) and Ladin and Romansh, minority languages of multilingual Switzerland.

The Germanic group of languages derived from the German peoples who, from their earliest known homeland in northern Europe between central Sweden and the Baltic lowlands of Denmark and western Germany, moved southwards to occupy areas both within and beyond the frontiers of the Roman Empire. This historic process, spread over many centuries, is called the *Völkerwanderung*, or Barbarian Invasions, and played a dramatic part in the collapse of Rome's Empire in the west, bringing distinctly named German national groups as conquerors, settlers and rulers into Italy, Iberia, Gaul and Britain as well as into parts of central and south-eastern Europe. The long history of the German people concerns us here in that their settlements and state-building and colonizing efforts had permanent effects, notably in the formation of the German languages, nations and states of the present map. German, English, Netherlandish (Dutch and Flemish), Norwegian, Danish, Swedish, Faeroese and Icelandic, as well as dialect variants, such as Austrian German, Swiss German and Luxembourg German, make up the count of Europe's Germanic languages.

The third of the language groups within the Indo-European family – indeed one which numbers about 40 per cent of the population of Europe and occupies fully one half of its area – is the Slav, which now includes Russian, Ukrainian, Byelorussian (White Russian), Polish, Serbo-Croat, Slovenian, Bulgarian, Czech, Slovak and Ruthenian. The Slavs, whose earliest history is by no means wholly clear, were a poor, semi-nomadic people, known to the Romans as Vends, who lived and moved within a wide stretch of the east-central European lowlands between the Baltic and the Black Sea, with their heartland situated amongst the marshes and woodlands of the Prypet river, a right-bank tributary of the Dnieper. They appear originally to have had no knowledge of agriculture and no means of transport, while linguistic evidence suggests their familiarity with an environment of woods and marshes, where they had eked out a living by hunting, fishing and trapping. Even so, the Slavs possessed remarkable powers of survival, mobility and colonization since, in the course of the Middle Ages, they became established widely in central, south-eastern and eastern Europe.

On linguistic grounds the Slavs of today are classified into western, southern and eastern groups. Those of central Europe (the western Slavs) are made up of Poles, Czechs, Slovaks, Ruthenians and a dwindling remnant of Sorbs in Brandenburg. The southern Slavs are now mainly, except for Bulgarians, contained within the federal republic of

6

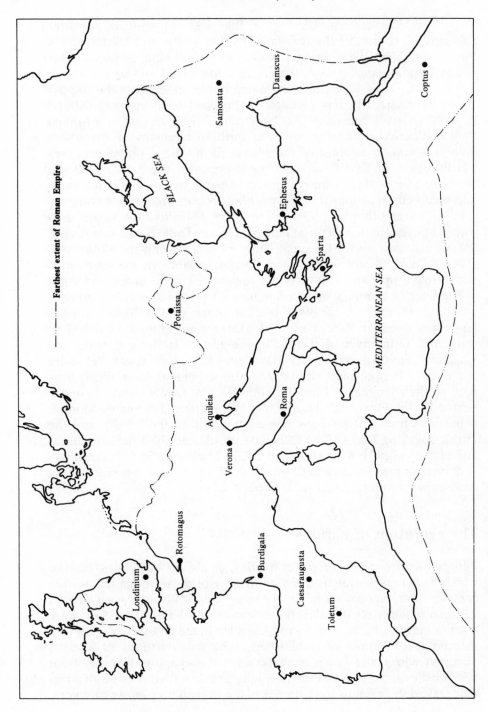

Map 2. Farthest Extent of Roman Empire about 2nd Century AD.

7

Yugoslavia. The eastern Slavs, by far the most numerous of the three sub-groups, consist of the Russians, Byelorussians and Ukrainians of the Soviet Union. Occupying an unenviable geographical position between Germans to the west, who sought to expand and colonize eastwards, and successively intruding nomadic horsemen from the steppes of western Asia, the Slav peoples had to yield territory marginally to superior coercive pressures, yet largely held their ground and formed their distinctive national groups. In northern Germany and northern Poland, Germans established themselves for a time in outposts of central Europe – in East Prussia, at the expense of the Balts, in Silesia, formerly Slav-settled country, and in Austria, which nomadic Avars had occupied. In European USSR the Slav peoples predominate numerically, although other peoples, who preserve distinctive features of their own language, nationality and culture, occupy Baltic coastlands (Lithuanians, Latvians and Estonians), lands on and beyond the Volga river (Tatars, Bashkirs and others), and Caucasian lands in the south-east, which make up part of the frontier region between Europe and Asia.

The lines of Europe's map of languages are thus mainly drawn with reference to nations speaking one or more of the Indo-European languages which include, besides the three main groups, Lettish (Latvian) and Lithuanian of the Baltic sub-group, Hellenic (Greek) and Albanian. Small numbers, we have already noted, speak yet older languages – Basque and Celtic. In addition, others, again relatively few, derived their languages from the Finno-Ugrian family, which is represented by the Finnic-speaking Finns, Hungarians, Estonians, Mordvinian and Chuvash (these last three living within the USSR), and the Turkic-speaking Turks of the Balkan peninsula and the Tatars and Bashkirs of the Volga-Ural region of the USSR. Maltese, a Semitic language, and certain place-names and words used in modern Spanish, recall Arab expansion into medieval Europe.

The evolution of nations

Europe has proved a nursery of nations, as also of languages, both of which have now a wide distribution in the world. Although nations are complex phenomena, each can be seen historically to have emerged within a separate territorial niche or 'core area' where it came to acquire a set of cultural traits, not least its own language or languages, and to become a community of recollections. The many nations of Europe, nurtured within their own habitats, appear ever more distinctly from later medieval times onwards as results of the settlements of invaders who staked their claims to territories of the Roman Empire, as survivors, like the Greeks, Albanians and Welsh, from pre-Roman times, and as pioneers and colonists who had taken over and developed lands formerly given over to woodland, marsh and steppe. In the formation of Europe's nations, as in the development of national consciousness which came vigorously to characterize them, internal struggles and external wars played major parts. Another marked characteristic has been the strong attachment to homeland territories, which tended to extend or contract in response to the strength or weakness of other national groups. One can envisage the growth of European nations as the outcome of a long-drawn-out process broadly achieved only in modern times, and should recognize them as highly mature societies when compared with the tribal groups which had long existed and remain dominant in many parts of the world today, as in most of Africa and in New Guinea. In the British Isles, for example, four major national communities evolved in post-Roman times. The Irish and the Welsh were descendants mainly of pre-Roman Celtic-speaking invaders and settlers; the English, and in part the Scots, resulted from the fusion of their Celtic populations with post-Roman invaders and colonists, Anglo-Saxons and Jutes in England and Scandinavian intruders, variously called Vikings, Norsemen or Northmen, into both Britain and Ireland. The English language, thanks in turn to emigration from the British Isles and to the impact of the United States on world affairs, now so widely spoken, was shaping in the time of Chaucer (fourteenth century) as the leading Anglo-Saxon dialect, replacing Latin, once spoken there, as a result of the colonization of southern Britain by Anglo-Saxon and other invaders of Germanic speech. In the emergence of national consciousness of the English, Scottish, Irish and Welsh nations, still so aware of their own distinctiveness, wars waged between them were clearly stimulants. We shall return to consider the significance of nations and nationalism in determining the European pattern of states.

Medieval Europe: some formative aspects

The thousand years following the collapse of the Roman Empire in the west and its fall into the hands of conquering barbarian peoples, eager to inherit its wealth and not unfitted or undesirous to learn its civilizing lessons, is the highly formative period known to historians as the Middle Ages. Although Europe was then thought of as Christendom and as the base for the defence and extension of this faith, its unity was undermined by continual armed conflict, the development of Christian heresies and separate languages and tribally organized peoples destined to crystallize into distinctive national groups. On the one hand, Europe acted as Christendom in repelling Arab-Moor invasions, notably of Iberia and Gaul and by co-ordinating offensive action in a series of crusading wars against Moslem-Arab conquerors of the Holy Land. On the other, the sheer difficulties of transport, despite technical improvements in sea navigation and shipbuilding and the use of horses by the few, enforced the regional restriction of political organization. In its best days the Roman Empire had sustained peace, security and relatively civilized life throughout an area overlapping three continents, and it even bequeathed in its eastern (or Byzantine) Empire, based on Constantinople (now Istanbul), a long-lasting and fairly stable Euro-Asiatic state. Now, most of Europe suffered periods of anarchy and became loosely organized by the feudal system. This was a complex system and meant above all 'an exact relationship between the tenure of land and military duty; and that duty was the duty of knight service.' In this sense feudalism had already appeared when Charles Martel, effective ruler of the Frankish kingdom, supported by knights on horseback, defeated the Arabs at the battle of Poitiers in 732 AD at the point of their maximum penetration from Iberia into Gaul. The feudal system, by linking land tenure to personal service from free and unfree alike, created a hierarchical structure of legal, political, economic and social relationships. At the apex stood the emperor – for the newly settled peoples, mainly Germanic, managed to restore some semblance of the integrated government of the fallen western empire which they had helped to destroy. This appeared with the empire of Charlemagne (AD 800–814), which stretched from west-central Europe through Italy and Gaul to just beyond the Pyrenees. It included the kingdoms of the Lombards in Italy and the Franks in Germany and Gaul, of which Charlemagne himself was king, and later became known to historians as the Holy Roman Empire, which disappeared formally only in 1806 during the Napoleonic Wars. This political unit was by no means a strong and unified structure. Rather it comprised a medley of political entities – kingdoms, principalities, duchies, counties, border fiefs called 'marks' or 'marches', and city-states, all of varying territorial scale. For long these fragmented the political map, breaking social life down into classes and setting obstacles to human mobility and trade.

Other aspects of medieval history also had lasting effects. The wide dispersal of peoples of Slav speech led to the colonization of regions both within and outside the limits of the Roman Empire, notably former imperial provinces in south-eastern Europe now part of Yugoslavia and Bulgaria, and relatively vast regions beyond, occupied today by European USSR, Poland and Czechoslovakia. Pressing against the Slavs on their western borderlands, German colonists intruded eastwards from the Rhine to settle parts of central Europe, including Baltic coastlands,

Map 3. Boundaries of Europe before World War I.

as far east as East Prussia, Brandenburg and Austria, which, as defended marchlands of German settlement and political organization, suffered then and later the threats and assaults of successive warlike invaders from the east – Avars, Magyars (Hungarians), Mongol-Tatars, and the Ottoman Turks, to name the chief. Another group of invaders, this time from Scandinavia, remarkable both for their seamanship and political ability, were the Northmen who, as raiders, traders and rulers, created the Russian state of Muscovy, ventured afar to Iceland, Green-

11

land and North America and, as Normans, conquered and organized southern Britain.

The organizational and civilizing efforts of Christian churches present another aspect of medieval times which gave reality to the concept of Europe as Christendom. In the western half of Europe the Roman Catholic Church, from its territorial base at Rome and the Papal States of central Italy, organized the faith by a hierarchical structure – the Pope, cardinals, archbishops, bishops, abbots and the lesser clergy. While, in the east, from Constantinople, the Orthodox (or Greek) church, with its differences of doctrine and ritual, held sway widely – in south-eastern and eastern Europe, therein including Russians, White Russians, Ukrainians, Greeks, Bulgarians and Serbians. In addition, so-called Uniate Christians, who accepted the authority of the Pope but practised the rituals of the Orthodox church, lay territorially between these, presenting another culturally divisive element in this continent. The Christian churches, by their services, courts of law, scholarship and monastic foundations, certainly helped to keep learning alive and to inculcate civilized thought and behaviour. Important, too, in this respect was the contribution, notably in Iberia, of Moslem peoples who had absorbed much of ancient Greek and Hellenistic learning. At the close of the Middle Ages, the migration, above all to Italy, of scholars, artists and others from the Byzantine Empire, as its capital (Constantinople) fell into the hands of the Ottoman Turks, brought to the west that revolution in thought, learning and art, known as the Renaissance. Lastly, we should note how, especially in western and central Europe, the later Middle Ages witnessed the birth and growth of numerous towns and cities, engaged above all in industrial and mercantile pursuits – manufacture and trade, domestic and international. As marine and river ports, as centres of manufacture and ecclesiastical and political organization, and as markets and fairs, these urban settlements depended on road and water transport and owed their origins to the protection of the emperor, kings, lords and bishops. In general, cities secured powers of self-government for their citizens and some, like Hamburg and Lübeck, flourished as city-states owing allegiance only to the emperor

The changing pattern of states

The modern state, loosely referred to as the 'nation state', which characterizes the map of Europe today, is largely a product of post-medieval times, often indeed of this century. The modern state marked a sharp reaction against the feudal dispersion of political power in favour of

12

more centralized royal control, as in England, France, Spain and Sweden. In some countries, as notably in England under Henry VIII and Elizabeth I, it marked the alienation of the wealth (in lands) of the Church and a revolt from Rome, so that the monarch acquired considerable powers formerly held and exercised by the Church. The Reformation so-called ushered in national Protestant churches and, as some believe, explains the new energies which were released and directed to overseas exploration, trade and colonization, and to industrial and commercial initiatives. Some of these modern states, like England, France, Portugal, the Netherlands, Sweden and Hungary, were national states, in that their populations were dominantly of one, self-conscious national group. However, this is only one of the types of states in post-medieval or modern Europe. On the one hand, Germany and Italy above all remained congeries of states – kingdoms, duchies, city-states and others – and on the other, large imperial states, such as the Austrian, Ottoman Turkish, and Russian Empires, essentially multi-national in character yet relatively strong and stable, occupied much of the continent. The Austrian Empire of the Habsburg dynasy, was a survivor after 1806 of the Holy Roman Empire, with its capital at Vienna, a focal point and an outpost against Turkish Moslem power until about AD 1700. The Ottoman Turkish Empire lost its Hungarian territory, but from its base in Asia Minor long retained its hold on south-eastern Europe, notably in the south-eastern (or Balkan) peninsula and in Cyprus. The territorially extensive Russian Empire, much expanded by 1815, had shared with its allies final victory over Napoleonic France. Although the Russian Empire was multi-national, it was predominantly Russian and politically organized as an autocracy, sustained by its armies, a national church and a bureaucracy, headed by the all-powerful Czar (i.e. Caesar), this title having been taken over from the Byzantine Empire after its extinction under Turkish assault.

As the 'political maps' so-called in historical atlases graphically show, the pattern of states in Europe changed continually during the centuries of modern history. Successive wars, started for a variety of reasons, invariably had claims to territory among their objectives. At the end of these wars territorial settlements adjusted the political map so that, especially in eastern and central Europe, individual citizens found themselves transferred from one ruler to another and thus tied by new claims to their loyalty.

Certain important political changes of territory occurred in the sixteenth, seventeenth and eighteenth centuries. France acquired territories on the left bank of the Rhine, notably on the Lorraine plateau, well placed for the defence of the Paris basin from attack from central Europe, and the Alsace lowland limited eastwards by the middle Rhine.

With the addition of further small territories during the Revolutionary wars, France could boast that its boundaries, like those of Roman Gaul, were aligned within the Alps and Pyrenees and along the Rhine. Attempts by France to secure also the Low Countries failed under Louis XIV but were achieved by the Emperor Napoleon, only to be lost in 1815 when they were joined as a kingdom of the Netherlands. In south-eastern Europe the Ottoman Turks made their furthest western penetration into east-central Europe. They were defeated at the gates of Vienna (1683) but managed to retain control of most of Hungary until 1699. In eastern Europe the early eighteenth century witnessed the reorganization of Russian administration and its army by Peter the Great, and Russia's territorial expansion in Europe continued. Peter the Great had acquired provinces on the Baltic and founded St Petersburg, now Leningrad. Then under the Empress Catherine the Great (1762–96) Russia expanded for the first time to the shores of the Black and Azov seas. Moreover, by a remarkable exercise in co-operative power politics, the empires of Russia and Austria, together with the kingdom of Prussia, partitioned the kingdom of Poland, then in a state of disorganized political weakness, effacing it from the map of Europe, by three annexations of its territory in 1772, 1793 and 1795. Although it had continually displayed remarkable military spirit in wars against would-be conquerors of Europe, such as the Tatar-Mongols in the later Middle Ages and the Ottoman Turks in the seventeenth century, Poland's still-feudal social and political structure and its geographical location between stronger powers led, despite its normal reliance on an alliance with France, to literal extinction as a state in which Poles formed a clear majority. Thus Russia, Austria and Prussia acquired further national groups, becoming increasingly multi-national, so that Poles came to serve in the armies of all three.

The French Revolution in 1789 and the Napoleonic wars which followed involved Europe in more than twenty years of war and, when these were finally ended in 1815, the statesmen of Europe after considerable labours at the Congress of Vienna redrew its political map. Surprisingly in retrospect they were never concerned to consider what were the wishes of particular national groups which were reallocated as territory changed hands, naturally to the advantage of the victors – the United Kingdom, the kingdom of Prussia, and the empires of Austria and Russia, above all. Interested in maintaining peace and stability, the statesmen of Vienna attempted to restore the political conditions which had been overthrown during the revolutionary wars. But national consciousness and activity, which had been aroused to add its strength to the coalition which defeated the emperor Napoleon, became stronger and more widely manifest during the nineteenth century. The Treaties of Vienna left the Austrian and Russian empires enlarged and strengthened. Italy, which had known two new kingdoms under.Napoleon's rule, became again 'a geographical expression', made up of many small states, including the kingdom of Naples in the south and the rich duchies of Lombardy and Venice in the north, which were held by Austria. A German Confederation, again a loose assemblage of member states, was created, as also a kingdom of the Netherlands in the attempt to restrain French expansion and to preserve the peace. Ominous, as later events showed, was the increase in 1815 of the territories and the power of the Prussian kingdom.

The sentiment and force of nationalism, on which nations based claims to independent political control of their fortunes, became progressively stronger during the nineteenth century and proved irresistible in the twentieth. Whereas 'patriotism' is the love of country and the will to defend it, 'nationalism' is a revolutionary force in international politics and 'national self-determination' so-called clearly threatened to undermine the stability of multi-national empires and indeed to disrupt them. However this movement was successfully resisted for many decades. The unification of Italy (in 1861) and of Germany, as the German Empire, in 1871, were signal nationalistic achievements, the fruits of both diplomacy and war. In south-eastern Europe Greece, Romania and Bulgaria, in turn and with foreign help, overthrew their Turkish masters and emerged as national states.

After the two world wars of 1914–19 and 1939–45, which Dean Acheson called the European Civil War, the oppressed nations finally won their liberation, thus adding substantially to the number of states contained within this relatively small continent. Although some of the new states, notably Yugoslavia and Poland, are by no means one-nation states, the nation state has become increasingly the European norm.

After the First World War the empires of Germany, Austro-Hungary (Hungary had been made a virtually equal partner with Austria in 1866), Russia and Turkey collapsed, though those of the western countries – the United Kingdom (which included Ireland wishful to break away), France, Portugal and the Netherlands survived intact. Already by 1917 czarist Russia, defeated in this war, fell to the Bolsheviks. They were led by Lenin, who believed that the Bolshevik revolution created a new world for the common man, although western observers, such as America's leading political geographer, Dr Isaiah Bowman saw this as a backward step from civilization to barbarism. The new Russia, despite Allied military intervention against its revolutionary Communist rulers, came to be organized under the Red Army and Party leaders as the Soviet Union or Union of Soviet Socialist Republics, but its territories in Europe were sharply curtailed by the hiving off of certain national

Map 4. Boundaries of Europe at the end of World War I.

groups – Finns, Estonians, Latvians, Lithuanians and Poles – who each attained national independence. The Austro-Hungarian Empire, which also broke down before the end of the First World War, was replaced by the small national states of Austria, with its outsized former imperial capital of Vienna, Hungary, the multi-national kingdom of the Serbs, Croats and Slovenes and, similarly multi-national, the republic of Czechoslovakia. The weak, though extensive, Ottoman Empire which had long held territories in three continents, finally disappeared, leaving

Map 5.   Boundaries of Europe at the end of World War II.

a republic of Turkey with a foothold in Europe – in eastern Thrace – and territorial control of the narrow seas which connect the Black and Mediterranean seas. In the Balkan peninsula Albania, the last to escape from Turkish rule, emerged in 1925 as a kingdom. In western Europe, Italy, which had joined the western powers in the First World War, acquired from Austria the Trentino, which included a German-speaking population, on the southern side of its Alpine border. Germany lost Alsace and eastern Lorraine, areas again with largely German-speaking

17

populations, which it had wrested from France in 1871 after the Franco-Prussian war which immediately preceded and facilitated the creation of the German Empire. Another German loss was the province of Silesia, which combined agricultural and mineral wealth (notably coal); this passed mainly to the newly constituted republic of Poland, but a small part was allocated to Czechoslovakia.

The political map of Europe again showed striking changes following the Second World War. The most momentous fact was the territorial aggrandizement of the Soviet Union since it succeeded in retaining or recovering most of the lost provinces of imperial Russia, notably Estonia, Latvia, Lithuania, eastern Poland, Ruthenia, Bessarabia and northern Bukovina, the two last being frontier territories which Romania had held, together with part of Germany's East Prussian provinces and marginal parts of Finland. Finland and Poland recovered their independent status, the former within restricted territory, the latter wholly refashioned: although it had lost to the USSR extensive eastern territories, these were less Polish than White Russian and Ukrainian in population, and Poland was well compensated by the additions of part of East Prussia (with Gdansk, originally the German seaport of Danzig), and German lands in Pomerania, Mecklenburg and Silesia – lands which had long been Slavic in population before the German colonization thrust of the later Middle Ages. The political and military strength of the Soviet Union was further consolidated by the demilitarization of Finland and by the creation of a tier of Soviet republics, formally independent but held tightly by their mighty neighbour, which lay on or just beyond USSR's western boundaries – Poland, Hungary, Czechoslovakia, Romania and Bulgaria. This allegedly defensive system, which Soviet leaders claim is necessary since their country has been attacked twice since the 1917 revolution, is reinforced by the bisection of Germany which enabled Stalin to organize as an ally Eastern Germany, now the Democratic People's Republic, which has become the most industrialized of the USSR's European allies or satellites. Note that by the territorial changes following the Second World War the Soviet Union obtained boundaries directly with Norway, Finland, Poland, Romania, Hungary and Czechoslovakia. Thus Russian military power extends far westwards into central Europe and this explains why the North Atlantic Treaty Organization, led by the United States, came into existence in 1949 as a western system of military defence. Symbolic of the division of Europe into two main parts, each with its opposed social, economic, political and military system, is the city of Berlin, Germany's old capital, which is still formally divided into zones of western and Soviet military occupation. The western zone is technically an 'international enclave', for it is islanded within the territory of the German Democratic Republic.

At the western extremity of Europe most of Ireland, comprising the bulk of the Roman Catholic population, managed at last to free itself from political association with Britain as part of the United Kingdom. Twenty-six of its counties were united first as the Irish Free State and then later (in 1949) as an independent republic, formally known as Ireland, with Dublin as its capital. However, this leaves the island of Ireland politically divided, for six northern counties, with a strongly Protestant population and a rapidly increasing Roman Catholic minority, with Belfast as capital, remain an integral part of the United Kingdom. Thus Ireland, only 40 per cent of the area of Britain, contains Irishmen of sharply conflicting political loyalties.

Europe as a whole

Natives of Europe when abroad may feel and appear genuinely 'European', but at home they become French, German, Italian, Russian or any one of the many national groups which make up this continent of concentrated diversity. The major national groups are broadly localized, living within states where their nationals predominate, yet the patterns of nationality distribution are by no means exact. In contrast, the patterns of states are surprisingly exact, for these, numbering over thirty and about one-fifth of the world's independent states, have surveyed and demarcated boundaries which are made largely visible on the ground by monuments, rivers, obelisks, posts and even barbed wire, as exists today between the Federal Republic of Germany and the German Democratic Republic. The effects of many centuries of migration, in part freely operative and encouraged, in part coerced, has meant that the boundaries of states do not, indeed cannot, be so drawn as to contain all of one national group within a single state. Thus commonly national 'minorities' so-called occur widely alongside majority populations of another nationality. There is a sizeable group of Hungarians within Romania; there are Austrian-German citizens of Italy; descendants of German-speaking subjects of the German Empire from 1871 to 1918 are now citizens of France; Spain is comprised of several national groups still conscious of their separate identities; and the United Kingdom countries, mainly English, with Scots, Welsh and even some Irish. To these groups must now be added those of African and Asian origin who have settled in large numbers throughout Britain. In addition migrant labour to the more prosperous industrialized countries – Germany, Switzerland, France and the Netherlands – has created the category of 'guest-workers', drawn from south European countries – Spain, Italy, Yugoslavia, Turkey and others – unable to absorb all their available labour at home. One element of the population of Europe throughout history, which made a contribution out of all proportion to its sheer numbers and is now greatly reduced because of Nazi decimation during the Second World War and because of the attraction of Israel, has been the Jews. Even in the USSR, where Jews still just exceed 2 million, and where Moscow is second only to New York as the world's largest Jewish city, freer emigration reduces their total.

2

France

Parish registers and state registers

The oldest parish registers in France date back to the first half of the
sixteenth century. As in England, they were kept by the parish priest,
but unlike the English counterpart the French curé had to make two
copies – at least from the eighteenth century and in most cases from
the seventeenth – one of which he had to deposit at the end of each
year with the Greffe du Tribunal (office of the clerk of the court). At the
time of the Revolution (from 1792 to be precise) the job of recording
births, marriages and deaths was transferred to the Mairie (town hall)
where parish priests were compelled by law to deposit all registers in
their possession. The new registers are known as Registres de l'État
Civil. Since that time all registration has been the responsibility of the
mayor and they can now be found either in the Bureau de l'État Civil,
the Mairie, or in the town library. Duplicates from pre-1792 have usually
been transferred to the Archives Départementales. For post-Revolution
registers there is sometimes, but not often, an alphabetical index by
surname or by christian name (in the older registers) at the end of the
volume or the year. Since 1792, except occasionally for the earliest years,
there are alphabetical indexes every ten years. The only exception to
this system is in the Comté of Nice, where the registers were returned
to the parishes when the territory was ceded to the Kingdom of Savoy
after the fall of Napoleon. Very few registers exist for the period before
the seventeenth century, though there are some outstanding exceptions, such as the register of Riom in Auvergne, which dates from 1530.

    In Paris, the original registers and their duplicates up to 1860 were
lost in the burning of the Hôtel de Ville and the Palais de Justice in
1871. A small number of reconstituted entries and all entries subsequent
to 1860 are in card indexes at the Archives Départementales de la Seine.
The first official reconstitution is at the branch office of these archives,
the second reconstitution and a few supplementary indexes are at the

head office. Extracts from pre-Revolution registers can be found in manuscript at the Bibliothèque Nationale and in other public libraries. Protestant registers, where they have survived, can be found in the Archives Départementales, with some copies in the Protestant Library.

Minutes of notaries public

Unlike England the probate of wills was a matter for notaries public, in whose archives they are to be found. It is no exaggeration to say that these archives contain more genealogical information than any other, for not only did the notaries deal with wills, but also with marriage contracts, deeds of purchase and sale and deeds of division of property. The inheritance laws in France differ markedly from those in England, especially in regard to property. Notarial minutes are to be found either in the hands of the successor in office of the notary public of the locality or in the Archives Départementales in the provinces and in the Minutier of the Archives Nationales in Paris. The volumes of minutes and transactions are usually indexed.

Registers of 'Insinuations'

Many notarial transactions had to be taxed. Summaries of these had to be entered into registers and handed to the Service de l'enrégistrement et du timbre, part of the Ministry of Finance. At Nice, the Italian registers of 'Insinuations' contain extensive copies of all notarial documents from about 1600 to 1789. Some of these are in the Archives Départementales for Nice (Alpes Maritimes), others in the Archives du Palais at Monaco.

Nobility

Families able to trace their descent without any known grant of nobility to 1400 or before were entitled to consider themselves the equal or peers of the king, whom they acknowledged as their feudal chief. These are known as the 'feudal families'. Quasi-feudal families are those which can prove an uninterrupted descent coupled with the possession of a fief from before 1560, but without any known grant of nobility. The descendants of such families were called gentlemen of rank, birth or blood and they could assume titles at their will. This immediately shows one of the many differences between the English 'nobility' and the

Map 6.   Internal Boundaries in France.

French 'noblesse'. In England the lowest rank of nobility was the 'baron', in France the 'écuyer' or esquire. The term 'seigneur', which is usually translated 'lord', is really the same as lord of the manor. Whether you were a seigneur or a 'duc' you owed your nobility to the fact that you were an 'écuyer'. In one sense, 'écuyer' was the lowest rank; in another it was the only one, for unless you were an 'écuyer' you could not be noble. Whether you called yourself baron, comte, marquis or duc depended upon the number of seigneuries, i.e. manors

23

or parishes you owned. Thus nobility derived from the size of your property, not, as today in England, from a grant by the sovereign. Francis I, King of France, is reported to have said 'Je suis né gentilhomme et non pas roi', by which he meant that his honour, or nobility, depended upon his being born a gentleman.

Below these great feudal families, who paid no taxes, but who were required to provide the king with military service – the 'impôt du sang' – there were people who were made noblemen by letters patent or through the exercise of certain offices, such as municipal magistrates of certain great cities, such as the mayors of Paris, Rouen, Niort, Angers, Bourges and to certain officers of finance. Such high officials obtained successively either nobility at the first degree or nobility at the third generation. The former (high officials) formed what became known as the 'noblesse de robe', the latter the 'noblesse de cloche'.

With the reign of Louis XIV, France for the first time became a unified kingdom, and in order to curb the power of local magnates and nobles, the' king conceived the idea of centralizing the administration of provinces under 'intendants' and of attracting the nobility to Versailles where he could keep them under his eye. In this way, the nobility tended to become time-servers and a privileged class, losing their former ideals of chivalry and duty. By the end of the eighteenth century their duties and powers had mostly vanished, though privilege remained.

By the beginning of the seventeenth century there were seven different ways of acquiring noblesse. The first was by 'extraction', which meant that the origins of the nobility were so old that they were lost in the mists of time. The second was 'noblesse uterine', which existed in certain provinces, especially in Champagne, and which meant nobility by descent in the female line. Noblesse uterine was divided into four classes, a) blood royal, b) feudal dignity, c) by letters patent and d) provincial custom. It was maintained that a noble mother could transmit noblesse to her son even if she married beneath her, though there were many disputes arising from this claim. The third, 'par chevalerie', was akin to knighthood and was conferred by the king on a non-noble person for public service on the field of battle or in a civil position. The fourth was by letters patent registered in the Cour de Comptes, without which they were not valid, and accompanied by the payment of a fee. The fifth was 'par fiefs', which meant acquisition by the investiture of a fief noble. The sixth was 'par office', which was the already mentioned noblesse de robe, i.e. those holding certain legal offices, 'par finance', i.e. those who held certain offices in the provincial treasury, and 'par la cloche', i.e. by holding municipal office. These did not confer immediate noblesse; in some cases it was after a certain term of years, e.g. twenty; in others after three generations, and also depending upon whether or not the person lived in 'noble fashion'. Finally, there was 'noblesse militaire' granted to a person in military service whose father and grandfather had served in the army for twenty years as a captain, lieutenant or ensign.

The mere acquisition of noblesse did not raise these newly made nobles to an equal social level with the older families. The honours of the court, such as the right to ride in the king's carriages, to hunt in the royal forests, or to have wives presented at court, were reserved for those who could show unbroken descent from 1400 without known 'anoblissement'. In the eighteenth century the same conditions were imposed for a commission in the king's bodyguard.

Titles under the 'Ancien Régime' derived from land and depended upon its quality. It was the land or 'terre' which was deemed to be a 'baronie, comté or marquisat', not the individual who possessed it. Up to the end of the seventeenth century there were no personal titles as such, though they began to be assumed in the eighteenth, sometimes by usurpation. There were a few instances of the king creating a personal title of duc by letters patent, but the title did not descend to the duke's posterity as in England. It is doubtful if, out of all those who called themselves marquis, comte or baron before the Revolution, more than a tiny fraction were actually seigneurs holding a terre of that particular quality.

With exceptions in different provinces, it did not follow in pre-Revolution days that the son of a marquis was a comte or the son of a comte a vicomte. For example, the eldest son of the Marquis de Thouars was called Louis Jacques de Cougnée (his family name), Marquis de Puissar, the name of his seigneurie. Thus if Alphonse de Bombard, écuyer, Seigneur Marquis de Champsneuf, was seigneur of a terre or fief which was a marquisat; and if the terre was alienated either by sale or by the failure of male heirs and subdivided among co-heiresses, the title passed to the next owner who was its seigneur. By subdivision it might lose its quality and become a smaller fief, such as a baronie or seigneurie. The composition of marquisates and baronies varied from period to period and province to province. Generally speaking a baronie comprised three parishes or manors.

Finally, there are those families or persons raised to the nobility under the First Empire, Restoration, the Monarchy of July, the Second Empire and by the Republic. On the eve of the Revolution it has been estimated that four-fifths of the so-called gentry had no real claim to belong to it. Today, it has been estimated that about 70,000 Frenchmen claim noble status, out of which not more than 8,000 or 9,000 have any real title to that quality.

The Revolution swept away the old feudal system and with it hereditary titles of nobility. Napoleon, however, created Imperial titles rather than a nobility. After his fall the old nobility regained its titles and the new kept theirs. The restoration of the old titles was at first confined to a personal title only, but later the right to transmit it was restored. Thus a duke, marquis or comte who had been one before 1790 regained his title, but no longer derived it from his marquisat or comté but by letters patent. In 1835, however, the law protecting titles against usurpation was repealed, with the result that today anyone who wishes to adopt a title in France may do so in principle but in fact would immediately cause a great outcry from all the remaining titled families. The Third Republic retained the 'Conseil du Sceau' which gave advice about the use of foreign and domestic titles, but there is no official body in France dealing with titles other than the Legion of Honour, which is not hereditary.

Heraldry

The first thing to be said about armorial bearings and the use of arms in France is that it has never been as strictly controlled as it has been in England. For centuries French families chose their own arms, and though from time to time attempts were made by the French kings to regulate the use of arms by compiling lists of those who bore them, nothing like the College of Arms existed, although the English heralds did have their French counterparts in medieval times. The first thing to note, therefore, is that armorial bearings were not always the privilege of noblemen. In 1696 Louis XIV instituted a General Armorial of France to register all the coats of arms of gentlemen as well as those of the noblesse de robe, ecclesiastics, burgesses of free cities and all those who, owing to the office they held, enjoyed certain privileges and public rights. The Armorial contained 40,000 coats of arms, noble and non-noble, but it was a registration designed chiefly to raise money by taxing the users of arms. In no way does the appearance of a family and its coat of arms in the Armorial imply anything like the grant of arms to an Englishman. The collection of tax was farmed out, and some 'farmers' imposed arms upon those who did not have them so that they might be taxed. Such coats of arms were turned out by the dozen. For example, at Marseilles the farmer of the Armorial turned out a shield per fess with an elephant in base and three stars or, a crescent between two stars, in chief, with every possible combination of colours and metals. Over 60,000 coats of arms are recorded in the 69 volumes of the manuscript *Grand Armorial de France* (often referred to as the 'd'Hozier' after the man who undertook the office of juge d'armes, or judge of arms) which is preserved in the Bibliothèque Nationale.

Bibliothèque Nationale and Archives Publiques

In addition to the General Armorial there are at the Bibliothèque Nationale thousands of manuscript volumes containing the papers of judges of arms of the reigns of Louis XIV, Louis XV and Louis XVI. Over 3,000 of these, known as 'pièces originales', contain original documents produced by the interested parties or the judges of arms. There are also 680 volumes headed 'dossiers bleus', 600 'carrés d'Hozier', 350 'cabinet d'Hozier', 350 'nouveau d'Hozier' and 220 'Chérin' filled with genealogical trees and copies of documents submitted to the judges of arms by people wishing to prove their right to nobility. The best index to these papers is the *Répertoire des séries généalogiques*.

After 1688, when James II went into exile in France, he took with him James Terry, Athlone Herald, who brought with him many heraldic and genealogical papers. Because it was necessary to prove noblesse before getting a commission in the army, many exiled Englishmen and Scotsmen applied to Terry to prove they were armigerous. Where he could not do so from his own sources he applied to the English and Scottish heralds. Many of his pedigrees from these sources have survived, especially valuable being those to do with Irish families. On Terry's death, his papers went to d'Hozier and are now in the manuscript collections associated with him.

Printed inventories of the Archives Départementales and Archives Communales have been published, and in most public record offices there are card indexes to help the searcher. Complete sets of these inventories are on public view in the reading rooms of the Bibliothèque Nationale and in most Archives Départementales. Series E in the Archives Départementales contains many documents relating to individual families.

Naval and military records are to be found in the Archives de la Marine and in the Archives de l'Armée de Terre. There are usually individual files for each officer for the pre-Empire period.

A letter of introduction from the Embassy of the searcher's country is required before admission can be gained to the Bibliothèque Nationale, Archives Nationales and to the naval and military archives. In the provinces admission is less rigorously controlled.

Huguenot records

Huguenot records vary according to locality; in some parts of France they have all been lost; in others much has survived. In the country as a whole there are few which begin much before 1660, but those of Caen, La Rochelle, Rouen and Nîmes are very extensive and begin at the end of the sixteenth century and continue up to the Revocation of the Edict of Nantes in 1685. They are to be found in the Archives Départementales, some at the Mairie among the parochial registers, and a few in private hands. A few stray volumes of various small churches are in Paris in the Archives Nationales, Série T.T, and some copies in the Protestant Library. The usefulness of French Protestant registers is not confined to English, American or other families of Huguenot descent. They contain many references to English, Scottish and Irish families resident in France, and especially to merchants trading between England and the French ports. The Protestant registers of Caen, Angers, Saumur, Tours, Nantes and Bordeaux have numerous references to English and Scottish residents, especially those who followed the Stuarts into exile.

3

Germany

Registration

Research in Germany is made difficult by the fact that the country was for so long divided into different kingdoms, and the religious divisions into Protestant and Catholic added a further complication.

Parish registers begin somewhat earlier in south Germany, in the sixteenth century, than they do in the north; the earliest date from about 1550. Civil registration was established in 1875 for the whole of Germany after its unification.

From 1 January 1876 every town of any size had to have a Standesamt (registry office) of its own, and these were grouped under a local Standesamt to which they were responsible. Birth, marriage and death records are kept in the Standesamt and duplicates sent to the local offices each year. There has been little attempt to centralize German records, mainly for historical reasons, since every city of any size possesses its own archives and every Province or Land its Staatsarchiv. This arises from the historical fact of the fragmentation of the country. For this reason it is important for the genealogical enquirer to know something about the area from which his ancestor may have come, but initial enquiries can be made to Der Herold Verein für Heraldik, Genealogie und Verwandte Wissenschaften, Wiesbaden, Dieselstrasse 24. There are likewise many genealogical societies concerned with the particular regions of Germany, and for those with ancestors from West Germany there is a society called the Deutsche Arbeitsgemeinschaft der Genealogischen Verbander (Union of German Genealogical Workers), Hanover, am Markt 4. For those of noble descent, there is the Deutsche Adelsarchiv, am Glaskopf 21, Marburg an der Lahn 16. The following German registries are likewise important:

Standesamt Berlin Mitte (Middle), Berlin C2 Elizabethstrasse 28–29
Standesamt I, Berlin (West), Berlin-Wilmersdorf, Fehrbelliner Platz 1
Standesamt I, Berlin (East), Berlin C2, Stralauerstrasse 42–43

Map 7. Internal Boundaries in Germany pre World War I.

Haupstandesamt Hamburg (Chief Registry Office), Hamburg I,
  Johanniswall 4
Berlin Hauptarchiv, Berlin-Dahlem, Archivstrasse 12–14
and for the archives of religious bodies:
Archivamt der Evangelischen Kirche Deutschland, Hanover,
  Militarstrasse 9
Kirchenbuchamt für den Osten, Hanover, Militarstrasse 9
Bischöfliches (Episcopal) Generalvikariat, abt.für Ostertriebene,
  Limburg/Lahn

The former German Empire, as has already been said, consisted of a
number of sovereign states, the archives of which still largely remain in
the chief cities of those states today. The following is a list of the
kingdoms and principalities and the capital city of each, as they were
immediately before the First World War. To go further back, the list

becomes intolerably long and exceedingly complicated, since through-out the nineteenth century the tendency towards unification developed piece-meal.

Kingdoms

Prussia–Berlin
Bavaria–Munich
Saxony–Dresden
Württemberg–Stuttgart

Grand duchies

Baden–Karlsruhe
Hessen–Darmstadt
Mecklenburg–Schwerin and Neu-Strelitz
Sachsen-Weimar–Weimar
Oldenburg–Oldenburg

The less important duchies were: Anhalt, Sachsen-Altenburg, Sachsen-Coburg-Gotha, Brunswick (Braunschweig), and Sachsen-Mein-ingen. Principalities, which were even smaller, comprised amongst others: Detmold, Bückeburg, Gera, Rudolstadt und Sondershausen, Greiz, Schleiz and Arolsen. In addition to these, there were the ancient Hanseatic cities which enjoyed certain freedoms and privileges; namely Bremen, Hamburg and Lübeck.

Between 1870 and 1918, Alsace and Lorraine, the chief cities of which were Colmar, Metz and Strasbourg, now part of France, were part of the German Empire; so, too, were the two Belgian districts of Eupen and Malmedy.

Generally speaking, the southern kingdoms were Catholic and the northern Protestant, but with the added complication that the Protest-ants were divided between Lutheran and Reformed churches. Each of these churches had similar, though different systems of registration. The oldest fragment of a German parish register is part of the baptismal register of Basel in Switzerland covering the years 1390–1407, and is now in the British Museum. Some South German parish registers date back fragmentally to around 1540.

Surnames

German surnames reveal more about the place of origin than British ones do. Local spellings and local names abound in Germany, thus helping the genealogist to narrow down his field of search. There are, of course, many surnames which occur throughout the country and which have the same spelling whether they be of families from Schleswig-Holstein in the north or Bavaria in the south. Such names and spellings as Schmidt and Braun reveal nothing about the place of origin of those families who bear these names. German surnames are, as such, comparatively recent. Hereditary surnames gradually began to appear towards the end of the Middle Ages between the twelfth and fourteenth centuries. The elements out of which they developed go much further back, and it is possible to detect three basic sources from which modern German names are derived.

1 Ancient indigenous heathen personal names such as Albrecht or Arnold.

2 Subsequently introduced Christian personal names such as Peter and Paul.

3 Locative names, patronymics, occupational names and nicknames, examples of which are Wittenberg, Ambach, Weber and Breitkopf.

When the population was scattered and life simple, there was no need for more than one name. But as trade and population increased and as towns and cities developed, the need for a more precise appellation developed. In Germany, by-names began to appear around 1100 in Cologne; 1145 in Zurich and 1168 in Basel, but in central Germany not until the thirteenth century. They first appeared later still in north Germany in the first half of the fourteenth century.

At first, most German names were patronymics, but gradually the genitive form was dropped. As in the case of English surnames, German names derive from occupations and places of origin. During the fifteenth and sixteenth centuries it became fashionable in some quarters to Latinize surnames so that essentially German names are disguised, as for example Curtius for Kurz or Piscator for Fischer. French and Slav changes occurred frequently in the seventeenth century and French Huguenot names likewise became Germanized.

German language boundaries never coincided with political frontiers, and they still differ today. Thus geographical variants play a more than usually important part in genealogical studies. For example, Metz, Strasbourg and Colmar, though linguistically German, are in France. Switzerland includes German, French and Italian speakers. From Carinthia in eastern Austria the boundary between German and Slav speakers generally follows the river Drava (or Drau in German). Northward the boundary is between German and Magyar speakers up to the confluence of the rivers Feistritz and Raab. The modern German/Polish frontier is wholly political. Until 1945 the whole of western Poland up to the Oder-Neisse line and east as far as Poznan and Bydgoszcz, north to Gdansk (Danzig) was all German; so too was the Baltic coastal area as

Map 8.   Internal Boundaries in Germany post World War II.

far north as the border of Lithuania, now in Soviet Russia. Not many Germans live there now, but many of German descent originate from this vast region.

In addition to the main bulk of German-speaking people, there were many isolated pockets of Germans in Hungary, the Ukraine and as far east as the Volga. Within Germany itself there is a further linguistic division between High German in the south and Low German in the north. Thus it is possible to divide Germany into four main areas: north-west = Low German: north-east = Low German/Slav; south-west = High German; and south-east = High German/Slav/Magyar

Jewish names

German Jews were ordered to take surnames in 1812. They had a choice of Hebrew Old Testament names, which were often taken in patronymic forms. Modern High German names were popular, especially if they sounded well. Jews also took the names of the towns in which they lived, especially in eastern Germany. Another popular category had to do with gold and silver, reflecting the Jewish interest in banking and money.

In the Austro-Hungarian Empire the ancient custom of using the patronymic 'ben' meaning 'son of' was officially regarded with disfavour, and there was much resistance on the part of Jews to take surnames. This led the authorities to impose surnames, often of a grossly insulting character such as Stinker or Eselkopf (donkey-head) to cite but two.

Internal registration of births, marriages and deaths in German Jewish communities*

In some countries a marriage oath had to be taken which conflicted with the Jewish religion, so that many chose marriage according to their own law, thus avoiding official registration. A further reason for avoiding official registration was due to the fact that the authorities forbade younger Jewish sons to marry in order to decrease the number of Jews who were born. The number of the Jewish population in a given town or village was often restricted, which resulted in many rules and regulations covering the movement of Jewish families. Second and subsequent sons were forced, therefore, to marry according to Jewish law.

The first laws regarding the registers of births, deaths and marriages appeared in most European countries after the French Revolution, together with the beginnings of Jewish emancipation which later found expression in the various Judenedikte in Germany. This form of registration ended in Germany with the introduction of the Standesamte in 1876, when all births, deaths and marriages had to be recorded irrespective of faith. Apart from the registers, so-called 'family books' were kept almost everywhere, listing every member of the household and often including the servants. During the Nazi regime, entries were made in the birth registers in various districts, particularly Bavaria, Brunswick and Holstein, regarding the additional Jewish private names

* Most information concerning German Jewry is to be found in the Jewish Historical General Archives in Jerusalem.

such as Israel and Sarah which were required by the government. Regulations in the following areas of Germany require particular attention:

Baden

In 1809 Rabbis were appointed to act as registrars, but two years later in May 1811 a further edict ordered that the registers be kept by the magistrates where, through insufficient knowledge of the German language, a Rabbi could not fulfil his duties. In 1817 the duty of keeping the registers was transferred to the clergy except in Karlsruhe, Mannheim, Bruchsal and Heidelberg. Twice a year the parochial offices had to send Jewish birth registers to a higher state authority. In June 1841 and October 1851 registration again became with certain exceptions, the responsibility of Rabbis. In 1869 civil registers and civil marriage were introduced in Baden. Register books were kept in three different sections, i.e. births, marriages and deaths, and a few communities compiled retrospective lists reaching back to the second half of the eighteenth century.

Bavaria

Up to 1807 there was no law in Bavaria regarding the keeping of Jewish registers. The early German written registers in the Jewish Historical General Archives come from Swabia, which in that period (1722–84) belonged to Austria. In Bayreuth regular registers as far back as 1799 and written in Hebrew continued far into the nineteenth century. These were later used as a basis for official retrospective registers. From about 1808 Jews began to carry out registration of births, marriages and deaths according to prescribed rules, which had to be verified by the heads of the Jewish community. Only in Würzburg, then under the jurisdiction of Ferdinand of Tuscany, does it appear that these registers were the responsibility of the parish priest. An edict of 1813 ordered the adoption of German family names by Jews, which were later entered into the official registers, and only a Jew who had a number in this register was recognized as a protected Jew or Schutzjude, and only if one family died out could another take its place. This law was abolished in 1861.

Brunswick

Registers of births, marriages and deaths for Jews, which began in 1809 in Wolfenbüttel and Seesen have survived only in the form of copies or extracts made in the second half of the nineteenth century. The registers of Wolfenbüttel beginning in 1855 contain information about marriages, banns, the name and domicile of the circumcisor, the Hebrew date and the Hebrew name of the child; and the death registers the place of burial and Hebrew date of death. These registers end in 1899.

Frankfurt-am-Main

The decree of the town council (Ratsedekt) of 1805 ordered the keeping of Jewish birth, marriage and death registers. These were written originally in Hebrew script. New registers written in German begin in 1808 and end in 1876.

Hamburg

Hamburg, being one of the Hanseatic cities, had its own government, which issued an edict in 1815 ordering all Church and Jewish congregations to keep registers of births, marriages and deaths. Duplicates were deposited in the town archives at the end of each year. For members of the Portuguese community there were special regulations, and all of these remained in force until 1865.

Hanover

The earliest Jewish registers date from before 1808, and appear to have been discontinued after 1813, until 1831, when new regulations regarding the Rabbinate were issued ordering the Chief Rabbi to keep two identical registers for each of the three districts. At the end of each year one of these two registers had to be sent to the Landdrostei. In 1832 the Landdrostei in Lüneburg authorized the Rabbi to appoint a Jewish registrar for every district. In 1843 special regulations were issued according to which registration was to be carried out by the head of the community, under the supervision of the district Rabbi.

Grand Duchy of Hessen

Registration in Hessen was never carried out by the Jews themselves. The parson, later the Landrat and his officials, and finally the burgomaster, were charged with this responsibility. These regulations date from 1732 with further amendments in 1787 and 1788, concerning the conditions for marriage licences to be granted to Jews. The earlier registers of births concerned only boys, though occasionally births of girls were entered. In 1808 it was ordered that Jews should adopt German family names, and the keeping of registers became the duty of grand ducal officers. The old registrations or extracts of them were handed over to these officials, who had to draw up special lists with the new names chosen by the Jews. Further regulations in 1823 decreed that future registration be carried out by the burgomaster, and finally regulations in 1837 ordered the use of printed forms for this purpose. These registers end between 1873 and 1876.

Hohenzollern–Hechingen

Birth, marriage and death registers of this Duchy are now in the Historical General Archives and begin between 1820 and 1828. They were drawn up by the Rabbis according to the instructions of the ducal commissioner for Jewish affairs. Most of the registers extend as far as the 1930s, and some are retrospective as far back as 1800.

Holstein

The Jewish Historical General Archives contain registers of the Jewish communities of Kiel and Elmshorn going back to 1841 and 1847 respectively. The Danish law on the conditions of the Jews in Holstein dating from 1863 contains some instructions regarding the keeping of Jewish registers. These were modified by the Prussian authorities after 1866 when the duchy came under German rule.

Lübeck

The first Jewish registers of Lübeck date from 1811, but these are only copies. Extracts from the death registers of 1812–28 also survive. Regular register books begin in 1848, and continue up to 1853, after which certain modifications appear. The birth and death registers end in 1876, and the marriage registers in 1918.

Mecklenburg-Schwerin

The earliest Jewish registers date from 1797. A decree of 1813 ordered the keeping of regular 'Jewish Church books'. These were kept in printed form, and have been maintained more or less uniformly ever since. In some places retrospective registers reach back to the 1780s.

Oldenburg

Copies of early Jewish registers dating from 1836 have survived, which refer to entries as early as 1814. New instructions in 1850 regarding Jewish births, marriages and deaths applied to the whole duchy, whereas formerly only the larger towns were involved. The first statistical survey of the Jewish population which served as a basis for later registers was made in 1840.

Prussia

The edict regarding the civil status of Jews in Prussia dates from 1812, but does not contain instruction regarding the keeping of registers. However, the police had authority to compile lists of births, deaths, marriages and divorces of Jewish citizens in Prussia, which were sent to central government at the end of every year. Under a decree of 1818 the illegitimate birth of the child of a Christian father was not entered in the Jewish register if the mother was Jewish. The birthdates appear in both Hebrew and German dating. In some districts the keeping of the registers was the responsibility of the Jewish congregation itself, though in others it was the responsibility of the mayor. Registration was usually carried out in German, but some registers were additionally completed in Polish as well as in Hebrew.

Sachsen, Weimar, Eisenach

The first regulations concerning Jewish registers date from 1823, and registration was to be carried out both by the parson and by the district Rabbi, and in small towns by the teacher or the reader in the synagogue. In 1873 further instructions ordered that in places where no Jewish community existed, the vicar should notify the district Rabbi at the end of the year of every Jewish birth, marriage or death in his parish.

Schleswig

The Jewish marriage registers of Friedrichstadt on the Eider from 1847–54 contain very detailed records not only of the bride and bridegroom and their legal status, but of their parents as well (whether alive or dead, the maiden name and birthplace of the mother). The birth registers, in addition to the usual particulars, also contain the date and place of the parents' marriage, and there are similar entries in the death registers. Dates are in both the Hebrew and the German calendars. New regulations came in in 1854, and ended in 1874.

Westphalia

Jewish registers in this former German kingdom date from 1809, and were supervised by the Rabbis who were also required to supervise the use of German family names.

Württemberg

Jewish registers date from 1807 and had to be completed by the synagogue warden, or where there were no synagogues, by the head of the municipality. Vicars until 1820 had to keep the Christian registers only, but in many cases they also include the registration of Jews. After 1820 it became the vicar's official duty to keep the Jewish registers, and the required particulars were supplied from the former registrars.

Wills

Unlike most other European countries, in Germany copies of wills are not deposited in local record offices. Testators file their wills with the local court if they wish, but there appears to be no compulsion in the matter.

4

Austria

The republic of Austria is a small neutral country in Central Europe with a population of about 7 million. It should not be confused with the great Austro-Hungarian Empire which had over 50 million inhabitants and which, since 1918, has been split into eight successor states. The whole of the former empire was often called Austria for short. Though information about people from the united empire can be found in Vienna, it is usually necessary to look for the origins of a family in the records of the successor states. These are as follows.

1 The Republic of Austria
2 Italy (South Tirol, Friuli and Trieste)
3 Czechoslovakia (Bohemia, Moravia, southern Silesia, Slovakia = formerly North Hungary)
4 Poland (Galicia)
5 USSR-Ukraine (east Galicia, north Bukovina)
6 Hungary
7 Romania (south Bukovina, Transylvania, south-east Hungary)
8 Yugoslavia (south Hungary, Croatia, south Styria, Dalmatia)

The names within brackets are those of the most important of the lost imperial provinces. It is important to note that with the exception of the republics of Austria and of Italy, all the rest of the former provinces are today under communist rule, and in these states genealogical research in general is almost impossible to pursue.

Archives

The Austrian Republic today consists of nine Bündesländer or provinces each with its own Landesarchiv, and genealogical enquiries can be made there about relevant source material. As well as the Länder, searches in the archives of the larger towns, old monasteries and episcopal records (Ordiniarate) can produce valuable results.

Map 9.   Austria pre World War I showing Austro-Hungarian Empire.

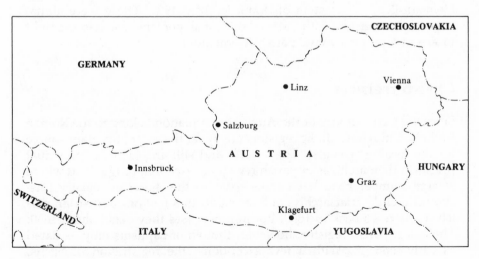

Map 10.   Austria post World War II.

41

The most extensive sources are to be found in the state archives in Vienna. Here, and especially in the sections known as the Haus-, Hof- and Staatsarchiv, are an abundance of important genealogical sources, including the remarkable collections of the Holy Roman Empire covering nearly 1000 years up to 1806, and the records of the Habsburg family from the thirteenth century to 1918. In the Allgemeines Verwaltungsarchiv of the general administration section are to be found copies of the Habsburg registers of arms and nobility (Wappenbriefe and Adelsbriefe) from the fifteenth century to 1918, and the files of the university professors for the whole monarchy. In the section known as the Hofkammerarchiv there is much material concerning financial and business affairs relating to the Habsburg crown lands, information concerning a large number of the officials and registers of German families which settled in south Hungary and Galicia from the eighteenth century. In the Kriegsarchiv or military section there are extensive records of personnel who served in the imperial army. These are complete from 1740. For officers there are alphabetical indexes; information about private soldiers can only be found if the name of the regiment in which they served is known. Particulars of sailors who served in the Austrian navy exist from 1790–1918.

Censuses

The records themselves no longer exist, having been made for statistical purposes only. There is, however, a good substitute to be found in the Heimatrollen, or registers of domicile, 1857–1939. These were alphabetical land registers with the vital data of all persons who had the right to live in a particular civil parish (Gemeinde).

Church registers

Since the vast majority of the Austrian population belong to the Roman Catholic Church, Catholic registers are by far the most important source for the local genealogist. They were, and still are, kept by individual priests in their archives or parish registries, except in Burgenland where a large number have been transferred to the diocesan registry (Bischöfliche Ordinariatsarchiv) in Eisenstadt. In a few cases Austrian parish registers go back to 1600, but in most cases they begin about 1650. The oldest parish register, however, though of baptisms only, is dated as early as 1542. With a few exceptions, the registration of births, marriages and deaths was ecclesiastical until 1938, and only after the

Anschluss with Germany did these become matters for civil registration. Thus marriage records date from the 1 August 1938 and those of births and deaths from 1 January 1939. A second feature about Austrian church records is that the age of records appears to decrease as one goes from west to east, so that the Tirol and Vorarlberg are the best documented. Records in the neighbourhood of Vienna date from 1684, after the second siege of the city by the Turks. Because of the lack of toleration for religious sects other than the Catholic Church, even after 1781, when private records were allowed, they had still to be included in the local Catholic parish until 1849. Some Protestant records from the sixteenth and seventeenth century do exist, however.

Since the nineteenth century, duplicate registers have been made, but in general these are not accessible. In Catholic registers before 1782, particulars of Protestant marriages can be found. Since that time, a few parishes have kept their own records. Since the nineteenth century, in a few of the larger towns, separate Jewish registers have been kept in some of the parishes. Most of these are kept today by the Jewish religious community in Vienna.

Civil registration

Since 1870 particulars of people with no religious affiliation have been kept in the registers of the chief executive of each district, or of the chief local officer of the town (Stadtmagistrat). The keeping of general state registers by registry offices has only been in force in Austria since 1939. In Burgenland, which joined the Austrian Republic in 1921, civil registration dates from 1895 when it was introduced in Hungary, to which country this province then belonged. Only limited access to state registers is allowed. There is no general public record office in Austria as there is in England.

Other genealogical sources

Among individual medieval documents, the granting of fiefs, estates, titles, etc., there are in the Landesarchiven large groups of estate books (Grundbücher), often dating from the fourteenth century, which give particulars of families who owned houses and estates as well as of craftsmen and peasants. The estate offices of the former landowners often contain originals or copies of wills and notes on the distribution of property to heirs after the death of the owner. Particularly worthwhile and interesting are the tax lists from about 1789 to 1819–25. Special attention is drawn to the 'Totenbeschauprotokolle', 1648–1928 in Vienna, the nearest English equivalents of which are the records of the coroner's court, in which full particulars of the deceased, cause and place of death are recorded. Hardly any notarial deeds from former times have survived. The distribution of property to heirs as well as of civil actions was in Austria not a matter for notaries, but for the officials appointed by the landowners; after 1850, they came under the jurisdiction of the state officials of the newly created state law courts.

Nobility

The rank of 'Landherr' or landowner originated with noble families and those who had held ministerial posts under the Babenburg rulers of Austria – the house which preceded the Habsburgs – in the thirteenth century. Within the representative bodies of the larger monasteries, of the nobility and of the cities, they constituted the families of the highest rank. Since the sixteenth century the nobility has been divided into Fürsten (princes), Grafen (counts) and Freiherren (barons) which together comprise the landed class of the high nobility (Herrenstand). Next come Ritter (knights) comprising the landed class of knights, or Ritterstand, corresponding to the English gentry. The emperors had a tendency to honour more and more families with hereditary titles, especially during the nineteenth century, when many received the rank of baron, to the extent that one can almost talk of a kind of 'inflation' of titles. After 1850 the privileges of the nobility were by and large revoked, so that these titles indicated no more than a superior position in society. Since then, the 'erste Gesellschaft', or what we might term the top people, consisted of the high aristocratic families of princes and counts, the higher officials and senior officers. Professional people and industrialists formed the 'Zweite Gesellschaft' or what in England might be termed the upper-middle class.

Under a law of 1919 Austrian citizens are forbidden to use titles. For this reason, on official documents, passports and even in civil registration, they do not appear. In purely private social intercourse, titles of nobility are often still used. As, however, there no longer exists any authority to regulate or establish the legality of such titles, their control has ceased, and many false titles have been assumed by parvenus who are not entitled to bear them. Information about Austrian noble families can be obtained from the state archives or the 'Adler Gesellschaft' in Vienna.

Heraldry

Arms were first introduced in the twelfth century at the time of the Norman Empire, and soon spread to Austria where they were adopted by the leading families as early as the fourteenth century. They were mostly taken from seals, while there are only a very small number of Austrian rolls of arms. Since the time of the Emperor Frederic III (died 1493), successive emperors and the independent archdukes of Tirol and Styria granted so many civic arms that their use became inflated. After 1625 application for new arms came to an end, and from that time onward it was necessary to exhibit the correct diploma of nobility before they could be granted. At any rate, from that time onward the unauthorized taking of new arms by non-noble families was strictly limited.

Although the official granting of family arms, just as of titles of nobility, was forbidden by the law of 1919, there exist today many families who are interested in the private use of newly created arms, so that since 1948 it has been possible to have these enrolled through the 'Adler Gesellschaft' in the Austrian roll of arms (Österreichischen Wappenrolle). Rich collections of material are to be found in the heraldic manuscripts of the Austrian National Library and in the Krahl Collection in the State Archives.

5

Switzerland

Political structure and history

In 1291 the three Swiss cantons of Uri, Schwyz and Unterwalden formed an alliance against the Habsburgs. It was not until 1848, however, that the Swiss Confederation was formally turned into a single political unit. Each Swiss canton – there are twenty-two, three of which have been subdivided, thus making twenty-five in all – has its own government, which runs its everyday affairs, administers its own justice and, to a certain extent, imposes its own laws. Switzerland has no single national language, its inhabitants speaking a German dialect in the north, French and Italian in the south and an ancient tongue known as Romansch in some parts of the east. Each cantonal government is responsible to the federal government in Bern. The following is a list of the cantons and the names of the chief towns in each of them. The language spoken in each canton is indicated as follows: F = French; G = German; I = Italian, R = Romansch.

Appenzell (Divided into Inter-Rhoden and Aüsser-Rhoden) –
   Appenzell and Herisau **G** (Roman Catholic and Protestant
   respectively)
Aargau – Aarau **G** (Protestant)
Basel (Basle or Bâle) (Divided into Basel-stadt and Basel-Land) – Basel
   and Liestal **G** (Protestant)
Berne (Bern) – Bern **G** (Protestant)
Fribourg – Fribourg **F** (Roman Catholic)
Geneva (Geneve, Genf) – Geneva **F** (Protestant)
Glarus (Glarus) – Glarus **G** (Protestant)
Grisons (Graubünden) – Chur **GR** (Protestant)
Lucerne (Luzern) – Luzern **G** (Roman Catholic)
Neuchatel – Neuchatel **F** (Protestant)
St-Gallen (St-Gall) – St Gallen **G** (Roman Catholic)
Schaffhausen (Schaffhouse) – Schaffhausen **G** (Protestant)

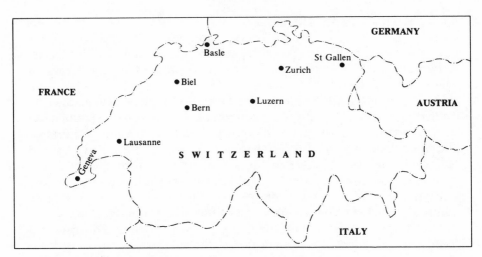

Map 11. Switzerland.

Schwyz (Schwytz) – Schwyz **G** (Roman Catholic)
Solothurn (Soleure) – Solothurn **G** (Roman Catholic)
Ticino (Tessin) – Bellinzona **I** (Roman Catholic)
Thurgau (Thurgovie) – Frauenfeld **G** (Protestant)
Unterwalden (Unterwald) (Divided into Nidwald and Obwald) – Stans
    and Sarnen **G** (Both Roman Catholic)
Uri – Altdorf **G** (Roman Catholic)
Valais – Sion **F** (Roman Catholic)
Vaud – Lausanne **F** (Protestant)
Zug (Zoug) – Zug **G** (Roman Catholic)
Zurich – Zürich **G** (Protestant)

Following the Pact between the Waldstätten in 1291, there was a continuing struggle against the Habsburgs throughout the fourteenth century. Pitted against the cavalry of the High German nobility, the confederated infantry won a series of battles in 1315, 1339, 1386 and 1388. Meanwhile several towns or länder joined the original nucleus. Luzern joined in 1332, Zurich in 1351, Glarus and Zug in 1352 and Bern in 1353. This group is known in Swiss history as the Eight Cantons. At the beginning of the sixteenth century the confederation acquired Fribourg, Solothurn, Basel, Schaffhausen and Appenzell. The territories of the 'allied countries' (Valais and the Grisons Leagues) and those of Thurgau and Ticino which were held in subjection by one or several cantons, fitted into the gaps between the Thirteen Cantons.

The Reformation preached by Zwingli and Calvin found fruitful soil for expansion in Switzerland. It spread throughout Romance Switzerland and struck deeply into the still imperfectly welded organization of

47

the Thirteen Cantons. The confederates, anxious to avoid disastrous schisms in their ranks, took care to refrain from religious strife. This gave substance to Swiss neutrality, which was fortified by the formal recognition of Swiss sovereignty by the signatories of the Treaty of Westphalia in 1648.

Under the French Revolution, the Directory imposed the status of a unified and centralized republic, known as the Helvetian Republic, on the Swiss people. Switzerland then became a battlefield for the French and their allied enemies, the Austrians, Prussians and Russians. In 1803 Napoleon imposed his Act of Mediation under which the federated nature of the country was recognized, but a triple equality 'of the cantons between themselves, of the town dwellers between themselves and of the people of the country and of the towns' was proclaimed. Six new cantons – Aargau, St-Gallen, the Grisons, Ticino, Thurgau and Vaud – were added to the political majority.

After the fall of Napoleon the accession of three new territories – Geneva, the Valais and Neuchatel – brought the number of cantons to its present twenty-two. At the Congress of Vienna the great European powers proclaimed the perpetual neutrality of Switzerland. The internal organization of the Confederation was not carried out without difficulty and the Constitution of 1848, which was established after several threats of secession by the Roman Catholic Cantons, and revised in 1874, defined the political organization which is still in force today.

Archives

The cantonal structure of Switzerland is reflected in the way its records are kept, there being no central organization or National Archives as in other countries. Before 1848, civil registration was a matter for each canton, with the result that the date for the beginning of registration differs from canton to canton. Since 1876 registration of vital statistics has been by the civil authorities; before that date it was the responsibility of the Church.

The Swiss system of civil registration records the date of birth, marriage, death, divorce or nullity of marriage, particulars of the children, change of place of abode. Access to these records is reserved to officials, though permission can be granted to private persons to consult the registers. Extracts can be made by officials on request and payment of a fee. Old church records have mostly been handed over to the state authorities.

There is a Swiss Heraldic Society (Schweizerische Heraldische Gesellschaft – Sociéte Suisse d'Héraldique) Zwinglistrasse 28, St-Gall.

Although there are no official heralds in Switzerland, it is necessary for anyone using arms to register them in the town archives.

Cantonal records

Cantonal records are to be found at the Headquarters of the Police, the departments of Communal affairs of the Chancelleries of each canton. The titles vary from canton to canton, so the simplest thing to do is to write to the head of the relevant department. The following is a list of the relevant department in each canton:

Appenzell – Gouvernement du canton. R.Ext.
Aargau – Direction de la Justice du canton
Basel – Département de la Justice du canton de Bâle-Ville
Liestal – Direction de la Justice du canton de Bâle-Campagne
Berne – Direction de la Police
Fribourg – Département de la Justice
Geneva – Département de la Justice et de la Police
Glarus – Chancellerie d'État du canton
Grisons – Département de l'Intérieur du canton des Grisons
Lucerne – Département des Affaires Communales du canton
Neuchatel – Département de la Justice
St-Gallen – Département de l'Intérieur
Schaffhausen – Direction des Affaires Communales
Schwyz – Département de l'Intérieur
Solothurn – Département de la Justice
Ticino – Département de l'Intérieur
Thurgau – Inspectorat de l'État Civil
Unterwalden – Chancellerie d'État du canton de Obwald, Sarnen
             – Chancellerie d'État du canton de Nidwald, Stans
Uri – Direction de la Justice
Valais – Département de la Justice
Vaud – Département de la Justice et Police
Zug – Direction de l'Intérieur
Zurich – Direction de l'Intérieur.

These supervisory authorities give their subordinate offices the authority to supply information when they cannot do so themselves. Under a Law of 1953 private individuals have no right to consult the registers of the état civil but only supervisory authorities and the tribunals have the right to consult them. The cantonal authority can, if it considers the request justified, give the right to other authorities and sometimes to private individuals. Article 138 of this law allows officials to give the following extracts from registers:

1 Special registers: births, deaths, marriages, legitimations and recognitions.

2 Registers of families: family deeds and certificates of civil status. People can obtain extracts from registers that concern them personally; apart from this, extracts are only given to relatives by blood or adoption, or to persons who can justify a direct interest, to a guardian or his or her appointee. As for ecclesiastical records, many still exist. In 1876, civil registers were introduced for the whole country and where church records have been deposited with the cantonal authorities, permission to examine them must be sought at the addresses given above. In general, genealogical research in Switzerland is not easy, and it is almost always necessary to consult an expert before attempting to embark upon it.

Liechtenstein

Liechtenstein is an independent principality of sixty-five square miles on the Upper Rhine between Vorarlberg (Austria) and Switzerland.

Two fiefs of the Holy Roman Empire, Schellenberg and Vaduz, were purchased in 1699 and 1712 by Prince Johann Adam of Liechtenstein, an Austrian noble, and the new territory recognized as an independent hereditary state by the Emperor Charles VI in 1719.

Church records are kept in the parishes and begin around 1640. Civil registration was introduced in 1878. Wills are proved in the principality's law court.

Genealogical enquiries should be made to:
Kanzlei der Regierung des Fürstentums,
Vaduz,
Liechtenstein.

6

Italy

❦

Surnames

Generally speaking Italian surnames derive from Roman sources, but the ancient custom of praenomen, nomen, cognomen and agnomen died out during the Dark Ages, and it was not until the tenth century, in Venice, that hereditary surnames once more began to come back into use.

The origins of surnames are sometimes easy and sometimes difficult to establish. They are, however, basically of ten different kinds in Italy. 1 *Surnames deriving from the father's name.* One of the most usual methods in the middle ages to distinguish a person was to cite his name followed by the name of his father. Thus: Antonius (*filius*) Petri, and Jacobus (*filius*) Gualterii. From these, the surnames Petri and Gualterii have been derived. Sometimes the word *filius* was itself incorporated into the surname. Thus: Filipetri, Filiperi, Filidolfi, Fililangeri, etc. Sometimes the father's name was preceded by the title *Ser*, thus producing such names as Serantoni, Sergiovanni, etc.
2 *Surnames deriving from the mother's name.* It is possible to distinguish certain names which derive from the mother. For example, d'Anna, d'Isa.
3 *Surnames deriving from the brother's name.* Some names are derived from brothers, for example Antonius frater Joannis, Frater Castorii, from which Fraggianni and Frascatori are derived.
4 *Names deriving from offices or titles.* Many surnames are derived from offices or titles of the more illustrious or more ancient members of a family. For example, Abati (abbot), Consoli (consul), Guidici (judge), Siniscalchi (seneschal), Conti (count), Baroni (baron), Marchesi (marquis), Capitani (captain), and so forth.
5 *Names deriving from professions and trades.* Names such as Maestri (master), Notari (notary), Fabbri (smith), Calzolai (shoemaker), Medici (doctor), Orefici (goldsmith) are self-explanatory.

Map 12. Italy.

6 *Names deriving from places or from the country of origin*. The custom of describing a person by his place of origin is very ancient and common. Thus one finds names such as Lombardi, Veneziani, Puglisi, Romani, Castiglioni, Trevisani, Pisani, Samminiati, Fiorentini, Veronesi, etc.

7 *Names deriving from feudal fiefs*. These are perhaps the most ancient surnames in Italy, because they refer to the ancient feudal families. Among these are Savoia, Spilimbergo, Colloredo, Acquaviva, Sanseverino, etc.

8 *Names deriving from topographical regions*. This very large category of surnames derives from places near which the family may have lived. For example, castles, churches, country districts, towns and rivers. It includes such names as Boschi (wood), Campi (field), Dalla Chiesa (church), Dalle Vigne (vineyard), Di Poggio (hill), Del Pozzo (well), Della Porta (gate).

9 *Names deriving from plants and animals*. Some families took names derived from plants and animals because they had taken their fancy. For example Peri (pears), Oliva (olives), Allori (laurel), Olmi (elm tree), Palma, Castagna (chestnut), Meli (apple) Leoni (lion), Cicogna (stork), etc.

10 *Names deriving from nicknames*. This is possibly the largest category of surnames and relates to particular actions, events or characteristics of the founder of the family. Such names include Buoncompagni (good companion), Buoncore (warm-hearted), Malatesta (literally sick-head), Mezzacapo (half-head), Quattromani (four-hands), Belli (beautiful), Gambacorta (short-legs), Arditi (ardent), Afflitto (afflicted), Clementi (merciful), Selvaggi (savage) and so on.

These are just a few examples of the commonest origins of Italian surnames. There are many other cases of corruptions, alterations and superimposition as well as many surnames deriving from Greek, Hebrew, Norman, Lombard, Gothic and German sources.

Some authorities believe that the use of surnames was definitely fixed for more modest families by the fifteenth century, though even as late as the sixteenth century many families did not have fixed surnames. The study of many parish registers of the sixteenth and early seventeenth centuries, will show that the births, marriages and burials of many individuals, especially in country districts, were entered with the single name of the father. The use of surnames developed during the centuries without any particular legislation and through the uninterrupted usage of the family concerned. With the institution of civil registration and the laws governing it the use of proper names and surnames has had a particular legal significance. Everyone has in effect the right to his own name and family surname, which is his own property and carries with it special rights and duties. The right to a name and surname and the right to keep it is regulated by articles 6, 7 and 8 of the civil law (Codice Civile). Changes, additions and corrections to surnames are governed by the Decree no. 1238 of 9 July 1939.

According to Italian law, any person has an absolute right to a name and surname. Changes, additions and alterations to names and surnames are not allowed without the formality of legal proceedings. If the right to the use of the surname is challenged, or if anyone is accused of damaging a family by using the surname of another, he has the right in law to defend this usage against the person who takes his name. As we have seen, the surname is no more than the legitimated usage of a simple right dating from antiquity. It is, however, also a piece of property codified and based on official documents having precise rights and duties linked to it. Because the characteristics of surnames are thus established, it follows that this is essential to genealogy, which is based on the study of surnames, and on the divisions of clans and families based upon surnames.

Church archives

The records of the Church are of course of fundamental importance in genealogical research. The Church is the only institution which has remained intact from its foundation to the present day, while the greatest political organizations have been supplanted and changed many times over. Church organization in Italy, as elsewhere in Europe, is based on the parish and the diocese. The bishops, who from the beginning of the Church's history, were the supreme governors of the diocese, soon became aware that they were not able to cater for the ever-growing spiritual needs of the faithful, and were therefore obliged to appoint missionary priests in both town and country to undertake the duties which they would otherwise have done themselves, especially in places where there were no resident bishops. From this beginning sprang the parish system. It is impossible to say exactly when Italian parishes were first established, but probably towards the end of the third century. As the centuries passed, there were great changes of organization within the Church, and the diocesan and episcopal institutions were developed as we see them today. The principal duties of the parish priest were to administer the sacraments of baptism, marriage and extreme unction. It is well known that in both Catholic and Protestant countries the citizens were obliged to follow the religion of the head of state in order to guarantee political continuity and security. To be the citizen of a state and to follow the religion of that state was one and the same thing. The parish priest, therefore, in baptizing and

54

celebrating marriages, was not only the representative of the Church but also of the state; thus in time he came to assume the role of registrar. This role was performed by the parish priest up to the French Revolution, at which time the union of Church and state was broken, after which the functions and attributes of the registrar were entrusted to the commune. This change came about naturally and by degrees between 1700 and 1870.

In the first centuries of the Church and throughout the Middle Ages, there are no records of the administration of baptism or marriage celebrated in the various parishes. It is only at the beginning of the fifteenth century (and then very exceptionally at first) that some parish priests, especially in the bigger urban parishes, felt the need to record in a particular register the administration of the sacraments. One of the most ancient registers – indeed perhaps the most ancient in Italy – is to be found in the archives of the parish of San Nicola in Guardiagrele (Chieti), and contains births, marriages and deaths beginning in the fourteenth century. In the diocesan archives of Fiesole, the baptismal registers of the parish of San Lorenzo a Diacceto begin in 1443. In Florence, in the archives of baptism, the most ancient register begins in 1425.

The Council of Trent, at its 24th Session on the 11 November 1563 established the canons of the Catholic doctrine of the sacrament of marriage and at its 25th Session on the 3 and 4 December 1563 ordered the institution of archives in each church to conserve the records, and especially in the parochial archives, the registration of baptisms, marriages and deaths of all Christians.

The most important parish book is the Status Animarum (Condition of Souls): 'Curae animarum Praefecti debent in primis, quemadmodum Tridentina Synodus docet (Sess. XXII, De reform, cap I) oves suas agnoscere, non solum in genere, quoad in earum numerum, sed in specie familias singulas.' The Liber Baptizatorum or book of baptisms, is that in which the names of all those who were baptized in church were recorded, together with the names of their godparents, and if they were born legally in wedlock, that of their father, together with the month and year of their baptism. The Liber Matrimoniorum, or marriage book, was to be established in order that those who contracted a marriage in a parish might do it publicly, so that there could be no doubts about it, and so that the faithful who contracted the marriage could have their names recorded in such a book. The Liber Defunctorum, or burial book, is that in which the deaths occurring in a parish were recorded. There was also the Liber Confirmatorum, or confirmation book, in which confirmations administered by the bishop are recorded. These record the name and surname of the person being confirmed, and the parish of the father and mother. Finally, there are the files of Marriage Allegations, that is to say, all those documents which it was necessary to produce in order to contract a marriage, especially if those who were parties to it came from different parishes. These have not always been preserved. Parish archives have in addition a number of other files and registers, such as inventories, donations, legacies, benefices and masses, etc.

As we have seen, the parochial registers are of great value not only in spiritual but also in lay terms. Amongst ecclesiastical archives are the Archivi Capitolari (Church archives), Monastici (monastic archives), Seminarili (seminary archives), which have great importance historically but are less important for genealogical research.

The archives of the episcopal court contain a great many records relating to parishes which have been either suppressed or abandoned, but whose archives or part of them have been amalgamated for various reasons in other diocesan archives. Often the archives of a parish are found partly in the parish itself and partly in the Diocesan court, and sometimes in the state registry or in the communal archives to which they came at different periods and for various reasons, mainly at the time of the formation of the state registry, when a good many parochial registers were transferred to the communal archives and finally handed over to the National Archives. A typical example of these transfers are the archives of Umbria where the parishes and the curie have hardly anything left of their registers which are deposited in the commune or in the National Archives.

In 1933 an Italian committee was established to study population problems, and a Commission for Historical Demography, which published an important list entitled *Archival Sources for the Study of Population Problems since 1848*, on the occasion of the International Congress for the Study of Population in 1933. A second edition was published in 1939/40. This is a very important work in which many leading historians collaborated, and the whole edition was published in eleven volumes. This lists a great many parochial archives of the major urban centres; unfortunately the war interrupted the work, which has not yet been resumed.

A full list of Italian parishes is published in the *Annuario delle Diocesi d'Italia* (Editore Marietti, Turin 1951), which describes the dioceses or episcopal seats (of which there are at least 280), and their division into parishes (amounting to about 25,000). This publication gives a description of each parish, and its year of foundation.

The Archivio di Stato exists in every major town and preserves all the documents concerning life and affairs of the population of the province or of the region. The Archivio Centrale dello Stato is in Rome and is concerned with matters of national importance.

Notarial records

Not less important than the Church archives for genealogical purposes are the civil archives, the most important of which are notarial records. Notaries first took on a precise character and definition in the twelfth century: 'Officium publicum quo varia hominum negotia, diversique actus, in publicam et authenticam forman scripti rediguntur atque ita plena dignaque fide a perpetuam posteriorum memoriam referuntur.' One cannot, however, consider the person of the notary apart from his archive. From the thirteenth century legislation of Italian communes was designed to ensure the conservation of all notarial acts. As each notary took over from his predecessor, the records gradually accumulated in private notarial offices. It was finally decreed that these should be deposited in special archives. After the unification of Italy, equal attention was paid to these records, although the laws under which they were deposited in central record offices differed from one commune or state to another. The new law of 17 May 1952, no. 629, art. 3 provides for the compulsory depositing of all notarial acts older than 100 years in the National Archives. This law is being implemented today with increasing effect. The importance of notarial acts for genealogical studies cannot be too highly emphasized.

Notarial acts often go back to 1200 or 1300, and permit studies to be undertaken as far back as this period. This would otherwise be difficult from a documentary point of view, and the homogeneity of the acts, drawn up in the same place by the same notary (in general by a man who was known to the family and to whom they could turn) often enables a search to be properly located and profitably developed. Purchases, sales, wills, and all other notarial acts allow genealogical research to be carried out from original documents, with an abundance of detailed historical and biographical information. Unfortunately such acts obviously only exist for those families who had property. For those who had none, it was difficult, if not impossible, to contract notarial acts, and for this reason it is inevitably necessary to confine one's research solely to parish records to find information about them.

National Archives

The National Archives contain an inexhaustible source of material for genealogists. There are not only the notarial records, in which are found all the documents relating to state property brought together from the individual states which existed before unification, but also those of the Signorie (city councils), principalities and communes.

With the unification of Italy, a commission was entrusted with the business of reorganizing all the various collections of archival material and to organize the National Archives of the Italian state. Out of the 17 state archives and 20 provincial archives which existed in 1875, by 1950 there were 60 archives and sections of archives, and it is proposed to institute sections of the National Archives in every provincial capital. The immense amount of material of such a varied nature preserved in these archives cannot be examined in detail, but of course they provide the most prolific sources for genealogical studies. The most obvious consist of parish registers, civil registers, levies, notarial acts, statements of income, censuses, licences of various sorts, contracts, professions and trades, colleges, registers of landed property, communal archives, administration records, taxes, hearth tax returns, feudal dues, family archives and many other kinds of miscellaneous documents.

Local archives

Communal archives are extremely interesting genealogical sources, and go back to the thirteenth century. Following the unification of Italy, various laws were passed culminating in the law of 1939 which is intended to establish the preservation of communal archives nation-wide. Of particular interest is the obligation to make inventories of material, one copy of which is to be deposited in the National Archives. Communal archives often contain, besides documentary material of their own, notarial archives and the files of notaries, parochial archives or part of them, judicial acts, acts of the corporation, and other documents of various regions within the jurisdiction of the commune itself. All these documents are of genealogical value, but they are often overlooked because of the lack of information about them, and because no guides or lists exist.

The Napoleonic conquest of Europe spread French ordinances and laws to every country, especially to Italy, Belgium, Holland and parts of Germany. The regulations of the Code Napoleon in matters of civil registration were applied by the new governments, who set up provincial registrar's offices and central offices for general registration. Parish priests continued to register baptisms, marriages, extreme unction and religious burials. There arose, therefore, a clear division between the registrar as a government servant and layman and the parish priest, whose registrations were those concerning the administration of the sacraments of baptism, marriage, extreme unction and of religious burial. This division of function between civil and religious authorities is the one which exists in Italy today.

The decree of 9 July 1939, no. 1238 lays down all the regulations concerning the registrar as well as the office and officials of the registry, the general rules relative to the register and deeds, what documents must be returned, how the deeds must be drawn up, how registers of citizenship, births, marriages and deaths are to be maintained, how civil marriage is to be celebrated, what the rules are for obtaining changes, additions or alterations to names and surnames, what authority is proposed for the periodical checking of registers, and how extracts of acts and the relevant certificates may be obtained.

The law of 31 October 1955, no. 1064 makes certain arrangements relative to the details of personal identification, short certificates, deeds and other documents, and modifications to the regulations regarding the registry and provides for the omission of paternity and maternity in these extracts and certificates and any other identity documents, by simply indicating the place and date of birth. It is obvious that the original deed drawn up by the official of the central registry will carry all the full information. The decree of 2 May 1957, no. 432 puts into effect all the foregoing legislation.

It is clear that the importance of the registrar and the relevant archives cannot be overstressed. In Tuscany, for example, there is a complete set of records beginning in 1806 preserved in the State Archives of Florence up to 1866, and at the commune for the succeeding period. In the regions which formed the ancient kingdom of Naples and Sicily, the State Archives contain the old archives of the communal registers from about 1806 to 1860 or 1870.

After the unification of Italy, the task of keeping the office of the registrar up to date was entrusted to the individual communes, who run them today. According to the *Annuario Generale dei Comuni e Frazioni d'Italia*, edited by the Touring Club of Italy (Milan 1968), there are 92 provincial capitals, and each province is divided into communes, of which there are 8,054 altogether. In their turn the communes are divided into frazioni, or hamlets. At present the territorial division of Church and State Archives do not always coincide, but normally each provincial capital is the seat of a bishop, with the relevant archives. In the communes, there are often one or more parishes, and often each hamlet (frazione) of a commune corresponds to a parish.

Jewish and Protestant archives

The presence of Jews in every Italian city witnesses to the fact of their persecution and expulsion from other countries. These Jews founded flourishing settlements in the cities, where they dedicated their lives to commerce and banking. There they followed strictly the customs, dress and religion of their race, and lived separately from the rest of the community. During the Dark Ages, when there were numerous persecutions, the Jews migrated to several cities in southern Italy and even to Rome, from where they were expelled in the sixteenth century. There was a large immigration of Jews from Spain where they had enjoyed greater liberty, and where they had come over the centuries to occupy important positions in various courts. Leghorn was the first Italian city to receive a large number of these immigrants, and they founded a community there with its own cemetery, but kept themselves apart from the other Jews, regarding themselves as somewhat superior and proud of their past greatness in Spain. Later there was an influx of Jews in the north of Italy from Germany and France, the former settling in Veneto and Piedmont and the latter in Piedmont only. These German Jews founded their own communities, so it is not uncommon to find synagogues following German, Spanish and Italian rites in different Italian cities.

The registers in which Rabbis entered births, marriages and deaths have found their way into the archives of the Jewish community. Registration however, is gappy for a number of reasons. Further difficulties in the way of finding Italian-Jewish certificates before 1870 are due to the destruction of the archives following the politico-religious persecutions and expulsions of the Jews as a whole. Also the events of World War II have contributed to the destruction of a great part of what remained of the archives of the Italian Jewish community. The genealogical documentation of Jewish families in Italy is therefore very difficult, and it is seldom possible to go back many generations.

Apart from the Jews, there are few non-Catholic communities in Italy. The most important without doubt is the Waldensian, the oldest Protestant sect in the world, whose original nucleus was in Piedmont in the region known as the Valli Valdesi. This consists of three large valleys, the Pellice, Chisone and Germanasca, and a number of smaller valleys. Its chief town was Torre Pellice, which the writer De Amicis has called 'The Italian Geneva', and which was the moral and intellectual capital of the 'Popolo Valdese'. The official buildings of the Waldensian Church are there, among them the archives and the central administration of the Church.

There are small Waldensian communities in Florence, Genoa, Trieste,

Pola, Venice and in some cities of Apulia and Sicily, but they are insignificant in size.

There are tiny Greek Orthodox communities in some of the cities of the ancient Magna Graecia and in Sicily, but they are very few in number. Of more recent formation is the Greek Orthodox community at Leghorn and in other Italian seaports, made up of people who have come over from the Balkans and the Greek Islands to trade.

Nobility

By the end of the ninth century the feudal system was firmly established. Bishops and lay fiefs or feudatories and groups of nobles had by means of barter and purchase, usurpation of feudal homages and burdensome donations gradually eliminated the lesser landowners who interrupted the continuity of their scattered lands, and had extended their own jurisdiction over them to make sovereign states of their own possessions. Royal grants made their appearance in the tenth and eleventh centuries when this work of consolidation was complete, and likewise saw the height of feudal power. In the twelfth century the need became apparent to give authority to certain customs which until that time had been the way in which the nation was governed, and Italy provided the first example of the compilation of feudal usage. This collection contains the rules of succession, rights and duties of sovereigns and feudatories, and matters which had until then been regulated by the particular custom of each kingdom and each city. It became in effect a kind of compromise between lords and sovereign.

The feudal contract gave birth to new links, modifying the political relationship between king and subject. The latter now no longer depended solely on the king, but on the feudatories, who were themselves only subject to the king. There were indeed grades, from the minor tenants or 'valvasini', who depended on the middling tenantry or 'valvassores', who in their turn depended upon the 'valvassores maiores' or 'capitanei', who alone depended directly upon the king, who alone was sovereign. The investiture of feudal rights transferred many functions to the tenants such as the administration of major and petty justice, the levying of taxes, the monopoly of water and mining, the right to mint coins, a seat in parliament, privilege to be judged in the court of peers. All this was in exchange for military service and contributions to the costs of the state. Within the boundaries of the fief, the lord maintained himself as a sovereign; there his word was law. His grant gave him all the prerogatives of public authority and the term feudatory became synonymous with the term sovereign.

In this way the nation split into many autonomous states of varying size, characterized and held together by the feudal contract. It was in this way that the feudal state arose, at whose head stood the king, a nominal and ineffective chief, because he did not have the strength to impose his authority on his vassals who exercised full control in their own feudal territories.

The ancient monarchy of Piedmont was feudally based; in Lombardy, Friuli, Veneto and Tuscany feudalism developed vigorously. In the Papal States until the ninth century the Roman nobility acquired power and received benefices from the Popes, but after that considered themselves true lords in their own right. In southern Italy, where the domains of the Longobard dukes were extensive, the growth of the fief was no different from what had occurred in the north. With the Norman conquest, the chiefs divided the territories among themselves, each considering himself sovereign in his own land, only subject to the overriding sovereignty of Duke Robert, to whom they swore fealty for the performance of military service. When then the Norman dukes conquered Sicily they made the same distribution of land, instituting there lay and ecclesiastical fiefs. In Sardinia, on the other hand, feudalism arose spontaneously, as in neighbouring Corsica, and consisted in the transfer of part of the public authority into private hands, and in the investing of rich land owners and ecclesiastics with the rights of administering justice.

The weakening imperial authority meant the decline of the Holy Roman Empire in Italy, and encouraged the rise in central and northern Italy of small and medium size states and independent cities, while a powerful monarchy flourished in the south.

But while the small fief was in the ascendant and was organizing itself politically, another force arose. The peasants themselves, starved of land and liberty, combined together and then rebelled. A profound change in the agrarian economy was set in motion among the disturbed rural population. Thus there began in the eleventh century written agreements with the barons fixing the quality and quantity of dues, and changing into ready money the rents which had hitherto been in produce. We are here at the start of the money economy, and can see the fief becoming freehold, barren uncultivated land brought under perpetual leases, the rights of usage becoming the rights of co-ownership of lands hitherto called common land. The free contracts led to greater prosperity: the small feudatories having more money to spend betook themselves to the cities where the count or bishop resided, and where the emperor stopped on his Italian progresses. The cities were attractive to these people, and they ended by transplanting themselves, some selling, others keeping their own old feudal lands and castles. They took part in the cities in those politico-religious movements which disturbed the cities in the eleventh century. They also took part in the election of bishops of whom they were nominally vassals. They made up the 'Curia Vassalorum' which dealt with the bishops as equals, and which formed the council for feudal questions, giving or refusing its own consent to the edicts of the episcopal family, passing judgments in lawsuits amongst equals, taking part alongside the original citizens in local disputes between the bishops of neighbouring dioceses or between the bishops and counts and great lay feudatories.

This movement enabled the peasants to acquire their freedom, for the small feudatories swarmed to the urban centres where they built their houses and towers. The towns were thus enriched with new forces and benefited by the influx of new money, thus becoming more and more different from the surrounding countryside, and placing themselves at the head of every movement against the past.

The commune materialized above all the work of the feudal middle class, which in the twelfth century led it to almost unrivalled heights. The commune took on many different forms, and coloured the political history of Italy, having no parallel elsewhere. Its variety was extraordinary, as well as its physical structure and the diversity of its social elements. In the same way the urban nobility, like the feudal nobility, found its origins in the exercise of sovereign rights. The concept of a civic patriciate, defined as a body or class of families whose members took part by inherited rights in the civic magistracy developed alongside the rise of free communes. The class of noble citizens came to constitute a privileged caste which tended according to time and circumstances to concentrate power in its own hands. This led to the formation in the communes of closed lists of families from among whom only councillors could be chosen, that is to say, the rulers of the civic government, families which alone enjoyed civil nobility and which became hereditary. In addition to this clique of noble citizens which did not admit outsiders, and which are only found in some cities, there existed in other communes a more open noble body to which recruits could be added by the deliberate acts of the councils or by the decree of the prince. Thus, while special conditions of time and circumstance induced the patriciate of certain cities to keep itself in splendid isolation, in others the classes of patrician families, united by the chains of common interest and often at odds among themselves for supremacy, allowed the opportunity within their own framework for the appearance of new elements. These newly admitted people were not necessarily their kinsmen, and the union of the old and new patricians did not always come about peacefully, but often following bitter struggles. These feuds signed the death warrant of the ancient nobility, and from their ashes a new nobility arose, that of the magnates who took the government of the Italian cities into their hands. This new class owed nothing to the blood of the former nobility, but excelled uniquely with its wealth in commerce and by the splendour of its arms and escutcheons and flags over its palaces, imitating in its dress the ancient nobility with whom it sought links of kinship in marriage, assumed public power in cities, and became their ruling class. It established the class of the aristocracy or gentry, opposed to the party of the people or the plebs. It established a new nobility, the civic patriciate, a privileged class, whose descendants are even now flourishing.

Titles in use in Italy are nobile, patrizio, barone (baron), conte (count), marchese (marquis), duca (duke) and principe (prince). They can be used with or without a predicate if the family had a fief and the title was granted with the fief. Today the nobility does not constitute a particular caste in accordance with Article 14 of the Provisional and Final Drafts of the Constitution of the Italian Republic of 1946, which says

Titles of nobility are not recognized. The 'Predicate' of those existing before the 23 October 1922 are valid as part of the name.
The Maurician Order is preserved as a hospital body, and functions in the way laid down by law. The law controls the suppression of the heraldic Consulta.

Titles of nobility therefore are not recognized officially by the Italian state, but are freely used by the families who have the traditional rights to them. There has been recently published the *Libro d'Oro della Nobiltá Italiana*, edited by the Heraldic College of Rome, which started this publication in 1910, and it is still being kept up-to-date.

Heraldry

It would be wrong to think that the insignia of gentility were exclusively the distinction of the nobility in Italy. In fact, if all those invested with a title of nobility had the right to arms, there are others entitled to them who have no title. Doubtless those men-at-arms or the founders of really noble houses were the first to adorn their shields with those emblems which later became hereditary, and served to distinguish their families, but it is no less true that in due course the civic nobility known as the 'nobiltá di toga' arose, which when they became a clearly defined social and political class, assumed the prerogatives of the nobility of the sword, 'nobiltá di spada'. Thus on the tombs of doctors and judges are carved arms such as one finds on those of knights of old. There are, furthermore, the arms due to ecclesiastical dignitaries (cardinals, archbishops, bishops, abbots and prelates) according to the customary usages and internal dispositions of the Church. There are also arms of citizenship, 'stemmi di cittadinanza', given to non-noble families, as a sign of courtesy. It must also be remembered that provinces, communes, political organizations, military units, are every day being granted arms, banners and standards by the Republican regime.

As regards the regulation of the right to arms, it is clear that it will be possible to carry this on in a civilized way only if it is governed by the same rules as those governing the rights to names and other personal rights. Before the Republican Constitution, the wrongful use of a coat-of-arms fell into the same category as the false assumption of a title of nobility. Today this is no longer the case.

7

Spain

General registration

General registration was introduced in Spain on 1 January 1870. Registry offices are situated in the municipal courts of those towns which have them, and in administrative and regional capitals and in foreign consulates for the registration of Spaniards born, married or dying abroad. Civil registers are in the custody of the respective judge or consul, and certificates of the records contained in their books are issued by the respective secretaries with the approval of those authorities. Birth certificates give the name and sex, place, date and hour of birth, name and surnames, nationality, age, abode and profession of parents, name and surnames, nationality and abode of paternal and maternal grandparents.

Marriage certificates give the names and surnames, age, nationality, abode and profession of both parties and of their parents, likewise place and date of marriage. Death certificates give the name, surnames, nationality, age, status, abode and profession of the deceased, and the place, date, hour and cause of death, including likewise the names and surnames of the parents of the deceased and of his or her spouse and children if they had any. In most cases registers are kept up to date and few have been destroyed.

Censuses

There have been many general censuses in Spain, the first of them being for the recruitment of nobles ordered by the Catholic monarchs for the War of Granada. Many of these have been lost or destroyed, and many contain little information of a genealogical nature. The only one of genealogical interest is that known by the name of the land census of the Marqués de la Ensenada, carried out between 1750 and

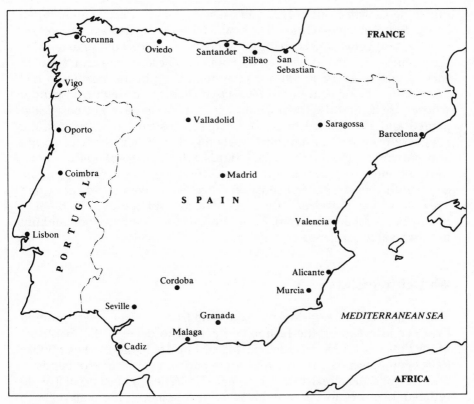

Map 13. Spain and Portugal.

1752. Its aims were primarily fiscal, but it did set out whether the individuals were noble or plebian. Three copies were taken, one of which was kept in the town hall, another was transferred to central administration of the respective provincial capital, and the third was earmarked for study and retained by the central services of the royal treasury. The first of these copies is still preserved in the corresponding municipal archives. The second is generally to be found in the local treasury offices of the provincial historical archives of each provincial capital, depending upon the circumstances; and the third was destroyed during the Civil War. The principal interest of the Ensenada land census, which is fundamental for the economic history of Spain, is due to the entries concerning laymen, giving date, age, social status and profession of all Spaniards living in the middle of the eighteenth century. The state of preservation and cataloguing is indifferent, and varies considerably from one area to another. In the general archives of Simancas there is another fiscal census less complete than the one just

67

mentioned, carried out in 1737 and preserved in the department known as the State Incomes Office (Dirección General de Rentas). Important censuses for genealogists are those which were carried out to determine the exemptions and privileges of nobility. These were carried out in each township every so often, a copy remaining in the local town hall and another being sent to the respective chancery or high court under whose jurisdiction the town came. Many of these have not been catalogued and are difficult to consult. These censuses, at least since the eighteenth century, group individuals together in families with names and surnames, giving the social status which corresponds to them. Most of those concerned were noble. From the last quarter of the eighteenth century general censuses have been taken in Spain, at first irregularly, but more recently every decade, but the data in them is mainly concerned with demographic and statistical information and not of much value for genealogists.

Church registers

The earliest church registers in Spain date from 1426 and were ordered by a synod called by the Bishop of León, who decreed that baptisms of all the faithful be recorded in his bishopric. None of these books have been preserved, although in some parishes certificates of baptism, marriage and death exist from the year 1500. The Archbishop of Toledo ordered registers to be kept in 1496, and some of these have been preserved, together with those of the parish of San Ginés in Madrid. Generally speaking, parish registers did not come in until after the Council of Trent (1560–3); most of them are complete, but the majority start from about 1650. Parish registers are in the care of parish priests who are responsible for issuing certificates from the entries contained in them. Parish registers in Spain consist of baptismal books in which the date of the ceremony, the names and first surnames of those being baptized and their parents are entered. In baptismal certificates written out since the middle of the seventeenth century, the names and surnames of paternal and maternal grandparents are also entered. Later, nationalities, abodes and professions were included. Parents, grandparents, godparents and witnesses are also included, but the degree of detail varies considerably according to the instructions issued by the bishop or the conscientiousness of the parish priest. Marriage books generally show the name and surnames of the couple and those of their parents; likewise the date. They become progressively more complete as time goes on. Burial registers only gave the name and surname of the deceased to begin with, but gradually the names and surnames of parents, spouses and children were entered, as was the place of burial, and in many regions whether or not the deceased had made a will, and even the town clerk or notary before whom he had made it, as well as the cause of death. Confirmation books are generally incomplete. They contain the names and surnames of the child confirmed and of his parents. These normally date from the beginning of the eighteenth century. The state of preservation varies from parish to parish. Fire, war, revolution and negligence have done their damage.

Cathedral archives

It was formerly necessary for anybody employed by Catholic chapters to prove non-Moorish, non-Jewish descent, and to show that they were not descended from heretics or those who had undergone penance on the instigation of the Inquisition. Consequently it was usual to preserve records of purity of blood of the canons of the cathedrals, incumbents, and such laymen who undertook specific work for the chapter. These proofs were required from the mid-sixteenth century to the middle of the nineteenth century. The records assemble the chief information about the person concerned, his grandparents and parents, and in some instances his great-grandparents and other relations. Most of these documents are of outstanding importance for genealogical research, especially as regards the regional nobility. The archives of León Cathedral are especially important, since they concern about 1,000 canons, incumbents, priests and lay employees. Other cathedral archives contain information going back to the Middle Ages, with particulars of tombs and cartularies, together with copies of the books of anniversaries and deaths. These are particularly important for the study of the genealogies of the great noble families between the ninth and fourteenth centuries. These archives are usually in charge of one of the canons of the cathedral chapter.

Diocesan archives

Diocesan archives are usually in the charge of a diocesan archivist. They contain marriage records of those marrying outside the diocese or when marriage required ecclesiastical dispensation. The records usually contain baptismal certificates of those marrying, and of their parents, and sometimes other documents of a genealogical nature. Diocesan archives also contain particulars concerning glebes, church livings and benefices, lawsuits concerning chaplaincies. The state of preservation and indexing differs greatly from diocese to diocese. There has recently been an episcopal conference to standardize indexing.

Some of these archives contain important information from the Middle Ages referring to nunneries suppressed by the First Republic.

Land records

Notarial records such as books in which the originals of wills, marriage settlements and other private docments were collected together were looked after in each place by the successive notaries who followed each other in office. Charles II ordered the calling-in of the most important of these books and required them to be preserved in the town halls of the principal cities and towns. In 1701 Philip V issued a further decree, and the Notaries Law of 1862 stated that the books or protocols belonging to the state should be lodged in the provincial capitals provided they were more than thirty years old. Individual decrees in 1931 and 1939 ordered the moving of the protocols of more than a hundred years old to the provincial capitals in order to create special archives for them. None of these orders was carried out very strictly, and those records which are preserved today can be found in provincial historical archives or in the care of the notaries of the first petition judges in the district capitals, where generally, through lack of the most elementary classification, they are extremely difficult to consult. The oldest are preserved in the territories which formed parts of the kingdom of León and Castile, and begin in the last quarter of the fifteenth century, and those in the kingdom of Aragón where they were conserved much better, in the middle of the fourteenth century.

Legal records of the civil courts

For the genealogical study of noble families belonging to the minor nobility, the numerous records preserved in the archives of the two chanceries of Valladolid and Granada are the most important. The jurisdiction of the first extended to all territories which made up part of the kingdom of León and Castile, including the domain of Biscay which were to the north of the River Tagus, and that of the second to those territories south of the Tagus. Because the nobles enjoyed certain privileges and taxation exemptions, the most interesting type of process from a genealogical point of view are those of a litigious administrative nature in which the noble status of an individual was debated. This required a great deal of genealogical information in support of each case. These records are well preserved and catalogued, and date from the mid-sixteenth century to the mid-nineteenth century. There are similar records for Aragón and Navarre in the archives of the royal high courts of both kingdoms. However, the first of these suffered irreparable losses during the Napoleonic Wars during the siege of Saragossa, but their absence can in part be made good through the information that the archives of the council of Saragossa provide through the lawsuits of entitlement to the lower ranks of nobility preserved in them.

Nobility

The present system of Spanish nobility originates from the early days of the Reconquest up to 1715, when a small number of Visigoth and Hispano-Roman people took refuge in the Asturian-Leónese mountains, which were in those days very sparsely populated. Others took refuge in the mountainous districts of Navarre and Aragón. The descendants of these Gothic nobles were at first of the same social rank, but they soon became diversified by obtaining court positions or acquiring territorial duties, or by being granted lands by the king. When the lands thus acquired were protected by the king in consideration of the various services of their proprietors, the feudal estates of the kingdoms of León and Castile came into being. Other nobles were favoured by the king with grants of tenancies or 'condado' (counties) over certain areas or provinces. In return for these tenancies they were expected to carry out the administration of justice on behalf of the king, and these were retained throughout several generations within one family in fact, though not always in law.

Fray Prudencio de Sandoval, in his *Historia de San Millan*, records the granting of such privileges as early as 903, and comes to the conclusion that society at the end of the Asturian monarchy consisted of the king, the counts (conde) and potentates or potestades, the lower nobility and the peasants or commoners. The titles of conde and protestade at that remote era were no more than a reference to the posts which conferred a higher personal rank on their holders. There did not appear to be an aristocracy of blood. The accumulation of lands or domains in one single family and the continuous occupation of tenancies by their most outstanding members for many generations, together with the distribution to those very people of large territories in New Castile and Andalucia from the twelfth and thirteenth centuries as a reward for their support during the Reconquest of Spain from the Moors accounts for the rise of the so-called grandees (ricoshombres). These were the most important noblemen who were able to supply considerable armed retinues in support of the king. Some of these were even as large as the royal army itself. These ricoshombres had the right to fly their own standards or flags.

In the fourteenth century the titles of conde, duque, marqués and vizconde were granted for the first time and made hereditary through primogeniture and by right of succession. Succession through the female line when males of the same line and of equal rank were lacking was permitted except when the patent of creation ordered otherwise. These titles, although personal and connected with the family and therefore not dependent on territorial seats, in fact were founded either on domains that already had titles attached to them, or on new territories granted by the king. The infanzones or lower nobility were the descendants of those with small estates who did not own serfs and who were bound to the king for war service, similar to the knights in England. This class of smaller nobility acted as a counter-weight to the power of the grandees. Because the kingdoms of Aragón, Catalonia and Navarre were, until quite late in the Middle Ages, separate Kingdoms, the origins of their nobility differ to some extent from those of Castile and León. In Navarre, for example, the right to use a coat of arms was only granted to 'registered nobles' or those with patents of nobility, whatever their rank. Charles I instituted the rank of grandeza or grandee. This rank was given to the most important families, but it did not carry with it any particular power over the rest of the nobility. At that period the Spanish nobility consisted of grandees, the titled nobility, the communities of lords in Castile and of barons in Aragón, and likewise of the non-titled nobility, to wit hidalgos in León and Castile and infanzones in Aragon and Navarre, nobles, gentlemen and honorable citizens in Catalonia and parientes mayores in Biscay.

The privileges of the nobility were severely curtailed in 1811 and again in 1837. In 1836 the requirement of nobility for entry as a cadet into the navy and the army was abolished. The Constitution of 1845 finally established that all public posts should be open to all Spaniards and not just to those of noble birth. The law of the 1st Republic of 25 May 1873 forbade the creation of new titles or the granting of privileges to the nobility. In 1874, this law referring to titles was repealed, and it was established that the authority to grant them should reside in Parliament (cortes). Finally, a law in January 1875 repealed two previous laws in so far as the king was exclusively authorized to grant titles. Under the present regime there is nothing to stop nobles who have no title from giving themselves one, or to prevent the king creating titles or giving privileges of nobility. Titles of nobility and 'grandee-ism' were abolished in 1931, but a law of 1948 re-established the position existing before the proclamation of the 2nd Republic.

Heraldry

The right to bear arms was restricted in the kingdom of Navarre to the nobility, and only those who could prove noble descent were entitled to claim and to have their arms recognized. In 1595 kings of arms were introduced by Philip II with the power to confer coats of arms when the king did not grant them directly. The power of this body was confirmed by a law of 1951, and it is therefore proper to deduce that anybody noble or not who obtains a certificate of arms from a member of the body of kings of arms has a perfect right to them legally. See also Appendix 1.

Public archives

The Historical Public Record Office is in Madrid; the address is Calle de Serrano, 117. It contains information of the greatest use concerning the great medieval families from the tenth to the fifteenth centuries, and much information concerning the clergy, military orders, Inquisition and treasury. Much of the information is well indexed and classified.

The Archivo de las Cortes or Parliamentary Archives, are to be found at the Calle de Fernanflor No. 1, Madrid. These contain the personal records of senators with interesting biographical information. In the Palace Archive, Plaza de la Armeria, Madrid, employees of the royal households are recorded, and information exists even during the revolution of 1868. In order to consult both archives special permission is required.

In the Library of the Academy of History, Calle de León 21, there is a well-catalogued collection, known as the Salazar y Castro Collection, dealing with Spanish families between 1250 and approximately 1600. These, however, are confined to high nobility only. The archives of the civil ministries are being transferred to a headquarters in Alcalá de Henares. These are important from a genealogical point of view, consisting as they do of personal records of professors, and including archives from the Ministry of Education. They also contain information about civil servants in the nineteenth century, hitherto kept in the Personnel Departments of the Treasury. In the archives of the Ministry of Justice, Calle de la Manzana 2, there are two departments known as the Departments of Titles and Nobility and the Departments of Ecclesiastics and Personnel; special permission is required to consult them.

The general archive of Simancas in the province of Valladolid, is extremely valuable for information concerning the kingdom of León and Castile between the fourteenth and nineteenth centuries. For genealogical purposes, its Royal Patronage, Ecclesiastical Patronage, House of Castile, Royal Council, Secretaries of State, Pardon and Justice, War and Navy Departments are of the greatest importance. Indexes and catalogues of the greater part of these records exist.

The general archive of the kingdom of Aragón is in Barcelona, and is similar to that of the archive of Simancas. There are also regional archives for the kingdom of Galicia to be found in the Jardin de San Carles de la Coruña. Likewise the original archives of Majorca and of Valencia are important, though the latter has been greatly damaged by flooding. The archive of the Assembly Hall of Guernica deals with the province of Biscay and possesses a considerable amount of genealogical information concerning Basques. Most of the material dates from the beginning of the seventeenth century and continues to the middle of the nineteenth.

The general archive of the Indies in Seville contains genealogical sources of exceptional importance for the inhabitants of Spanish America and the Philippines, the most important of these being the departments known as the Patronato (Casa de Contratación), the Department of Justice, Department of Government and the department of Titles and Nobility. Guides and catalogues for these various departments exist.

Military archives

In addition to records to be found in the Public Historical Record Office and in the General Archives of Simancas and of the Indies, there is also a General Military Archive in Segovia, and also an Admiralty Archive. The first of these can only be consulted with the express authority of the General Under-Secretary of the War Office. It contains the personal and matrimonial records of officers in the Spanish army, and of some sailors who served, from the middle of the eighteenth century to the present time. There is likewise information relating to a large number of people directly or indirectly connected with the War Office. The second is mainly established in El Viso del Marqués, Ciudad Real. However, in the Admiralty Museum there are interesting records regarding naval and marine personnel which can also be consulted. Indexes and catalogues for both archives exist, and the information is well classified.

8

Portugal

Parish registers

The oldest parish registers in Portugal belong to the municipality of
Loures and date from 1507. However, there is a record of D. Alfonso
Nogueira, Archbishop of Lisbon, on his visitation to the church of
Santiago de Óbidos (9 June 1462) referring to the marriage registers of
the fifteenth century. By the 1563 Diocesan Constitutions of Lisbon the
keeping of parish registers of baptisms and deaths was made obligatory,
whereas previously it had been voluntary.

Such a measure was already traditional practice in Portugal when it
was adopted and enforced during the third phase of the Council of
Trent (4 December 1563), at the suggestion of a Portuguese, Dom Frei
Bartolomeu dos Mártires, Archbishop of Braga. Moreover, the Secretary who recorded the Council's proceedings was also a Portuguese,
Frei Francisco Foreiro, a Dominican. From this it is obvious that the
Portuguese delegates to the Council exerted a considerable influence on
the decision-making In Portugal the law enacted by the Council was
promulgated by a patent of 12 December 1564.

Until the decree of 16 May 1832, these registers were solely the
responsibility of the Church. The 1832 decree was the first attempt to
establish a civil registry of births, marriages and deaths, but by the
decree of 9 August 1859, the keeping of registers became once again
the responsibility of the parishes. This measure was reinforced by the
decree of 28 November 1878 whereby the civil registration was strictly
for non-Catholics. However, the decree of 18 February 1911 set up two
registries, one civil and one ecclesiastical.

Nevertheless, even though the ecclesiastical registers continued to be
kept alongside the civil ones, both old parish and other books were
taken over by the State Archives. By the decree of 30 May 1834 the
property of religious orders was secularized and article 4 of the government regulation of 4 June 1834 established the terms of its enforcement.

Since the sixteenth century the ecclesiastical registers record a person's profession, civil status, parents' names and place of birth. From the eighteenth century the names of the grandparents and nationalities were added. As from the end of the seventeenth century, the parish registers of the Protestants of Lisbon, à Estrella, have been kept by the vicar.

All parish registers more than a hundred years old are deposited with the district archives, and so, too, are all notarial records of more than thirty years old. There is no public access to these books more recent than thirty years old. These are kept at the civil registry and the office of the public notary of each municipality.

Virtually all the legal records and cases of the Holy Office (Inquisition) and the criminal cases from the seventeenth century until the nineteenth century are to be found in the National Archives of the Torre do Tombo. Detailed information concerning families can be obtained here.

Civil registration

The civil registry books, recording wills, estate purchases, majorat patents, marriage contracts, donations, etc., constitute a valuable source of information, and so do the records of bequests, donations, etc. found in the registers of the ecclesiastical courts.

It should also be noted that, since the right of tenure did not exceed three lives, the copyholds containing the entries of admission of every tenant provide an inexhaustible source of genealogical information from the fourteenth century on.

Another important source of genealogical information is the records of the Church's sanctions of marriage between members of the same family, since unlimited data can be obtained from the inquiries held to prove consanguinity.

By law all these registers and records are kept in the district archives or in the National Archives of Torre do Tombo in Lisbon.

In Portugal each district has an archive which has the right to demand the compulsory deposit of records. There are, however, exceptions such as in Bragança where the records of the Ecclesiastical Court have not yet been deposited; the records of Viana do Castelo are in the district archives of Braga; those of Guimarães in the municipal archives 'Alfredo Pimenta'; the archives of Vila Real are shut; and in the Azores only the district archives of Angra do Heroismo are properly organized.

Academic and professional records

The General Archive of the University of Coimbra keeps the records of all its bachelors, licentiates and doctors, and these include information concerning parents, place and date of birth. More recently the universities of Lisbon and Oporto have set up their own archives.

In the Historical Military Archives the record of every serviceman is kept – such records include details of parentage, place and date of birth, marriage authorization, and name of future wife, as well as details of the military career. The Ministry of Naval Affairs has its own archives.

The records *de genere* concerning priests and those who took minor orders are kept in the district archives. These records include the names and places of birth of the parents and grandparents and information concerning each one of these members of the family. Furthermore, there are the seminaries' registration books, which date from the fifteenth century, and in which records of parentage and places of birth are to be found. Finally the dossiers of foreigners applying for Portuguese nationality are kept in the National Archives of Torre do Tombo.

Genealogical and heraldic institutions

There are three institutions in Portugal which carry out studies in heraldry, two of these dealing also with genealogy. The Conselho de Nombreza, set up by a decree of 8 April 1945, is the only institution recognized by the Ministry of Justice and the Ministry of Foreign Affairs, and the only one granting patents of coats of arms and titles. It publishes *Boletim Oficial do Conselho de Nombreza*.

The Instituto Português de Heralidca (Largo do Carmo – Lisboa, 2), which publishes a quarterly bulletin, *Armas e Troféus*, is a cultural institution where studies of Portuguese heraldry and genealogy are carried out. Its statute received official approval in 1930.

Another cultural institution, set up officially in 1864, the Associaçâo dos Arqueológos Portugueses has a heraldry department founded in April 1910. It carries out studies in civil heraldry for the Ministry of Home Affairs.

9

Holland

History

By the middle of the sixteenth century the Netherlands were ruled by the Habsburg kings of Spain. Since the Reformation had taken a firm hold upon the minds of Dutchmen, the imposition by the Spanish governor of the Inquisition provoked the rebellion of 1566 led by William, Prince of Orange, which resulted in eighty years of bitter warfare. During this war, in 1579, the northern and southern Netherlands were separated from each other, but in 1588 the Republic of the United Netherlands, with the princes of Orange as stadtholders appointed by the states general, was founded. This lasted until 1795. For the next eighteen years, until 1813, the Netherlands were occupied by France, but with the fall of Napoleon, the kingdom of the Netherlands was proclaimed that still exists today.

Both the Scots and the English had many connections with Holland. There were colonies of merchants in Dordrecht, Middelburg and Rotterdam from the sixteenth century; likewise, there were Dutch colonies, with their churches, in London, Norwich and Kings Lynn. The earliest English church in Holland was founded in 1607 at Amsterdam, and others followed at Rotterdam (1621; Scots), Middelburg (1624), Dordrecht (1625: Scots), The Hague (1627) and Delft (1645).

Civil registration (Burgerlijke Stand)

There is no central registration of births, marriages and deaths as there is in Britain. Civil registration was introduced by the French in Belgium and the southern Netherlands in 1796, and in the rest of the country in 1811. Each municipality, of which there are approximately 1,000 keeps its own records of births, marriages, divorces and deaths. For the period 1811–92 duplicate records were kept in the provincial archives of which

78

Map 14. Holland, Belgium and Luxembourg.

there are eleven, but there are no central indexes. However, each register (usually covering one year) of births, marriages or deaths is indexed
alphabetically, and there are decennial indexes for each municipality.
For the period since 1892, copies of records can only be obtained from
the registrar of each municipality (Ambtenaar van de Burgerlijke Stand),
and these have to be paid for.

   Since the mid-nineteenth century population registers (Bevolkings-
registers) have been kept locally. These records give information about
a person's birth, parentage, occupation and children. When someone
leaves the country, his card is sent to the Central Population Register,

where it remains. People moving about within the country have their cards transferred to their new home, but a record remains on the files of the previous place of abode. When a person dies his card is sent to the Central Bureau for Statistics and each year records of all those who have died are sent to the Central Bureau for Genealogy. The system has been likened to a running census.

Parish registers

Church registers are kept by the ministers of the different denominations in their own churches. Between 1588 and 1795 the Dutch Reformed Church was the state church, and as in England, people who dissented from it had to marry there or before a magistrate as well as in their own churches. Marriages of Roman Catholics, Jews and other Nonconformists, therefore, can often be found in Dutch Reformed Church registers. The vast majority of the ancient registers were handed over to the civil authorities in 1796, and are now in the custody of the municipal archives (Gemeentearchieven). A guide to the whereabouts of Dutch parish registers before 1796 – the *Reportorium DTB* – with English explanations, was published in 1969 by the Central Bureau for Genealogy.

Notarial and judicial records

Wills, transfers and divisions of property, marriage contracts, tax rolls and the administration of orphans' estates were all matters controlled by notaries, just as they are in France. The language, of course, is Dutch, so that it is necessary for those who do not speak the language to employ the services of a professional genealogist. A general survey of the contents of the notarial records has been published in *De Rijksarchieven in Nederland* (1973).

Wills in Holland are generally notarial deeds and are to be found in bound volumes of notarial deeds executed by a particular notary. These volumes are housed in the various record offices up and down the country. If, at the period in which the search is being undertaken, there were only one or two notaries active in a particular town, then searching their records is not very difficult. In large cities, such as Amsterdam, it is, of course, a much bigger undertaking. The names of the notaries and the towns where they practised are to be found in the *Register der protocollen van Notarissen in Nederland* by F. L. Hartong (1916). The list covers the period from 1550 to 1916. In places where there were no notaries, of which Groningen was one, notarial duties were performed by the leading functionary of the town. Once the correct notarial register has been found, a great deal of information about the family, apart from its wills, will be found, for all sorts of miscellaneous financial transactions were conducted by notaries. The registers of the following notaries of Rotterdam and Amsterdam, for example, contain much information relating to trade with Virginia and other English colonies in the seventeenth century.

Amsterdam notaries

Frederick van Banchem; C. Pietersz; Jan Warnaertsz; C. Touw; J. Volkaerts Oli; J. Franssen Bruyningh; J. de Graeff; J. van de Ven; l'Hommelie; Pieter Carelsz; J. Steyns; H. Schaeff; A. Eggering; B. Coop van Groen; F. Uytenbogaert; J. Verhey; D. Doornick; J. van Zwieten; J. Hellerus; P. Capoen; G. Borselaer.

Rotterdam notaries

J. van Aller; A. Huysmans; W. van Aller; J. Delphius; A. Kieboom; J. Duyfhuysen; J. Troost; V. Mustelius; G. van der Hout; Nic. Vogel; Pieter de Paus; B. de Gruyter; J. Grimes.

All the above practised between 1621 and 1664.

One of the most valuable sources for information about English merchants is to be found in the lists of freemen burgesses of Rotterdam and other cities published in *Gens Nostra*, the organ of the Dutch Genealogical Society.

The Central Bureau for Genealogy (Central Bureau voor Genealogie)

Founded in 1945 as a semi-official institution, the Central Bureau for Genealogy is located at Nassauplaan 18, The Hague. Its chief purpose is to house the national genealogical collections, and to be a documentation centre for family history. The Bureau has a sizeable staff, who can undertake, for a fee, some research. Here can be found information on more than 15,000 Dutch families, including a card index of over 1½ million baptisms, marriages and deaths as well as details of membership of the Walloon churches in France and Germany as well as the Netherlands. Indeed, this is probably the largest source of information on French or Walloon Huguenot families in existence. The Central Bureau for Genealogy has a large collection of descriptions of coats of arms and the names of those who are entitled to use them. Anyone may have a coat of arms if he wishes. There is no official registration of arms except to those granted to the nobility. Noble arms are regulated by the Hoge Raad van Adel, which advises the sovereign on municipal arms and admission to sundry orders of knighthood, such as the Order of Malta and the Order of Teutonic Knights.

University records

A list of university towns appears in the *Genealogisch Repertorium* by Jonkheer van Beresteyn, which contains information about alumni and graduates of the universities concerned. In these lists of alumni are to be found many Huguenot names. In this connection it should be pointed out that not all Huguenot names appear as French ones, for a number of Huguenots, who later settled in England and the colonies, went first to the Netherlands, and so their names appear in a Dutch form. A most valuable collection of Huguenot data is at the Bibliothèque Wallonne at Leyden. This consists of copies of baptismal, marriage and death entries to do with refugee families taken from the registers of churches in France before the Revocation of the Edict of Nantes, of the Walloon churches in Holland itself, and of Huguenot churches in Germany. Enquiries should be written in French and addressed to the Secrétaire de la Commission de l'Histoire des Églises Wallonnes, Pieterskerkhof 40, Leyden.

Names

One of the great difficulties of Dutch genealogy is, that until 1811, real surnames were few and far between, for people used personal patronymics not surnames. Napoleon decreed that everyone should take surnames and register them, so that there are now about 87,000 family names in Holland. Sometimes the name itself gives a clue to the district of origin. According to Dr T. G. Fahy (*Genealogists Magazine*, vol. xiii, no. 12), names ending in 'ma' and 'ga' are generally Frisian; names ending in 'donk' are generally of Brabant origin, while names ending in 'ink' tend to originate in the east of Holland.

Addresses of Record Offices

Rijksarchief in Drenthe, Brink 4, Assen
Rijksarchief in Friesland, Turfmarkt 13, Leeuwarden
Rijksarchief in Glederland, Markt 1, Arnhem
Rijksarchief in Groningen, St. Jansstraat 2, Groningen

Rijksarchief in Limburg, St. Pietersstraat 7, Maastricht
Rijksarchief in Noord-Brabant, Waterstraat 20, 's-Hertogenbosch
Rijksarchief in Noord-Holland, Ceciliastraat 12, Haarlem
Rijksarchief in Overijssel, Sassenpoort, Zwolle
Rijksarchief in Utrecht, Alexander Numankade 201, Utrecht
Rijksarchief in Zeeland, St. Pietersstraat 38, Middelburg
Algemeen Rijksarchief, Bleyenburg 7, 's-Gravenhage

Full details of the record offices of the Netherlands and the type of
records which they possess can be obtained from *Gids voor de Archieven
van Gemeenten en Waterschappen in Nederland* (van de Koning, The Hague,
1945), or *Repertorium van Inventarissen van Nederlandse Archieven* (Van der
Kamp, Groningen, 1947).

10

Belgium[*]

Parish registers

Before the end of the eighteenth century registers were kept by the
Roman Catholic parish priests in the different parishes. Most of these
have now been transferred to provincial archives, though some are kept
in the state archives and a few still remain in the custody of incumbents.
The addresses of the various state archives are as follows:
Antwerp: 5 Door Verstraeteplaats
Arlon: Place Léopold
Bruges: 14–18 Akademiestraat
Ghent: Geeraard Duivelsteen
Hasselt: Bampslaan
Liège: 8 Rue Pouplin
Mons: 23 Place du Parc
Namur: 45 Rue d'Arquet

Civil registration

Dating from 1795, these records are now kept at town halls.

Wills

Wills proved before 1795 are usually to be found in state archives in the
provincial capitals. Some notarial acts are in the possession of modern
notaries but as a general rule the Chambers of Notaries publish indexes
of the original notarial acts according to *arrondissements*.

* Note: Records in Belgium are in either French or Flemish. Modern records
   are usually in both languages.

General archives

The Archives Generales du Royaume (Het Algemeen Rijksarchief) is situated at 78 Galerie Ravenstein, Brussels. A full guide exists describing the extent and whereabouts of Belgian archives from the Middle Ages to the present day. Note that due to the vicissitudes of history, some Belgian records are to be found in French archives and some in Holland. A few are still to be found in the Austrian and Spanish archives.

Heraldic archives and genealogical societies

L'Office Genéalogique et Héraldique de Belgique, 37 Rue Bosquet, Brussels
Le Conseil Héraldique, 85, Rue du Prince Royal, Brussels
L'Association de la Noblesse du Royaume de Belgique, 96 Rue Souveraine, Brussels
Antwerpsche Kring voor Familiekunde, 25 Moonsstraat, Antwerp
Service de Centralisation des Etudes Genéalogiques et Démographiques de Belgique, 26 Rue aux Laines, Brussels

Luxembourg

A 1,000-square mile grand duchy, independent since 1815, bounded by Germany, France and Belgium. The permanent population of 357,000 is swollen by temporary migrant workers, mainly from southern Europe. Emigration has been principally to North America; there are sizeable communities of Luxembourgeois in Chicago and Pittsburgh.

The principal genealogical and heraldic sources within present-day Luxembourg are:
Archivists de la Ville de Luxembourg, Hôtel de Ville, Place Guillaume, Luxembourg
Conservateur aux Archives du Gouvernement, 4, Boulevard Roosevelt, Luxembourg
Le Conseil Héraldique, 25, rue Bertholet, Luxembourg

11

Sweden

Names

Many emigrants of Swedish origin found it necessary when settling in an English-speaking country to change their name. Although in many respects Swedish and English names are not dissimilar, the spelling differs considerably. Names such as Sjöstrand or Sköld are difficult for English speakers to pronounce correctly, so often become translated as, for example in the former case to Seashore, or transliterated in the latter to Shold. Names such as Johnsson, Jansson, Jeansson, Jonasson, Johansson, Johannesson and Jonsson all fuse into the form of Johnson. Many female emigrants of the last century used the old female patronymic ending in -dotter (daughter), as for example Andersdotter, Persdotter, Jansdotter and so on. Often these women changed their names to the easier form ending in son.

Personal documents

The flyttningsbetyg was the official exit permit issued by the pastor of the parish in Sweden which the emigrant took with him when he left home. It is important since technically no Swede could leave his home parish without one. It gives the person's full name, date and place of birth, character reference, knowledge of the catechism and Bible, the name of the parish to which he moved or, if he went directly to America or elsewhere, the name of the country of destination. Unfortunately many of these documents have been lost by those who emigrated, but where they survive they are of immense value to genealogists.

Certificates of naturalization were obtained by most Swedes who settled in America and the English-speaking colonies. They may not always give the place of birth, but they always give the date of entry

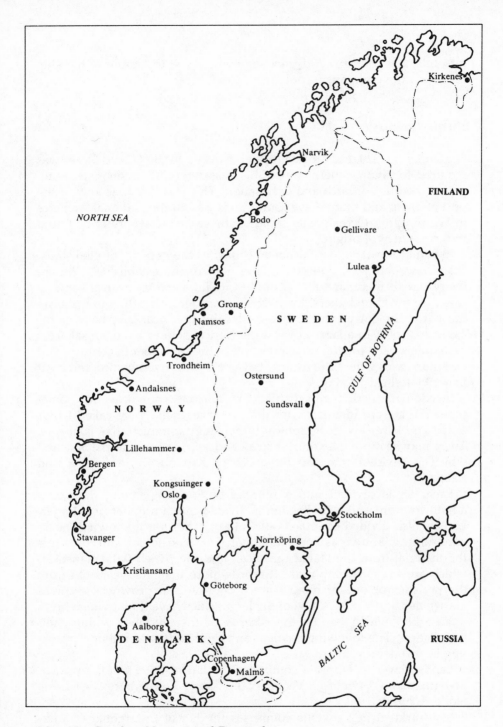

Map 15. Sweden, Norway and Denmark.

87

into the new country, and they sometimes give the name of the ship on which the emigrant travelled.

Public records

Beginning in 1820, each master bringing a ship to the United States was required to divulge the names of his passengers, their sex, age, occupation, country of birth and destination. This manifest was kept at the port of entry and many have found their way to the National Archives in Washington. Occasionally copies of these manifests are to be found in the country of origin.

In common with most European countries the keeping of vital statistics in Sweden was, and still is, the duty of the established Church. Every parish maintains the records of its inhabitants, even if some of these are not churchgoers. Every birth, marriage or death, removal from the parish or entry into it, is recorded by the vicar or pastor or his assistants, or if in a large city, by the clerical staff at his disposal. This system has been in effect since the end of the seventeenth century, and except in cases where the records have been destroyed by fire, the great majority still exist today.

Sweden is divided into districts or divisions known as län. Sometimes the län are identical with the provinces, which are called Landskap. The latter are geographical rather than administrative concepts. There may be more than one län in a Landskap, as for example Småland which is divided into the three län of Kronoberg, Jönköping and Kalmar.

Each län is divided into a number of Fögderi, having their own administration, and each Fögderi is divided into a number of Härader. Län are also divided ecclesiastically into parishes, once known as Socknar and now known as Försammlingar. For genealogical purposes it is the material from the Härad (juridical) and the parish (vital statistical) which are the most important. Records more than 100 years old from the parishes of one or more län are deposited in provincial archives known as Landsarkiv. A few of the larger cities have their own archives (Stadsarkiv) which handle the records of the churches within their jurisdiction. The following archives and their addresses are now operating in Sweden:

1 Landsarkivet in Uppsala comprises the län of Stockholm, Uppsala, Södermanland, Örebro, Västmanland and Kopparberg. Address: Slotte, Uppsala.

2 Landsarkivet in Vadstena comprises the län of Östergötland, Jönköping, Kronoberg and Kalmar. Address: Slottet, Vadstena.

Parish records

In addition to registers of births, marriages and deaths, the Swedish clergy were required to keep lists of those being confirmed, and records known as Husförhörslängder, or household examination rolls, originally established to see how the spiritual and physical needs of parishioners were faring. These contain miscellaneous information about the educational standing of people, their character, their reliability as parishioners, whether they were alcoholics, mentally deficient or criminals. They also contain information about lodgers such as aged parents, servants, tradesmen, military personnel and poor-house inmates. Taken together, the Husförhörslängder are probably the most important single source for family historians, since they give an overall picture of a family and its place in parish society. The earliest go back to the 1620s (in the diocese of Västerås), those in Linköping diocese in 1714, and there are several in Växjö diocese dating back to 1717, but the majority begin about 1750 when the Swedish Central Bureau of Statistics was founded.

In 1895 the character of the Husförhörslängder was changed, and they were re-named Församlingsböcker. In 1946 the system of keeping vital statistics was changed. In addition to the information supplied in parish registers, each person was given a Personakt (personal record) which contains an extract of all the pertinent dates appearing in the parish registers. When a person moves to another parish he takes the Personakt with him. If he dies or emigrates, his Personakt is sent to the Central Bureau of Statistics at Stockholm. Here two series are kept, one of deaths and one of emigrations.

For information more than 100 years old, one has to go to the Landsarkiv or Stadsarkiv depending upon where the parish records are stored. A few parishes, principally in the Landskap of Dalarna, retain their old records. There are about forty of these and enquiry at the nearest Landsarkiv will usually elicit their whereabouts.

Probate records

In addition to the parish records, regional and district archives also contain inventories of estates of deceased persons (bouppteckningar), somewhat similar to American Probate Court records; records of court depositions and judgments (dumböcker); estate transfers, marriage settlements, and guardianships grouped together under the title of småprotokoll.

Censuses

Mantalslängd or census returns are housed in landsarkiven. These were made annually, and although incomplete for earlier periods are very useful. Here also are the jordeböcker, or lists of real property, with the names of owners and certain tax information. Some of these records date back to 1630, and ante-date parish registers. A copy of every mantalslängd and jordebok was sent to the Kammararkivet in Stockholm, some of the material going back to as early as 1540.

Public and military service records

For those holding official positions in Sweden, including the armed forces, much material can be gleaned from the records in the Krigsarkiv and Riksarkiv. Information about Swedish diplomats and Swedes who served abroad, or about whom the Swedish Foreign Office may have enquired from the Swedish representatives abroad, will be found in the Kungliga Utrikesdepartementets arkiv. Members of the Swedish house of nobility have their genealogies recorded in the Riddarhusets arkiv.

Finally, it should be pointed out that Statistiska centralbyråns arkiv in Stockholm has excellent collections of extracts from registers of births, marriages and deaths for each year from 1860–1947, and extracts from the husförhörslängder and parish registers for each ten-year period from 1860 to the present day. From 1860 one can also find here details of Swedes who emigrated, listed by parishes. Each migrant is listed, together with his age, occupation, and the country to which he emigrated.

Research aids

Apart from the difficulty for English speakers in undertaking research in a country whose language they do not speak, there is a further complication in the fact that many pre-1800 Swedish records are written in old German script. Thus the services of a professional genealogist must nearly always be engaged.

For American students, there are two institutes in the United States which may be of help. The first is the Genealogical Society of the Church of Jesus Christ of Latter Day Saints at Salt Lake City, and the other is the National Genealogical Society in Washington, D.C. In Sweden, two societies have for many years furthered genealogical research. They are Personhistoriska Samfundet, Stockholm, and Genealogiska Föreningen, Stockholm. Both these publish excellent quarterlies in Swedish. The latter has a library which can be consulted by the public.

12

Norway

Whereabouts of sources

For Americans of Norwegian descent, possibly the first step to take in tracing ancestry in Norway would be to consult the Supreme Lodge of the Sons of Norway, 1312, West Lake Street, Minneapolis, Minnesota 55408, or one of the many other organizations fostering Norwegian/ American relations. Amongst many useful books are those published by the Norwegian-American Historical Association, St Olaf College, Northfield, Minnesota 55057. These publications, as well as other Norwegian and Norse/American literature, can be consulted at any major library. There is a considerable Norwegian collection to be found in the Genealogical Society of the Church of Jesus Christ of Latter Day Saints, in Salt Lake City, Utah, and printed family histories can be found not only in American libraries, but also in the principal libraries in Norway, among them the Universitetsbiblioteket i Oslo, Oslo 2; Universitetsbiblioteket i Bergen, N–500 Bergen; and Videnskabsselskabets bibliotek, N–7000 Trondheim. The Norsk Slektshistorisk Forening (The Norwegian Genealogical Society), Øvre Slottsgate 17, Oslo 1, will also be able to provide information. The society is, moreover, the publisher of the chief genealogical magazine in Norway, *Norsk Slektshistorisk Tidsskrift*. The Norwegian bygdebøker (rural chronicles) are the best source of information about farming families. They often devote space to farm and family histories, and a recent survey of this literature is given in *Norsk lokalhistorie. En bibliografi* by Harald Andresen (Oslo 1969).

Norway is divided into districts roughly corresponding to British and American counties. They are known as fylke, but before 1919 they were called amt. There are at present nineteen fylker (some of the old amt names being given below in parentheses): Østfold (Samaalenene), Akershus, Oslo (the capital, before 1925 called Kristiania), Hedmark, Oppland (Kristian), Buskerud, Vestfold (Jarlsberg og Larvik), Telemark (Bratsberg) Aust-Agder (Nedenes), Vest-Agder (Lister og Mandal), Rogaland (Ryfylke, also Stavanger), Hordaland (Søndre Bergenhus, including the city of Bergen), Sogn og Fjordane (Nordre Bergenhus), Møre og Romsdal, Sør-Trøndelag (Søndre Trondhjem), Nord-Trøndelag (Nordre Trondhjem), Nordland, Troms (Tromsø), and Finnmark. There are also many administrative sub-divisions such as Kommuner (municipalities and townships) and prestegjeld and sokn (parishes). Farm names are important, as will be seen later, and a list of them is given in *Norske Gaardnavne* by O. Rygh, and in *Norsk Stedsfortegnelse*, published by Postdirektoratet, 1972. Use of both these works can help identity the parish in which a particular family originated.

Names

As in the other Scandinavian countries, the use of patronymics ending in -son or -søn, and -datter or -dotter, was the usual practice until comparatively recently. In addition, a third name was very often used, usually the farm name. This by-name did not necessarily identify the family or the relationship, for it signified the dwelling place. When a farmer Ole Olsen Li moved from Li to another farm, say Dal, he became known as Ole Olsen Dal. This practise is comparable in modern Wales, where the number of surnames being small, people are identified by their trade or profession, as for examples Jones the Milk, Jones the Post, Jones the Baker, Jones the Stationmaster. Similarly a farm labourer in Norway could be named in the same way, without in any way being related to the farmer. Sometimes the preposition på (at) is placed between the patronymic and the farm name, which indicated that the person concerned worked at that particular farm. Similarly, a tenant farmer or cottager (husmann) was very often recorded in official registers under the name of the farm to which his cottage belonged, sometimes with the preposition 'under' before the farm name. Thus a cottager connected with a farm called Lunde might be called Hans Peterson Lunde, and sometimes Lunde-eie (eie = possession). A surname or by-name in addition to the forename and patronymic is therefore not always the same as a modern family name. Family surnames in Norway are in fact of very recent growth, except amongst the higher classes such as the clergy, military and civil servants. Immigrants, therefore, either bore these local names, or adopted a third name when they arrived in America. This was usually the name of the farm from which they had immediately come, but in many cases they preferred to take the name of another farm where they had lived at some time or another, or they might even take the name of their home parish. Some immigrants dropped the old name and adopted the patronymic as the family name. As in the case of Swedish and Danish families, many Norwegian names were transliterated into a form more easily pronounced in English, i.e. Håkonsen might become Hawkinson, and Gulbrand – Gilbert.

Parish registers

Parish registers are kept by the parish clergyman, usually the pastor or parish minister (sokneprest), but sometimes by his curate (kapellan). They record baptisms, births, confirmations, marriages, burials and deaths, and since the beginning of the nineteenth century have recorded movements into and out of the parish, similar to the system adopted in Sweden. These lists, however, are often very incomplete.

Some parish registers date from the 1600s, but most from after 1700, and it was not until about 1800 that they were given a standardized form. Parish registers are transferred to the regional archives eighty years after the last entry; thus all recent registers are in the care of parish ministers.

In rural areas as well as in some towns and cities, duplicates of parish registers have been made by deacons, and are known as klokkerbøker. These are sent to the regional archives as soon as they are completed. Registers less than sixty-years old are not accessible for genealogical research without special permission.

Abstracts of the parish registers of 1873–77 and since 1921 are held by the Central Bureau of Statistics (Statistisk Sentralbyrå, Oslo 1). For the periods 1866–72 and 1889 to 1920, the abstracts are to be found in the National Archives. Registers with details of Church proceedings are also kept by the leaders of recognized Nonconformist Churches. With a few exceptions, these have not yet been transferred to regional archives. Up to the end of the nineteenth century, however, practically all Norwegians were members of the Lutheran State Church.

Censuses

Official censuses were taken in 1769, 1801 and every tenth year from 1815 up to and including 1875. From 1890 a population census has been taken every tenth year, and all returns from 1900 and earlier are available for inspection in the National Archives. The census returns for 1875 and 1900, however, are kept in the regional archives. From a genealogical point of view, the best is the 1801 census which gives the name, age, occupation and family status, and the returns from 1865 onwards, which also give information about each person's place of birth. The 1769 census, however, includes some lists of names, mostly from north Norway.

The National Archives contain a number of records dating from before the introduction of national censuses, known as manntall. The most important of these are the rolls of 1664 to 1666, covering rural districts only. These are entered in two parallel series, one of which was completed by the parish minister and the other by the local law officers. Apart from women engaged in farming, only men and boys over a certain age are listed. The population rolls of 1701 list only males in rural districts, and records for large parts of south and east Norway are missing.

Probate records

These, known as skifteprotokoller, show the registration, valuation and division of real estate and property of all kinds left by deceased persons. They give the names of heirs and guardians and much other family information, as well as data of an economic and cultural nature. The oldest registers go back to about 1660. They were kept by the probate court, i.e. by the stipendiary magistrate (sorenskriver) in the rural areas, and by the corresponding official (magistrat, byfogd, byskriver) in the towns, and are now preserved in the regional archives. Quite a number of these have been indexed. These probate registers do not cover the estates, of all deceased persons. Only in certain cases, when the heirs were under age, was the estate administered officially. Special clerical and military probate registers are also to be found in National and Regional Archives.

Court records

Assize Court proceedings (tingbøker) are deposited in regional archives. They contain reports of civil and criminal cases, and in some instances contain information about entire families through several generations. Some of the books go back to the early seventeenth century, but most are un-indexed.

Registers of conveyances and mortgages

These books contain information about real estate conveyances, mortgages and other encumbrances on property, agreements and contracts, and often much biographical material. They rarely date back earlier than 1720. Early deeds are in the custody of the regional archives, although more modern deeds are held by the local magistrate or town council clerk (sorenskriver or byskriver).

Real estate books

These records, called matrikler, give the names of owners and occupiers of farms dating from 1665. They are to be found in the National Archives. More recent matrikler from about 1838 have been printed. There are also quite a number of jordebøker, some of them dating from the Middle Ages. Particularly important ones are Statholderarkivet's jorderbøker 1624–6, and Landkommisjonens Jorderbøker 1661, both now in the National Archives.

Emigrant lists

Since the end of the 1860s, the police in a number of districts have kept lists of emigrants with their name, home address, date of departure, destination and name of ship. They are kept at the local police station, but the oldest lists of Oslo, Kristiansand, Bergen and Trondheim have been transferred to the regional archives. The regional archives in Oslo also have emigrant lists from the White Star Line's agent for the period 1883–1923. The Stavanger emigrant lists have been destroyed by fire. In this connection it should be noted that domicile is frequently not identical with place of birth.

Tax records

Various accounts dating back to the sixteenth century, including tax lists and real estate registers, which help to trace the owners and occupiers of farms, are deposited in the National Archives (lens- and fogedregnskaper).

Military records

Lists of officers and other ranks for each military unit exist from about 1650. The eighteenth and nineteenth-century lists give much personal information. The preservation of these lists, however, has been very much a matter of chance, and for certain periods and districts or units they are completely lacking. Those that have been preserved are to be found in the National Archives, and partly in the regional archives, especially of Bergen and Trondheim. Useful biographical and genealogical information is to be found in the military probate and trustees administration records.

Miscellaneous records

Newspapers contain much personal and family information, and most newspapers are filed at the Universitetsbiblioteket, Oslo 2. The use of coats of arms in Norway has been restricted to relatively few families, in particular the nobility, state officials and the upper-middle class. The so-called bumerker, used to mark tools and as signets and signatures, are not coats of arms. Their initials and emblems, however, can sometimes help to solve genealogical problems.

A register of population (folkeregister) is now kept by all municipalities. It is intended as an administrative aid, but can also to a certain extent help answer enquiries from the public. It can supply genealogical information and data about emigration, but its usefulness is limited because it was not made compulsory until 1946. Before that date, only the largest municipalities kept population registers, and even the oldest only go back to the beginning of the present century.

The Statistisk Sentralbyrå, Dronningens gate 16, Oslo-Dep., Oslo 1, is the central agency for all official statistics. It is charged with the supervision of civic registration, and thus receives a large amount of personal data. Generally speaking, it is duplicated by local information to be found in parish registers and elsewhere.

In some communal archives, school registers giving the names of children, their date of birth and also their parents' status and name, have been preserved. These records must be studied in the town itself, and have practically never been transferred to regional archives.

In rural districts, the lensmann (district superintendent of police or sheriff) has traditionally played a central role in local administration. Where his archives are preserved, they are very comprehensive and yield much useful information, especially about emigrants. These also have to be studied in the town itself, since only a small number of them have been transferred to the regional archives.

Finally, it should be recalled that all pre-nineteenth-century Norwegian documents are liable to be written in old Gothic lettering, and therefore hard for the non-professional searcher to read.

13

Denmark

General information

Two important facts must be noted when attempting to trace ancestry in Denmark: First, until 1900 all documents were written in Deutsche Schrift (German Hand) and many printed documents in Gothic type; second, before 1850 the majority of the rural population of Denmark did not use surnames; instead sons used their father's given name plus the suffix -sen (son), and daughters added the suffix -datter (daughter). Thus Peter Olsen's son and daughter would be called, for example, Ole Petersen and Karen Petersdatter.

It is certain, therefore, that Peter Olsen's father had been given the name Ole, but there are no means of knowing what his surname was. The number of names, however, in actual use was comparatively small, and this therefore makes the danger of mistaken identity even greater. A further difficulty arises from the fact that many names underwent changes after emigration: thus Jørgensen, Johansens and Jensen might all have been changed to Johnson.

It can be seen from the foregoing that it is of the greatest importance to establish the original name of the ancestor in question, his precise age, and above all his birthplace. If the latter is not possible, then his last permanent address in Denmark may be of help. Indications such as 'of the county of Aalborg' or 'from Jutland' are of no use, for it is essential to know the name of the town or parish in which registration took place. As a rule the available source material makes it extremely hard to trace Danish ancestry further back than 200 or 250 years. Only in the case of noble families or of families with employment within the administration is there much chance of getting farther back.

Family documents

Oral or written information is usually the starting point from which investigations can begin. However dubious these traditions may be, old stories about the family in Denmark may contain elements of the truth, and should therefore be checked by such written evidence as can be found.

The following are among the more useful items worthy of investigation:

1 *Conduct books*. From 1832 and well into the present century all Danish domestics were required to possess conduct books, in which comments on their behaviour could be made by their employers. The flyleaves of such books usually carry information about the birth date and home parish of the servant in question.

2 *Letters from Denmark*. It is probable that modern emigrants of Danish origin no longer understand the Danish language, but old letters from relatives may still exist and upon them may be written addresses, or even postmarks, which can be helpful in suggesting the best starting point for an investigation.

3 *Books and documents brought from Denmark by emigrants*. The principal documents of this kind are usually family bibles, though diaries are an equally important source. There may also be draft papers, or service records, together with old photographs of relatives left behind in Denmark. These sometimes will include the name and address of the photographer indicating the town of origin. Such material should not be destroyed, and those who possess such documents should deposit them with the Danes Worldwide Archives (Udvandrer Arkivet), 2 Konvalvej, DK 9000, Aalborg.

4 *Naturalization documents*. Immigrants to a new country often keep their naturalization papers carefully. Such certificates may contain information about the immigrant's birthplace, and usually state when and where the immigration took place, and so leads to the relevant official records. This also holds true for wills, social benefit applications, deeds, etc. For Americans of Danish origin there is considerable information to be found in the National Archives at Washington.

Emigrants

Among the most valuable sources of information to emigrants from Denmark are lists compiled by the Commissioner of the Copenhagen Police. These lists have been deposited in the Provincial Archives of Sealand (Sjaeland), 10 Jagtvej, DK 2200, Copenhagen N. Copies are also available at the Danes Worldwide Archives. These lists contain information about the dates of emigration and the home parishes of emigrants, the name of the vessel that carried them and their destinations.

A knowledge of the relevant locality is a vital prerequisite to establishing contact with relatives who may still be alive. Advertisements in local newspapers are useful, or enquiries at the municipal archives will elicit the required information. If the names of persons who have died since 1923 or of persons still living can be established, the National Registration Office may prove of use. In view of the language difficulty it is, however, advisable to make the first approach through the Danes Worldwide Archives, who for a small fee will arrange to place advertisements in the relevant local newspapers.

State Archives

The Danish State Archives comprise the National Archives in Copenhagen and four provincial Archives. Their addresses are as follows:
Rigsarkivet, 9, Rigsdagsgården, DK 1218, Copenhagen K.
Landsarkivet for Sjaelland m.m., 10 Jagtvej, DK 2200 Copenhagen N.
Landsarkivet for Fyn (Funen), 36 Jernbanegade, DK 5000 Odense
Landsarkivet for Nørrejylland (North Jutland), 5 Ll.Sct.Hansgade, DK 8800 Viborg
Landsarkivet for de sønderjyske Landsdele, 45 Haderslevvej, DK 6200 Åbenrå.

The Danish National Archives keep the records of the central administration. The most important genealogical sources among these are the census returns and the draft lists. The latter are lists of men conscripted for compulsory national military service. The oldest censuses date from 1787 and there were further censuses in 1801, 1834 and 1840. From 1845 quinquennial and decennial returns contain information about places of birth. The draft registers begin in 1788. Originally the conscripts were exclusively the sons of peasants and they were registered at birth; from 1849 onwards, compulsory service was extended to all males, who were registered at the age of 15.

Records to do with local administration were divided geographically among the various four provincial archives. The provincial archives of Sealand contain not only those from the province of Sealand but also from Copenhagen and the islands of Lolland, Falster, Møn and Bornholm. The Funen provincial archives contain the records of the province of Funen and the adjacent islands, including Aerø. The provincial archives of North Jutland cover Jutland as far south as the Danish-German border, established after the 1864 war. The parts of Schleswig that were reunited with Denmark in 1920 have their own archives in Åbenrå in which are also the records of the Prussian local administration up to 1920. Sources from Holstein and from the parts of Schleswig that remained German must be looked for in German archives, and in particular the Landesarchiv Schleswig-Holstein, Schlossgottdorf, D/2380 Schleswig, or with Church authorities. However, some central administrative records such as the census returns for 1803 to 1860 are found in the National Archives in Copenhagen.

Danish provincial archives contain records pertaining to both secular and ecclesiastical administrations.

Parish registers

By far the most important genealogical sources are parish registers, especially since the majority of the population belonged to the Lutheran National Church. Registers of other denominations have been deposited in the provincial archives. The earliest parish registers date from 1660 or thereabouts, but as quite a number of rectories have suffered from fire or other damage during the centuries, there has been considerable destruction of parish registers. From 1814 all parish registers were kept in duplicate and from that time onwards, all are extant. In addition to births, deaths and marriages, the registers contain information about confirmations, and from 1815 to 1874 (1850 in the case of town registers) they also include lists of those who left and those who arrived in the parish. However, such lists are often incomplete or missing altogether. One copy of the parish register was deposited in provincial archives thirty years after completion, while the other remained with the local clergyman for a hundred years to facilitate the issue of certificates of various kinds.

Land records

Another much-used source is state inventories. These books contain information about the financial status of deceased property owners, and frequently state the names and addresses of the heirs. Sometimes distribution of property was made out of court, in which case information about heirs will not be available. Estate books from 1919 onwards are normally to be found in the offices of local magistrates.

Tracing the history of a particular property owned by a family for several generations can provide valuable genealogical information. The main source for this is the register of deeds which is normally deposited in provincial archives together with the land register containing title numbers. If the title number is not known, it is difficult, if not impossible, to locate an estate owned or inhabited by a given person. In such instances, the local archives may be helpful. It might be desirable even to contact the present owner, for he often keeps copies of the deeds containing this information. In the cases of copyhold property, the records of the manor (in most cases deposited in the provincial archives) yield information about tenants as far back as the early eighteenth century.

Nobility and heraldry

The best source of information concerning the Danish nobility is Denmark's *Adels Aarbog* (1884) and subsequent editions, and the Nyt Dansk Adelslexicon 1904. Since 1849 no new noblemen have been created in Denmark.

Every Dane has in principle the right to use coats of arms without any registration. For information concerning the arms of noble Danish families, the following is a useful book: *Danske Adelsvådaner* by Sven Tito Achen (1973). Further information concerning genealogical subjects can be obtained from the Dansk Genealogi og Personalhistorie, Stenshøj 12, Bruunshåb, DK 8800 Viborg, and the Heraldisk Selskab (Societas Heraldica Scandinavica), Degnemosealle 26, DK 2700 Brønshøj.

Iceland and Faeroe Islands

Iceland was an independent republic until 1264 when it became part of Norway. In 1380 it passed, with Norway, under the crown of Denmark where it remained until 1944, since when it has been once more an independent republic. Like other Scandinavian countries, records of births, marriages and deaths have been kept by the clergy, but parish registers date from 1746 only in unbroken series. The clergy are required to submit annual returns to the Statistical Bureau of Iceland and all parish registers no longer in use are deposited in the capital, Reykjavik, in the Nationalarkivet (Thjodskjalasafn Island) which was established in 1899. All Icelandic enquiries should be addressed there. Wills, census returns and many other sources of genealogical interest are to be found in the National Archives. For Americans of Icelandic descent the *Almanach Fyrir*, published in 1895 by Utgefandic and written by Olafur S. Thorgeisson is of major importance. For those of Faroese descent, information can be obtained from the Landsarkivet (Föroya Landsskjalasavn), Torshavn, Faeroe Islands.

14

Finland

Parish registers

Church registration is as important as civil registration, and most people will find records through the Evangelical Lutheran Church. As Finland has been variously united with Sweden and Russia, there are gaps in records of the eighteenth century. Since 1918 civil registration has been a possible alternative to Church registration, but all religious congregations are authorized to keep registers and there is no central register for the whole country. Certain chronological lists are available before 1850 in the Central Archives, but it is usually necessary to know the parish or commune in which a person lived.

Finnish registers contain chronological lists of births, marriages and deaths as well as removals in and out of the parish and lists of members of families. The member lists are kept up to date and include information from the chronological lists. The oldest date from the mid-seventeenth century. The National Archives (Riksarkivet, Fredsgatan 17, Helsinki) holds copies of all chronological lists before 1850.

Wills

These were fairly infrequent, and enquirers should use 'estate inventories', which list information on property, claims, debts and heirs. They may be found in town archives or district archives, dated from the seventeenth and eighteenth centuries.

Genealogical society

Genealogiska Samfundet i Finland,
Snellmansgatan 9–11, Helsinki

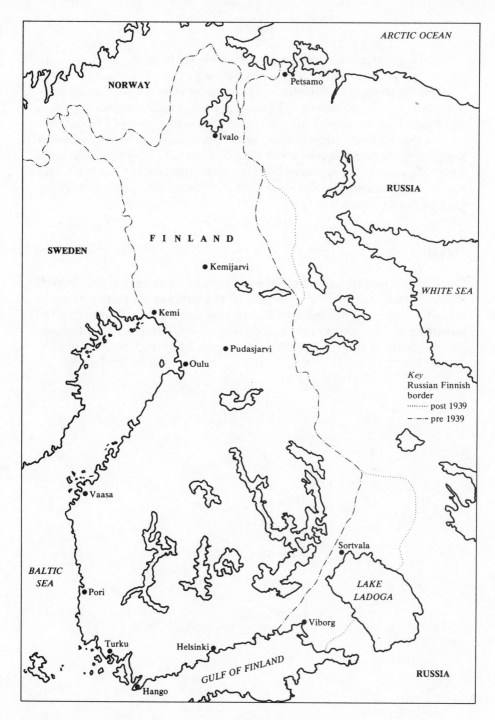

Map 16.   Finland.

Certain publications are largely available in libraries of similar societies in the United Kingdom and USA, e.g. a complete set of copies of births, marriages and deaths registers of all parishes in Finland until 1950. The *Statistical Yearbook* of Finland is published in English, Swedish and Finnish and is useful for preliminary investigations in Finland. So, too, is the *Finlands Statskalendar*, which contains list of all Lutheran congregations and those of other religious bodies. Also available are a series of personal tax registers from the sixteenth century onwards with names and households; and also court records which sometimes fill the gaps of the eighteenth century.

Heraldry

There is no official body in Finland to grant or record arms, though formerly there was a Finnish house of nobility similar to the Swedish riddarhus. During the period of Russian occupation, some families were ennobled by the Tsars. Information regarding Finnish noble families can be obtained from Riddarhusgenealogen, Riddarhuset, Helsinki.

15

Poland

History

A few comments on Polish history and social structure, and the peculiarities of Polish genealogy are, perhaps, useful as an introduction to tracing the ancestry of families which originated in Poland.

From the early fifteenth century Poland was a united kingdom of multi-national and multi-denominational character. This kingdom included, apart from Poland proper ('The Krown') also Lithuania, Byelorussia, part of Livonia (Kurland) and parts of Silesia, etc. From 1572 Polish kings were elected by the nobility which by that time had gained a dominant position in the state. Members of this large social group (amounting to 10 per cent of the whole population) were, at least in theory, all equal and enjoying the same privileges.

The use of titles was forbidden by law, except for a few families of dynastic origin and those with titles confirmed by the Sejm (the lower Chamber of the Polish Parliament). A large majority of the families using titles today received them from the foreign monarchs, and in particular from the partitioning powers, after Poland was divided between Russia, Prussia and Austria in three partitions which took place from 1772 to 1795. The country remained divided until 1918.

All children of Polish nobility inherited their parents' status. All nobility were entitled to use coats of arms. Often a large number of families use the same arms. These arms have their own names and are inherited from generation to generation without any change. The main religion in Poland is Roman Catholic, but other religions (and also other ethnic groups) always enjoyed considerable freedom.

As the Polish nobility was politically and socially by far the most important class, a large majority of the genealogical publications and also unpublished documents of the pre-partition period are devoted to it.

The most important and reliable genealogical information can be ex-

Map 17.   Poland pre World War I.

tracted from birth, marriage and death certificates, but legal documents
such as wills, marriage contracts or property conveyances, tombstones
and monuments, memoirs and diaries, lists of civil servants, professional directories can supply much important information. Work on the
Polish *Dictionary of National Biography* (*Polski Słownik Biograficzny*) is in
progress. Twenty-two volumes (from A to M) are already published.

106

There are also many biographical dictionaries of specific professions such as a dictionary of architects and builders (S. Łoza, *Architeksi i budowniczowie w Polsce*), dictionary of the medical profession (S. Kośmiński, *Słownik lekarzow*), and many others. The old dictionaries of artists (E. Rastawiecki, *Słownik malarzów polskich*, *Słownik rytownikow polskich*) are now gradually being replaced by the dictionary of the Polish artists (*Słownik artystów polskich*, of which two volumes are already published: from A to G).

Public registration

Records in this group for Roman Catholics in Poland were usually integrated with the parish records. Parish priests from the beginning of the nineteenth century were also acting as civil servants responsible for the registration of births, marriages and deaths. The official state registers are kept only for the period after the partition of the country, in the grand duchy of Warsaw from 1808 and in the so-called congress kingdom of Poland from 1825. In the Russian-occupied territories documents were written at first in Polish, later in Russian. Each document was prepared in two copies – one to be kept in the parish records, another to be sent to the appropriate civil courts. In the Austrian- and Prussian-occupied territories documents were prepared in Latin. From 1874 in the Prussian-occupied part of Poland secular state officials were introduced and they prepared all documents in German. Documents of the Evangelical-Reformed Church in the parts of Poland which belonged to Russia were written in Polish up to 1868, and thereafter in Russian; in parts which belonged to Prussia and Austria – always in German. The documents of Augsburg Confession in all three partitions were from the start prepared in German. The documents of the Orthodox Greek Catholic Churches, in Russian. Documents of all other religions were written as the Roman-Catholic documents.

These documents contain the basic biographical information about the newly born, married and dead, names and first names of parents, with the maiden names of mothers, sometimes also the ages of the parents. In the death certificates, the name of the surviving wife or husband is also added. In all documents names of witnesses are mentioned. Some documents have additional information on the social class, occupation, address, property, cause of death of the deceased, etc.

Birth, marriage and death certificates, when less than a hundred years old, are kept in the appropriate registration offices attached to the town or county administrative offices (Urzedy Miejskie, Uzędy Gminne). These Offices are also responsible for current registrations. Older

Map 18.   Poland post World War II.

documents are kept in the appropriate state county archives
(Wojewódzkie Archiwa Państwowe) located in the county towns
(miasta wojewódzkie) and in the central state archives for smaller
places. Some documents, although of secular character, are kept in the
Church diocesan and archdiocesan archives.

It is possible to obtain genealogical information from these birth,
marriage and death certificates and other documents kept in the Polish
State Archives by using the services of the Central Office of the State
Archives in Poland (Naczelna Dyrekcja Archiwów Państwowych, Warszawa, ul, Długa 6), or the appropriate county public record offices.
Only members of public record offices make genealogical enquiries; no
private persons may do so.

Copies of the certificates can also be obtained by contacting the appropriate Polish consulates.

Parish registers

Roman Catholic parish registers of baptisms, marriages and deaths were sporadically kept in Poland even before the ruling on the matter at the Council of Trent in 1563. The earliest preserved *metrica copulatorum* from St Mary's Church in Kraców contains entries from 1548 to 1585. Regular registers of baptisms and marriages started in Poland towards the end of the sixteenth century and registers of deaths from the seventeenth century. Up to the beginning of the nineteenth century entries are in Latin. They are often irregular and summary. More scrupulous are the seventeenth and eighteenth-century registers of the Protestant Churches. But from the middle of the seventeenth century to approximately the middle of the eighteenth century dissenters were often using the registers in Catholic parishes when their own parishes were inconveniently distant. From the beginning of the nineteenth century parish priests were also instructed to keep the state registers. The character and the amount of genealogical information which can be found in the Church registers is similar to that from the state registers, sometimes with additional information of a religious character (e.g. dispensations in the case of marriages between cousins).

A large amount of parish registers are still kept in the Catholic parishes. Some of them are deposited in the archdiocesan and diocesan archives (in particular those in Kraców, Póznan, Plock, Lódź and Pelpin). Many Parish registers of denominations other than Roman Catholic (e.g. Protestant, Orthodox, Jewish) are preserved in the territorially appropriate State Archives. Some are also kept by the town or county registration offices. It is worth while bearing in mind that a large number of the parish registers were destroyed in Poland during the Second World War.

Some of the parish registers of all denominations from the territories which belonged to Poland up to 1939 (the Eastern Territories) but which were transferred to Russia after the war, were handed over to Poland. The older of these (up to 1850) are now kept in the State Archives (Archiwum Główne Akt Dawnych, Warszawa, ul. Długa 7), while the more recent (after 1850) are kept in the public register offices attached to the district offices, Warsaw-Centre (Urząd Stanu Cywilnego przy Urzędzie Dzielnicowym Warszawa-Śródmieście, Warszawa, Nowy Świat 18/20).

Some of the parish registers from the Roman Catholic and the Protestant parishes from the territories which up to 1945 belonged to Germany, and which were transferred subsequently to Poland, are now kept in Germany. The list of these registers with the added information of where they are now kept is published by W. Klytta, *Die Bescheffung*

*von Urkunden. Handbuch der verlagerten Personenstandregister und Kirchen-
bücher der ausländischen Konsularbehörden und der Standsämter mit Son-
deraufgaben* (Frankfurt am Main, 1953). Compare also: J. Kaps, *Handbuch
über die katholischen Kirchenbücher in der Ostdeutschen Kirchenprovinz öst-
lich der Oder und Neisse und dem Bistum Danzig* (München, 1962). Microfilms of many parish registers of several denominations from Poland,
particularly those which are kept in the State Archives, are owned by
the Genealogical Society of the Church of Jesus Christ of Latter Day
Saints in Salt Lake City. The genealogical information from those parish
registers which are kept in the State Archives in Poland can be obtained
on the terms already described in the chapter devoted to public registers. As for the parish registers kept in the archdiocesan and diocesan
archives, all enquiries should be addressed to: Ośrodek Archiwów,
Bibliotek i Muzeów Kościelnych, Lublin, ul. Chopina 27.

For information preserved in the parish offices, it is necessary to
address enquiries to the parish priests in question. When enquiring, it
is customary to send a donation for the Church funds. For supplying
a copy of a certificate (e.g. baptismal), the fee is 200 zl. Perhaps better
results might be expected if the parish (or parishes) in question were
approached for information by somebody living in Poland, and if the
enquiries were in Polish.

Land records

Older documents dealing with the transfer of property (purchases,
sales, donations, cessions, marriage contracts, last wills, inventories,
plenipotentiary powers, authorizations, etc.) are kept in the State Archives. In the period from the fourteenth to the eighteenth centuries
these documents were recorded in the town and district judiciary books
(Księgi Sadowe Grodzkie i Ziemskie) of the appropriate district or town.
The largest collection of these books is preserved in the central archives
in Warsaw (Archiwum Główne Akt Dawnych, Warszawa). Unfortunately the war damage to the contents of this Institution was considerable, and in the county state archives (Wojewódzkie Archiw
Państwowe) in Kraców, Poznań, Lublin and Przemyśl. For the nineteenth and twentieth centuries these documents can be found in the
notarial and hypothecary (mortgage) records. The notarial records up
to 1808 are kept (under the names of the notaries) in the appropriate
state archives (e.g. a sizeable collection in the State Archives of the City
of Warsaw). The records after 1808 are kept in the state notary offices
(Państwowe Biura Notarialne). The hypothecary records up to 1818
connected with property are usually kept by the State Archives, and

the more recent by the state notary offices (in some cases, as in Warsaw, older records are kept there too).

Nobility and heraldry

The Polish aristocratic families are listed and described in a number of publications devoted to the subject. The most reliable is S. Konarski, *Armorial de la Noblesse Polonnaise Titrée* (Paris, 1958). A sort of continuation of this book, for selected families only, has been published by E. Borowski but so far only four parts have appeared. The value of these genealogies is diminished by some notable omissions of persons who died unmarried.

A considerable number of works have been published on the subject of the genealogy of the Polish nobility (*szlachta*).

The records of the heraldic offices of the 'congress kingdom' (Akta Heraldii Królestwa Polskiego) for the period 1836–69 were destroyed during the last war in Warsaw. Similar documents for the rest of the Russian-occupied territories for the years 1870–1915 are preserved in the Central State Historical Archives in Leningrad, Russia.

The most extensive book on the coats of arms of the Polish nobility is J. Ostrowski, Ksiega Herbowa Rodów Polskich (Warszawa 1897–1906). Unfortunately it was never completed. It covers coats of arms, alphabetically arranged, from A to Sz. The new, enlarged edition, completed and supplemented by a list of the families entitled to use armorial achievements is now in the advanced stage of preparation. For the time being the most complete published list of the noble families is that by E. von Szeliga-Zernicki, Der Polnische Adel, (Hamburg, 1905).

Professional directories

In Poland the systematic documentation of the professional structure of society before the nineteenth century does not exist. In the nineteenth and twentieth centuries, however, lists of civil servants, clergy, university professors and lecturers, members of the legal and medical professions, etc. were often published. A comprehensive collection of these lists is owned by the national library in Warsaw. To establish the profession of a given person before the nineteenth century special research is needed. This can be facilitated by the use of a considerable number of biographical dictionaries of specific professions, some of them of very specific character.

16

Russia and the Balkans

USSR

It goes without saying that countries with Communist governments put every possible difficulty in the way of those who wish to undertake family historical research. This is in tune with Marxist philosophy which sees in family life and family institutions a threat to the brand of Utopia it seeks to purvey.

There is reason to believe that records in Communist countries dating from before the establishment of the present regimes have been well preserved. The head of the Russian National Archives in a speech delivered to the World Conference on Records at Salt Lake City in 1969 indicated (perhaps for the benefit of his Mormon hosts) that genealogical enquiries would be sympathetically considered. Nevertheless the experience of the author is to the contrary. Following this lecture he wrote to the speaker after his return to Moscow reminding him of what he had said in America, and asking for details concerning an Englishman who had served in a Russian guards regiment in the last century. After four months he received a reply in Russian stating that no such records existed.

Nevertheless a certain amount of information is held by émigrés in Western Europe and America. Enquiries directed to George A. Federoff, 42.33 Saull Street, Flushing, New York, NY 11355 will elicit information about the Russian Monarchist Societies in America, and to the Bureau Généalogique, Union de la Noblesse Russe, 8 rue Gabrielle d'Estrées, (92) Vanves, France, may likewise be useful.

Civil registration in Russia was introduced by the Bolsheviks in 1918, and at the same time the Church was not only separated from the state, but suffered considerable persecution. All information relating to births, marriages, deaths and occupation are kept by the Ministry of Internal Affairs. Before the Revolution, such matters were the responsibility of the Church authorities. The registration of civil status was introduced

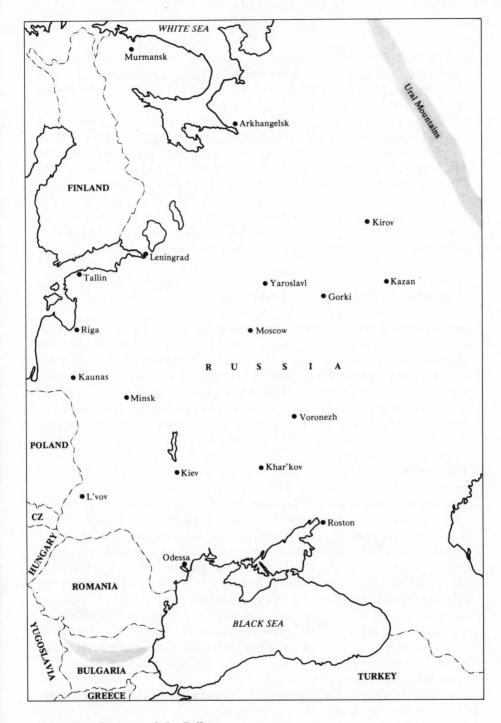

Map 19.   Russia and the Balkans.

by Peter the Great in 1722 for all citizens, while the priests and ministers of minority religions, i.e. Roman Catholic, Lutheran, Moslem and Jewish, kept similar records of their own. Proscribed religions such as the Baptists had their statistics kept by the police.

Russian nobility derived from two sources: ancient feudal lines and nobles created by the Czars according to the civil or military rank held by individuals or their predecessors. A register known as the *Barhatnaia Knega* or Velvet Book was made in 1682. Though modern books on the Russian nobility and their arms are very hard to come by, *La Noblesse Titré de l'Empire de Russie*, by R. J. Emerin (1892), and *Les Principales Familles de la Russie* by Prince Peter Dolgoruky (1859) can still be found. Some further information can also be gleaned from the *Almanach de Gotha*, though only for the very grandest families.

Yugoslavia, Bulgaria and Albania

Large areas of modern Yugoslavia were for centuries under Turkish rule, and have no surviving records. Territories under former Austro-Hungary were administered from Vienna, similarly to the rest of the empire. Enquiries by the author to the Yugoslavia Embassy in London while this book was being written, asking for information about access to records in Yugoslavia, did not receive a reply. Similarly, enquiries to the embassies of Bulgaria and Albania were likewise non-productive.

Romania

Registration of civil status was introduced in 1831 in Walachia and in 1832 in Moldavia. These registers were held by the Church. Other religious bodies kept registers of births, marriages and deaths since the second half of the eighteenth century. After 1861 registers of civil status were passed over to offices of civil status, part of the mayoral departments of local authorities. The priests were, however, obliged to continue keeping registers in their parishes. Before these became compulsory, the Churches had their own registers. In Transylvania, registers of civil status were introduced in 1895. Prior to this date, acts of civil status appeared in parochial registers. Roman Catholics, Reformed, Lutheran and Unitarian churches in Romania had the right to keep their own registers from 1791.

Wills are found in the state archives of the region to which the courts in which they were proved belonged.

The State Archives of Romania are in Bucharest, and the address is as follows: Directia Generala a Archivelor Statului, B-Dul, Gheorghe Gheorghui Dej 29, Bucharest.

Greece

Church registers have been kept in Greece for a fairly long time, though no informatioin is available as to when the earliest were introduced nor how many ancient registers have survived. Civil registration dates from 1856, but only covered part of the country, mainly the larger towns. Since 1931 it has been extended throughout Greece.

Wills are kept in notarial offices, and notaries are obliged to send copies of wills on the death of their clients to the Court of First Instance. Copies of some wills have to be sent to the Court of First Instance at Athens, where they are held.

Information relating to records in Cyprus, which until the middle of this century was a British colony, can be found in London in the records of the Colonial Office.

Information concerning genealogical sources in Greece can be obtained from G. Thevaios, Director General, Ministry of Culture and Science, Directorate of Archives, Aristeidou 14, Athens. The Heraldic and Genealogical Society is to be found at 27 Halcocondyli Street, Athens.

17

Islam

History and background

Sometime around the year AD 615 Mohammed heard the call to establish the religion God had enjoined upon Abraham, Moses and Jesus. Islam, which means submission to the will of God first took root amongst Arab merchants living around Mecca and is firmly based upon a set of rules laid down in the Koran. Instead of a hierarchy of priests and a complex structure of churches and cathedrals, the Muslim depends only on the teaching of holy men and can pray wherever he may be with nothing more cumbersome than a prayer mat. He worships not the mysterious Trinity but the one true God, Allah. In this great simplicity of Islam lay its strength. Within fifteen years of the death of the Prophet, Islam had conquered the whole of the Middle East: within a century the Muslim faith stretched from Pakistan to Spain.

Although the Arab tide of conquest was turned at Poitiers in 732, the cultural legacy of Islam to European thought was considerable and enduring. In the first chapter of his *History of Civilization in England*, T. H. Buckle wrote in 1857: 'The political and military annals of all great countries in Europe, and most of those outside Europe, have been carefully compiled. In regard to the most civilized people, we are now acquainted with the rate of their mortality, of their marriages and the proportion of their births.' In one respect he was right. The touchstone for the recording of vital statistics consists in the accurate keeping of census returns. Once this is done on a national scale, genealogy and demography become potentially sciences, a part of history, subject to the disciplines of historical evidence, as they are now.

It is in the light of this fact that Islamic genealogy is to be examined. There are three stages in genealogical development. The first is the period of oral tradition, then that of committing pedigrees to writing, and finally, from the sixteenth century onward, the attempt to record all members of a people and not merely the higher classes. The first and second stages apply to Islamic pedigrees as they do in all great civilizations. It is when we come to the third stage that there is bound to be disappointment, though for perfectly understandable reasons.

Islamic genealogy today

The foundation of records of vital statistics lies in the taking of a census. Mooted in 1751, it did not happen in Britain until 1801, but maintenance of vital statistics followed in 1837. In the Ottoman Empire, the greatest of Islamic states, and the first to be propelled from medievalism into modernity, regular censuses of rural populations were proposed by Lüfti Pasha in the reign of Suleiman the Magnificent (Sultan 1520–66). Lufti's idea was to institute by means of such records a control on the competence of provincial governments.* Nothing occurred, however, until 1927 when Turkey under the regime of Kemal Atatürk began to make national records. The population was then found to be 13½ million; in 1935, 16 million, and in 1965, more than 31 million, a remarkable increase. With Atatürk, then, records of the Turkish people, the ordinary men and women, begin. And before Atatürk? No formal record; only oral tradition.

Of the lords of the Ottoman Empire, the sultans, the last Islamic rulers to be styled caliphs of Islam, parentage and ancestry of course are known, though direct blood connections with the ancient Arab caliphs the Ottoman sovereigns did not possess. They were, incidentally, dominated by their women-folk, who were of Circassian, Russian or Italian origin.

At the time of Atatürk's death in 1938 many of the Islamic states were still under European rule, or close to some form of tutelage to the West. The colonial governments usually desired a record of the numbers of their subjects. 'There went forth a decree from Caesar Augustus' – but not always. Egypt had its first census in 1897, under British suzerainty, and the process of record has continued ever since, the figures at 1947 showing an increase of 400,000 a year. This, combined with frequent military service, has required maintenance of records as in European countries. In other European-ruled lands, the estimates of population were based on general conceptions, somewhat similar to those deduced in England of the eleventh century from the Doomsday Book. Thus in Algeria, the first census occurred in 1966 after independence. In Libya there was an unofficial estimate in 1968. For Tunisia the same rough estimate has been made. In Syria the population was

* See *The Emergence of Modern Turkey* by Bernard Lewis, 1961.

thought to be nearly 6 million in 1967. From this vagueness, the maintenance of other records does not appear to be likely.

More precise figures may now be available, but it is clear that an emigrant from the Arab states to Europe or the USA or Canada is not likely to be able to give precise information beyond his own birth, possibly his parents' marriage; further details will be based on memory, or general information, e.g. that his father was born about 1910.

Difficulties in research in Islamic records arise from:

(1) the extremely common forenames in use. Anyone who travels in Islamic lands, and who finds himself in the middle of a crowd, will note how many of the bystanders are called Mohammed or Fatima (the name of the Prophet's daughter);

(2) the problem of surnames. If these vary, as they do in European families, it can easily be understood how much this is so in Moslem lands. Thus the Turks have taken surnames in many cases quite recently. Many surnames are common, having been thus taken on lines similar to those of the Welsh in the sixteenth and seventeenth centuries;

(3) the seclusion of women in the past has not assisted enquiries into maternal lines of descent.

Ancient Islamic ancestries

Must then the man or woman of Islamic origin abandon hope of tracing ancestry? Not if he or she should belong to one of the ancient Arab lines. It must be remembered that of Islamic lands no fewer than eighteen are designated as being Arab. We may not dwell too long on the Arabian nature of some of them, but in the homeland of Saudi Arabia, in Iraq, in Syria and in parts of North Africa, the old Arabian stock has taken deep root. Long before the time of the Prophet Mohammed the tribal system prevailed in Arabia and with it its pride of ancestry of the leading families. The Prophet himself belonged to a notable Meccan tribe, the Khoreish, and many of the genealogies (be it added also the sectarian controversies) in Islam spring from that fact. The collective work of the Arab genealogists is based on the assumption that the tribe is a family on a larger scale. In pre-Islamic days there appears to have been in Arabia a cult of the dead, and some scholars contend that there have been traces of it still. Such a cult would, as in China, encourage the memory of genealogies.

In pre-Islamic days we find in Arabia, particularly in the south, genealogies based like those in Genesis and other parts of the Old Testament on the Patriarchs. Such family lines were known in cherished traditions. The form in which they have reached us shows the influence of the Koran. The Arabs had two lines of descent from a common ancestor, Sam b. Nub, i.e. Shem, son of Noah. The Arabs of the north, a fiercer and less settled breed deduced their descent from Adnan, descended from Ishmael. Their southern brethren traced themselves back to Qahtan, identified as Joktan, son of Eber. There is nothing surprising in these affiliations, for the Old Testament is consistently clear as to the kinship of Israelite and Ishmaelite. The genealogies both Hebrew and Arab, are telescoped with a few generations covering 700–1,000 years. In addition, as with all tribal genealogies, the clan is held to descend from an eponym. Adopting the standards of western Asia, then, we find princes of the Arabs who can rehearse their pedigrees through Adnan from Ishmael, the elder son of Abraham, numbering until we reach the seventh century AD no less than eighty generations. The Seyyid ancestry is of the blood of the Prophet from his only surviving child, Fatima, and the Caliph Ali, tracing thus for 1,300 years.

When the Islamic revolution occurred, and the most marvellous (to the Muslims) of all books, the holy Koran was in their hands, the Arabs began to study the traditional genealogies which had been handed down to them. Thus their study of the Koran and of Biblical history led to the introduction of the patriarchs who stand at the head of their lists.

Reynold A. Nicholson (*A Literary History of the Arabs*: 1953), giving a genealogical table of the early pre-Islamic descents, writes:

Nor can we accept the national genealogy beginning with Adnan as entirely historical, though a great deal of it was actually stored in the memories of the Arabs at the time when Islam arose. On the other hand, the alleged descent of every tribe from an eponymous ancestor is consistent with facts established by modern research. It is probable that many names represent merely a local or accidental union.

In other words, the Arabian tribes resembled those of the Scottish Highlands, where a chief's 'umbrella' opened to protect persons called by his name but not of his blood.

With the Koran and the Arab conquests there began an era of brilliant civilization. Inevitably, genealogy formed one of the subjects of enquiry. In fact an interesting parallel exists between the work of the Arab genealogists and their counterparts about the same period in the British Isles. All over the latter there existed in pre-Christian times lists of eponymoi, Irish, Highland Scots, Welsh and Anglo-Saxon. With the advent of the monks, these memorized lists were joined to the Biblical genealogies of the patriarchs. So, too, with the Arabs; thus they who had always recounted the pedigrees of their wonderful steeds, along with their own, were now able to go back to the patriarchal race.

The evaluation of these pre-Islamic genealogies of the Arabs is a matter for the philosophical genealogist. That they must contain some facts ought to be obvious. Who would invent a string of names? We are reminded of Lord Macaulay's remarks about the discussions on abstruse and intricate subjects which at the distance of 3,000 years took place among Idumean Emirs; this being so, as anyone can see from the book of Job, why should not the speakers have been equally well informed about their ancestry, which they cherished?

Genealogy in Islamic literature

With the growth of a vast literature in Islam, genealogy found its place. The chronicler al-Tabari (AH 310, AD 923) included the genealogies of the pre-Islamic Arab tribes, but Ibn Durayi (died AD 934) who was a distinguished philologist and poet, wrote a treatise on the genealogies of the tribes (*Kitabu 'l Ishtiqaq*). Moreover, as the Arabs progressed in their amazingly swift conquests, they encountered civilizations superior to their own. Persia was overwhelmed by them in three days' battle, and the Sassanid dynasty overthrown. But the Arabs had taken over a civilization older than their own in cultural achievement. The Iranian noblemen cherished their genealogies with the same care as did the Arabs, so that these boasts which so offended the Arabs may in many cases have been well founded. Even in the genealogies of the Arabs they were better instructed than the Arabs themselves*. The 'boasts' were, for example, the words of a poet:
Princes were my ancestors, noble satraps of high breeding,
generous, hospitable,
Comparable to Khursraw or Shapur.
In the Iranian instance the descents went back in some cases to the time of the old Persian monarchy, which was ended by Alexander.

The Islamic Revolution encouraged the pursuit of Arabic genealogy in three ways. It naturally supported those of the conquerors who belonged to the more distinguished tribes, to further their original and traditional genealogies. These were now joined to the very ancient written traditional sources. Anyone therefore who considers that he or she belongs to one of these most ancient tribes can feel a pride of ancestry going back some millenia.

Second, the career of Mohammed in itself gave rise to a considerable growth in the study of family history. He did his best to avoid the controversies which he saw were involving both Jews and Christians. There are no priests in Islam – *pace* some Englishmen who should know

* E. G. Brown, *A Literary History of Persia*, vol. 1, 1928, p. 267.

better – hence no ecclesiastical divisions. The Islamic creed being limited to two articles, there is no place for the great Christological controversies. But human nature loves diversity, and Islam found in the question of succession to the Prophet ample cause for difference. The first three caliphs – successors – Abu Bekr, Omar and Othman, reigned without disturbance, though the last two were both murdered. But on Othman's death, four candidates came forward for the office. Of these, one was Ali, the Prophet's cousin and son-in-law, being husband of Fatima. The fourth candidate was Moawyah, governor of Syria. To this day the Shiites of Persia are the Moslems who uphold the claims of Ali. But Moawyah was successful, and founded the Umayyad dynasty. Genealogical knowledge was necessarily advanced as the various dynasties proliferated. The Umayyada gave way to the Abbasids who were descended from the Prophet's uncle, whose genealogical table was of course well preserved in writing by this time. Then came the Marwanid or Umayyad Spanish dynasty (from a solitary survivor of the senior line). A great deal about these dynasties appeared in the remarkable work of Ibn Khaldun, *The Muqaddimah*, a thirteenth-century fore-runner of Toynbee's *Study of History*. This work contains a good deal of genealogical information, which was necessary for the historian, in view of the numerous dynasties which arose. Very often a provincial governor (the famous Saladin was one such) became so powerful that the nominal ruler, the caliph, had to grant him virtual autonomy. This feature repeated itself in Ottoman times in the Egyptian dynasty, now in exile.

Despite the above concern with the genealogies of the high and mighty, exemplified too, in the grandiloquent style – Sublime Porte – of the Ottoman sultans, there has been a third strand of genealogical fact in Islam. All men are brothers who are True Believers. The proudest sultan has as much chance of paradise – and no more – than the humblest believer. That lowliest believer may be a descendant of the Prophet and thus entitled by his 1300 years of descent to an honoured place.

18

China and Japan

Names

In a paper delivered to the World Congress on Records held at Salt Lake City in 1969, Thomas W. Chinn stated that Chinese genealogy traces its beginnings to the reign of the Emperor Fu Hi about 2852 BC. This enlightened monarch, who seems to have had at least a theoretical knowledge of Mendelian genetics, ordered all Chinese to take surnames so that families could be distinguished from each other and to prevent the inter-marriage of kith and kin. At first all families adopted a single-character name, but in time, double-character names became more common.

Chia Pu

Nearly all Chinese families kept a genealogical record of 'Book of Generations' known as a Chia Pu. This recorded the family's origin, its collateral lines and vital statistics of its male members. Periodically members of the family or clan met together to up-date it under the chairmanship of the eldest living member of the clan. The nearest European and American equivalents to this are the lineage or single-name societies which have appeared in ever increasing numbers over the past three or four decades, or the Scottish Clan Societies, which have an even older history in Britain and throughout the Commonwealth and America.

Since veneration for one's ancestors formed part of Chinese and, incidentally, Japanese religious practice, it was not only a pious duty to preserve the family history, but the existence of the system itself led to the settlement of family disputes before they could reach the courts of justice, as well as the arrangement of marriages and funerals and the care of widows and orphans. Attempts were made by Chinese emigrants to America and Europe to maintain this system and Chia Pus were started, though not always kept up as they were in China itself.

With the fall of the empire the custom fell into decline with the establishment of state departments, and genealogies were relegated to an inferior position and kept in clan halls in the charge of clan chieftains.

Destruction of records

Under Communist rule these genealogies were regarded as perpetuating feudalism and ruthlessly destroyed. Records going back hundreds, if not thousands, of years were ordered to be burnt wholesale with the result that the accumulated genealogical and genetical knowledge they contained has been lost for ever. According to official Communist sources, more than 230 tons of genealogical and historical records were burnt in Shanghai alone in 1951 and 1952.

Family customs

Every Chinese has the right to three names. First came the family or clan name – let us say Chiang; the second is a generation name – Kai; and the third a given or forename – Shek. The middle name was adopted about 200 BC and indicates the number of generations from the beginning of the pedigree as shown in the Chia Pu. The system by which the generation name was given was a complex one, deriving from a poem relating to the family and peculiar to it. These poems usually allowed for twenty generations and were composed of twenty characters, and the words themselves used in that order, thus forming a kind of easily memorized code. No two persons in a family were allowed to have the same name, and since the first two were allocated according to the principles just described, the third, or given, name allowed families a wide choice of characters to choose from, since there were virtually no limits to what could be used. Few emigrant Chinese, however, continue this practice, which enabled a complete record to be kept from which it was possible to establish almost at a glance any individual's place in the pedigree. This system enabled one to tell beyond doubt whether people were related or not. It also enabled people to place strangers, who might be kin or not, in their correct generation, and thus enabled their rank in the family hierarchy to be established.

These records enabled demographers to establish, for example, the rate of fertility, the number of sons reaching puberty, life expectancy and the average age of marriage. So detailed were some of the Chia Pu, it is or was, before their destruction, easy to establish the inheritance of genetical characteristics.

In matters of inheritance all children were treated equally, though primogeniture existed in some cases for ritual purposes. Although in general it was the custom to take only one wife, the children of concubines were recognized, and where the son of a concubine was the oldest surviving male issue, he was allowed to become the ritual head of the family who performed sacrifices to the ancestors. In cases of childless families adoption was not uncommon, but the child had to be a member of the same family.

Genealogies from north China tended to be scarcer than those from the south, and since most Chinese in Europe and America today come from the south, this is of less importance than it might otherwise be. However, these ancient customs have largely died out among overseas Chinese, although family associations among the inhabitants of Chinatowns in Europe and America do exist, and some have kept records going back more than a century. In recent years large numbers of Chinese from Hong Kong have come to Britain, and while many families try to keep up the traditions of the past, pressure to conform to British customs is great. The race relations legislation, coupled with the obligation to send their children to British schools will ensure that the majority, not only of Chinese, but of all Asian, African and West Indian immigrants will be absorbed into British society, and that they will cease to practise their ancient customs, wherever these conflict with British practice and usage.

Owing to linguistic and other difficulties, the tracing of Chinese and Japanese genealogies now presents formidable problems to the average amateur genealogist. The Genealogical Society of the LDS Church at Salt Lake City has an oriental section, and readers who are interested should apply there for help.

Japanese historical background

Japanese historical records are extensive but largely inaccessible to any but specialists. The Historiographical Institute of Tokyo University and the records in the National Diet Library are open to researchers, and records, mainly of aristocratic families, of temples and of merchants are to be found in public and private libraries. The Japanese Academy of Science published a guide to the location of private historical collections in 1952, two years after the Ministry of Education had opened a historical archive. The latter is not a national archive, but encourages research for the period 1600–1868, sometimes known as the Samurai period. In the same year a Council of Research in Local History was also formed. This publishes a journal and a guide to local history.

Family registration

According to Toshiyuki Yanese, who delivered a paper on the extent and preservation of Japanese historical records to the World Conference on Records in 1969, Japanese family register systems, known as Koseki, are said to date back to 86 BC. Registration was required primarily for military and taxation purposes, and was superseded in 1898 by a modern civil code which vested certain powers and responsibilities on the heads of families. This was replaced in 1947 with a new code curtailing the authority vested in the heads of families, but the system of registration remains virtually unchanged from ancient times.

These registers have certain similarities to some European family books, and include among other important data the permanent domicile of the family, name of head of family, birth-, death- and marriage-dates together with places where these took place of each member of the family, information about adopted children, relationship of family members to the head of the family, illegitimate children and details of people not biologically related to the family, but who may be living with them. Records of servants and their service are also kept by the head of the family.

There exist a number of national biographical dictionaries in Japan, mostly concerned with military men, businessmen and government officials since the Meiji restoration at the end of the last century. There are however many biographies of Samurai who died in battle in the sixteenth and seventeenth centuries and of those who committed Harakiri or succeeded well in the social life of the country.

PART TWO

PART TWO

19

Ships and shipping

A knowledge of the movements, ownership and hirers of vessels plays an important part in colonial genealogy. Unfortunately, little work has been done to collate such information as there is, which is scattered among a large range of sources. Passenger lists as such are few and far between, so the genealogist must first find out what he can and piece it together to form some kind of consistent background for his research.

In the early years of the seventeenth century the distinction between men-of-war and merchantmen was not exclusive and clear-cut. It was as necessary for a ship to fight as to float. It was the responsibility of merchants, supported by governments, to build stout ships and to arm and man them well, with the double purpose of securing national trade and maintaining a supply of large ships from which a navy could be improvised when the need arose.*

Before the middle of the seventeenth century, however, the English navy became highly professionalized with the introduction of the heavily armed fighting ship. This tended to exclude armed merchantmen from the line of battle, and gradually reduced them to more humble employment as victuallers, convoys and fire ships. The Navigation Acts of the seventeenth century gave preference to English shipping by bonuses to the owners and remissions of customs duties, by prohibition to sell ships of fighting capacity and by penalties for such masters as should surrender their ships without fighting. Although the English were reminded of their patriotic duty to build large and dependable vessels, this was not always acted upon, for the greater part of the merchant marine consisted of vessels of less than 100 tons burthen.

Until the beginning of the eighteenth century ship-owning was a minor function of people whose more important interests and investments lay elsewhere. Most ship-owners were merchants, most mer-

* *The Rise of the English Shipping Industry in the 17th and 18th Centuries*, by Ralph Davis, 1962.

chants were sometimes ship-owners, but ship-owning claimed only a small proportion of each man's capital and received only a correspondingly small share of his time and attention. The seventeenth century merchant might describe himself, for example, as a Turkey or a Russian merchant, yet he was ready to take part in a wide range of business affairs outside his special field. Bankers advised their clients to invest in the silk or wine trades, perhaps, but to those people who took part in business enterprises at all there was a big difference in investment in trading operations and investment in shipping.

Before the days of the limited liability company there were two normal forms of business organization. On the one hand there were the sole traders and on the other the partnership in which the partners were sufficiently few for all to be actively engaged. Joint stock companies were uncommon in English business until the late seventeenth century, and the large unincorporated partnership was developed only slowly with uncertain legality, and for a narrow range of purposes, in the eighteenth century. The character of ship-owning groups, however, was entirely different from that of the ordinary partnerships of the day. It often consisted of ten or twelve, and sometimes as many as twenty members with their affairs managed by one or two partners, and in some cases by the ship's master who was not a partner. In this dissociation of ownership from management, ship-owning was an important exception to general commercial practice. Property in a ship was divided into equal parts or shares – usually, but by no means always, divisions of four; eighths, sixteenths, thirty-secondths and occasionally sixty-fourths. The shares were usually distributed fairly evenly; a particular owner might own one or two thirty-secondths but the very large individual holding was as uncommon as the ship with a single owner. Many ship-owning partnerships were organized by mariners, both active and retired, but the majority of them were organized by merchants.

The active mariner had a strong incentive to put his money into a ship, because this was the simplest way of securing all the prequisites of a ship's master. The retired mariner who had settled ashore with a small fortune might feel he could best use his resources by turning his maritime experience to account in organizing and managing shipping partnerships. If the need to secure capital was one motive for taking partners by ships' managers, it is not a sufficient explanation for the formation of ownership groups, particularly that very large number which owed the first impulses to a merchant. The large ship of the early seventeenth century outside the Levant and East Indies trade was of some 200 tons. The capital resources of merchants were not so small that it was imperative to divide the ownership of such vessels which

130

might cost no more than £2,000 to set out. Cargoes were often worth nearly as much as the ship itself. Even the financing of the great East Indiamen was well within the capacity of the individual magnate who in fact owned only small shares in them.

The practice of selling parts is in fact most often associated with the problem of risk. Losses of ships by storm, bad navigation, piracy and privateers, fire and runaway crews were high, even when England was at peace with Europe. The individual investor could reduce the likelihood of total loss by spreading his investment over several ships. The chances of partial loss were of course increased, but these could be borne. This system of division into shares was the original means adopted to spread the risk of ship-owning, and is much older than the practice of insurance. As late as the seventeenth century when the insurance of goods carried by sea was becoming regular, the ships were more often than not uninsured.

The step towards a concentration of ownership and the professionalization of management led in time to the separation of merchant from ship-owner. Until this division took place, shareholding in ships provided an outlet into which a typical merchant fed some of his capital, and many merchants engaged in trade by sea found it convenient to organize the buying of one or two ships, spreading wide the owning partnership but keeping management in their own hands.

One of the greatest assets a merchant possessed were his kinsmen, the most important of whom were his agents and factors in various ports at home and overseas. Almost as valuable were his contacts with fellow merchants and with reliable master mariners. Shipping offered the merchant a further opportunity to exploit these connections by using capital, most of which was put up and risked by other people. He was encouraged to embark on shipping enterprises in the hope that in spite of fierce competition his friends and kinsmen would do him favours. If his trading connections tempted a merchant to buy a ship he would not usually use it for his own cargoes. As a trader he was an individual seeking to have his goods carried at the lowest price; as a ship-owner he was acting for a group of partners who were entitled to ·expect that he would seek out the highest freights. Even before the beginning of the seventeenth century, there was a well-established market for shipping services at the Royal Exchange in London and the Tolsey in Bristol. Merchants came to both these centres expecting to find a ship which would carry their goods at the right time, or ships they could charter for a round voyage, to bring home cargoes of colonial produce on behalf of themselves and their business associates.

Ship-owning partnerships got round the practical difficulties which under English Law faced attempts to set up and operate large unincorporated partnerships. All the members of an ordinary partnership were liable to the extent of their whole individual estates, if need be, for the debts of the whole of the partnership, so that the prudent man avoided partnership except when he intended to take a close continuous interest in the management of its affairs. They could only withdraw from partnership with great difficulty, and at the risk of ruining the remaining partners by leaving them short of capital. The death or bankruptcy of a partner, too, required the withdrawing of his capital at whatever inconvenience or loss to the other partners. A new partner could not be introduced without the unanimous consent of the other partners and on terms they agreed to. It was impossible for a partner simply to sell his shares and thrust the purchaser into partnership. Finally, the large partnership faced practical inconveniences when it became entangled with the law; all its members had to be joined in formal legal processes such as the conveyance of property, and in lawsuits, whether as plaintiffs or defendants.

The legal status of the ship-owning partnership, however, was quite different. Because it was an ancient institution, it was regulated by a special body of law, administered by the High Court of Admiralty. Admiralty law centred not on the person but on the ship, and the effect was to create a corporation centred on each ship. Shares in a ship were transferable by simple execution of a Bill of Sale, without reference to the other part-owners; thus a degree of limited liability existed.

No part-owner could avoid the risk of loss. Investors from outside the business world were perhaps less willing than others to accept the failure of some of their enterprises. To the risks of loss due to incompetent, unfortunate or fraudulent management must be added those of fraud in the sale of parts. There was nothing to prevent the reckless or unscrupulous from selling twenty or thirty sixteenths in a single ship, and the courts were many times faced with disputes between pretending part-owners arising from such frauds.

In North America the New England colonies created farming settlements, grew their own food and eventually had more than they needed. They developed towns and merchant communities and even industries in endeavouring to achieve self-sufficiency. New England was also the home of American ship-building, and American ships soon began to carry a considerable part of the limited volume of trade then available. This trade was totally different from the trade in tobacco and sugar from Virginia and the West Indies. The principal function of English shipping before the American Revolution was the supply of slaves to the West Indies. The plantation colonies of North America had few slaves before the beginning of the eighteenth century, and when they did begin to import slaves on a big scale, much of the traffic was

132

handled by American ships sailing from American ports. Because the slave trade required the maintenance of fortified trade stations on the African coast, it was for the last half of the seventeenth century monopolized in theory by companies operating under Royal Charter. The last of these companies retained control of the forts and the right to levy a duty on all English participants in the trade until 1713, and subsequently until 1750 received a subsidy for the upkeep of them. The main destination of the slaving ships until about 1680 was usually Barbados; after that date Jamaica rapidly overtook it as the chief market, for it became a slave-trading centre for the whole Caribbean, as well as a great employer of labour in its own plantations. Churchill's *Collections of Voyages and Travels* (1732), describes the ideal timing of slaving voyages. He writes:

I am of the opinion that the properest season to render the Guinea voyages most prosperous and safe is to depart from Europe about the latter end of September, to enjoy the longer there on that coast, and to have a sufficient time to carry on the trade there, so as to reach the Leeward Islands of America by the latter end of April following, which is the time when they make the sugar there, and sail thence to Europe again before the season of hurricanes, and arrive here before the boisterous weather, which usually reigns on our coasts about the beginning of October.

After the middle of the eighteenth century, the rapid expansion of the shipping industry was a reflection of the accelerated pace of growth of the English economy. There is no reason to suppose that the shipping industry was one of the pacemakers of advance, however. It seems possible that in capital and output the industry reached a peak in relation to national wealth and national income before the end of the seventeenth century. The shipping tonnage of 1775 was double that of 100 years before. This reflects the number of emigrants who travelled from the Old World to the New as well as the volume of goods imported from the New to the Old.

Note: Since this chapter was written P. William Filby's and Mary K. Meyer's valuable index of ships and passenger lists has been published in the United States, thus fulfilling a long-felt need for a consolidated reference work in this field.

20

Anglo-Saxon settlement of America

Man is and always has been, a nomad. History is the record of the movement of individuals, families, tribes and nations from one part of the globe to another. A knowledge of how, when and why these movements took place is of great importance to the genealogist, for without it the task of identifying emigrants and their origins becomes much harder.

For an American of European descent trying to identify his emigrant ancestors there is much preliminary work to be done before searches can begin in Europe. He must discover when his ancestor's name first appears in American records; who were his closest associates and what they did; whether he was a planter, trapper or professional man; to what religious or ethnic group he belonged; whether he remained in one city or state all his life; whether his children married within the local community or outside it; if he was a man of property, can any clue to his origin be gained from knowing the name he gave his home or plantation; to whom was he related by marriage and blood? These and other seemingly trivial questions must be answered in order to make the task of identification easier. Furthermore, the problem of finding these answers varies from state to state and from century to century; thus a knowledge of the way in which the American states were settled is essential.

North America from the Gulf of Mexico to the Arctic has been populated by migrants who came over a period of approximately four hundred years beginning in the late sixteenth century. Broadly speaking, those who settled on the Eastern coastal plains between latitudes 35° and 50°N were English, Dutch, Scandinavian and French in origin, and at first they occupied a fairly narrow belt of land bounded on the west by the Appalachians and the Great Lakes. South of latitude 35°, which embraces Florida and the West Indies, the settlements were mainly Spanish, interspersed with settlements of French, Dutch and English. The Mississippi valley was a French preserve, to the south and

134

west of which ranged the vast Spanish empire of Central America, consisting not only of modern Mexico and all the states to its southeast, but also Texas and California as far north as latitude 40°. Not until the nineteenth century was the remainder of the land-mass settled by Europeans in a movement of population which is still continuing today.

Within this huge area of space and time, the pattern and rate of migration has been regulated by economic, political and religious factors operating not only within Europe itself, but also within its individual countries and their provinces. These have influenced the motives which made people uproot themselves to seek their fortunes in a new continent. Migration is hardly ever a matter of free, unfettered choice; there are always factors that drive as well as attract, and their relative strength changes from time to time and varies with every individual. The main encouragement to the well-to-do and enterprising before 1775 was the opportunity America offered to the commercial adventurer. To the less well off it was the inducement of land and work which convinced the emigrant that he went of his own free will. To the poor, or to the petty criminal, there was virtually no choice, unless it was one between death or prison at home and exile abroad. During the past two hundred years, however, most European migrants have gone to America under some kind of duress. If it was not the threat of persecution, as it was for Central and Eastern European Jewry, then it was the threat of famine or unemployment for the Italian or Irish peasant. Two quotations illustrate the difference; the first appeared in the *Frankfurter Allgemeine Zeitung* in 1818. It describes emigration as 'a form of suicide because it separates a person from all that life gives, except the material wants of simple animal existence.' By contrast, the promoters of the London Virginia Company proclaimed in 1610 the virtues and advantages of colonization and emigration as being three in number: First, to preach and baptize into the Christian religion the native populations; second, to provide and build up for the 'publike Honor and Safety of our gratious King' an empire by transplanting 'the rancknesse and multitude of increase in our people'; and lastly, 'the appearance and assurance of Private Commodity to the particular undertakers by recovering the possessing themselves a fruitful land, whence they may furnish and provide this Kingdome with all such necessities and defects . . . under which we labor and are now enforced to buy and receive at the courtesie of other Princes.'

To settle colonies not only leaders but also labourers were required; however, the motives of those who command are very different from those who obey. So the attraction of America to the French Huguenot or English Brownist was quite different from that which motivated the Dutch or English merchant. Genealogists, therefore, must be aware of such differences when they attempt to identify particular emigrants. Because most emigrants were from humble stations in life, and because, in England especially, there were numerous people bearing identical names, it is probable that identification will only be by means of circumstantial rather than direct evidence.

Virginia

In early Virginia, for example, an emigrant's name may first appear in a list of headrights supporting a planter's grant of land. In order to encourage settlement, the Virginia Company, and later the Crown, decreed that everyone who went to the colony should be entitled to 50 acres of land – with, of course, certain qualifications. The man who paid his own passage was automatically entitled to 50 acres, and if he paid the passage of his wife, family and servants, then he got 50 acres for each of them too. In time it became the custom for merchants and ships' captains to bind young men and women for service in the colonies, and to transport them to Virginia, where they could be sold to the planters, and with them their entitlement to 50 acres. Established planters were used to buying one or two servants at a time, and when they had collected a number of headrights, they would apply for a grant of the relevant number of acres. A list of these headrights had to accompany the application for each grant. In the earliest years of Virginia, servants were recruited by the chief entrepreneurs, and because most of these came from London and south-east England, the majority of those who migrated during the first thirty years were recruited in this part of the country.

Under the Charters granted by James I, the London Virginia Company was allocated territory between 34° and 40°N., roughly between what is now North Carolina and the city of New York. The Plymouth Virginia Company, on the other hand, was allocated territory north of this as far as the borders of Maine. The latter Company, which consisted of West Country men, was unable to establish a permanent settlement in 1607 unlike its London counterpart, with the result that New England's development started later and differed markedly from Virginia's. By 1620, when the Pilgrim Fathers set sail, Virginia had firmly established a thriving commercial economy based on tobacco. The failure of the Plymouth Company to establish a comparable economy left the way open to settlers of another stamp and outlook. The exploitation of timber, fish and furs, the staples of New England commerce, require a different type of labour force and individual effort from the cultivation of tobacco. Furthermore, from the beginning, New England attracted groups of religious dissidents of a much more independent turn of mind than the indentured servants who were sent to Virginia. John Winthrop's Massachusetts Bay Company and John White's Dorchester Company of 1630, while for practical reasons insisting on commercial profits, were far less interested in establishing business enterprises than in affording themselves and their followers a refuge in which to practise their particular type of non-conforming religion. Similarly, Maryland, whose natural resources and economy had much in common with Virginia's, nevertheless shared with New England the distinction of being a refuge for religious refugees, in this case Roman Catholics. Later in the century, Pennsylvania was founded as a home for Quakers, and throughout American history such links between religion and commerce have occurred again and again, culminating in the mid-nineteenth century with the foundation of Utah as a refuge for the Mormons.

With these differences in mind, it is easy to understand why the northern colonies in the seventeenth century attracted men and women from all over Britain, for their common interest was a dislike of the Established Church. This means that the genealogist must search among sectarian records rather than among the archives of a particular region, though even in New England, and particularly in Massachusetts, the majority emigrated from the south-east and East Anglia, because John Winthrop and his associates were from these parts and the port of departure was London.

The English Civil Wars of the 1640s completely changed the patterns of migration. By the time the Cromwellian Protectorate was established, the colonies of Virginia and New England had developed their own political outlook. The former, under the governorship of Sir William Berkeley, remained loyal to the Crown and to the Established Church, although even in Virginia there was a strong Puritan faction. New England and the West Indies, on the other hand, supported Parliament and Cromwell. For the first time in its history Virginia began to welcome political refugees, not only from England but also from other transatlantic colonies. Another effect of the Civil War was the ending of London's monopoly in the tobacco trade and the growth of Bristol as a port of entry for both tobacco and sugar. Hitherto, Bristol mariners had traded mainly in fish and wine, which took them outward to Newfoundland, thence south-eastward to France, Spain and the Mediterranean, then back home to Bristol. From about 1640 this pattern changed to embrace the southern trade whose routes lay south-west towards the coasts of North Africa, thence west to the Lesser Antilles and north-west to the Chesapeake and so back home. Between 1654 and 1685 more than 10,000 indentured servants left Bristol for America, by far the largest majority of them destined for Virginia and Barbados. During the same period emigration to New England dwindled to a mere trickle, partly as a result of deliberate exclusiveness, but also because of an ever-increasing demand for labour in the southern settlements. With this shift in the pattern of trade from London to Bristol, the recruiting ground for emigrants switched from the south-east to the Severn Valley, South Wales and those regions of Wiltshire, Somerset and Dorset lying within a radius of fifty miles from Bristol.

In spite of what Canon Law says about marriage, the union of man and wife has usually had to do with the conservation of capital, the maintenance of influence, power and wealth, the furtherance of commerce and the preservation of status rather than the mystical union betwixt Christ and his Church or even the love of a man for a woman. The development of colonial trade was firmly based on family ties. From the leading aristocratic entrepreneurs to the humblest indentured servant there were countless examples of brothers, cousins and more distant kinsmen emigrating or working together in transatlantic enterprises. Indeed the colonies could not have been established at all without such enlightened nepotism as then prevailed. At every turn bonds of kinship linked men and women across thousands of miles of ocean, and because of this, the task of the genealogist today is made easier.

It is a common though erroneous belief that once an emigrant had left Europe he never returned. There is also a belief that if a name is found, say, in Barbados, it cannot possibly belong to an individual of the same name living in Virginia or New England at about the same time. While it is indeed true to say that the majority of emigrants stayed where they were once they arrived on the far side of the Atlantic, nevertheless mobility between one colony and another, as well as back and forth across the ocean, was by no means rare, or confined to the rich, to seamen or to traders. There are numerous instances of men and women of modest means, even of servants, returning home to visit relatives or to attend to family business, in particular to matters connected with the inheritance of property. The pattern of transatlantic trade made the movement of people and goods from one colony to another comparatively simple. As the seventeenth century wore on, sailings from London and Bristol became remarkably regular and reliable. Fleets of twenty ships and more would leave the Thames or the Avon in September or early October reaching Virginia in November or December. Those that were not involved in the slave trade would trade either with Newfoundland for fish, or with the West Indies for sugar, and return to Virginia in time to load the tobacco crop before the end of March, returning to England by May or early June. Unless something untoward happened it was possible to calculate to within a week or ten days how long a voyage would take; delays of more than two weeks were exceptional, and anything longer than that might lead to a court action for negligence against the ship's master. The cost of a passage to America remained at £6 for the first thirty years of the century, and rose slowly to about £7.10s. by its end. Passengers had, in addition to their fare, to provide themselves with food and drink, or, as often happened, the poorer passengers worked their passage as auxiliary members of the crew. This meant that after about the first decade of settlement there was constant and regular contact between the three main groups of colonies themselves – the West Indies, Virginia and New England – as well as with Europe. In addition there was an increasing coastal trade between Virginia and its neighbours to the north and the south.

Merchants trading with the colonies – and this applied as much to the Dutch and French as to the English – sent out apprentices, who were more often than not their young kinsmen, to learn the trade by acting as factors or agents there. Some of these young men stayed abroad for long periods, and many established themselves permanently as planters or traders in their own right. Others returned home to Europe after five or ten years to carry on the family business in London, Bristol or Amsterdam, sending out in their turn other kinsmen to replace themselves as factors abroad.

New England

In New England it was different. For one thing, tobacco demands more land and labour than fishing, salt manufacture, trapping and shipbuilding; for another, New England society had always been more urban and bourgeois than that of Virginia. In the south, planters settled on widely separated plantations which, as time went by, they consciously modelled on the large, aristocratic landed estates of England. Furthermore, geography played an important part in moulding the two societies. Massachusetts Bay is a compact, semi-circular gulf at the head of which, as at the centre of a fan, lies Boston, with small concentrated settlements spanning out from it to the north, west and south. From its very foundation it was a natural focus from which communications radiated inland in all directions. Not so Jamestown; in Virginia the settlements, mainly isolated estates, not urban centres of population, were strung out along the banks of the five great rivers which run parallel to each other and empty into the Chesapeake Bay. Even after the administrative centre of Virginia was moved from the Jamestown/ Williamsburg area to Richmond, the latter never became the communications centre of the state in quite the same way that Boston had always been. Due also the philosophic and religious outlook of its pioneers,

New England established its centre of learning – Harvard College – within a decade of its foundation, whereas William and Mary College was not founded until eighty years after the first settlers had come to Virginia. This meant that boys from the New England colonies could be educated near home, whereas Virginians, who wanted to ensure that their sons had a first-class education, were obliged to send them home to England well into the eighteenth century.

Forced emigration

Even though emigration in the earliest years was on the whole voluntary, nevertheless forced transportation as a punishment began as early as 1615. It has been estimated that more than 30,000 convicts were transported from England to America and the West Indies between that date and 1775. As Peter Wilson Coldham writes in his *English Convicts in Colonial America*, it is 'one of the ironies of Anglo-American genealogy that the lives and movements of those who were deported for their crimes are, on the whole, better chronicled than those of the good men and true who sat in judgment upon them.'

An Elizabethan Act of 1597 providing for the banishment of rogues and vagabonds constituted the legal framework under which convicts were despatched as slave labour to the colonies. The crimes of which they were convicted were usually robbery or felony, and many were of a nature so trivial that today they could hardly merit a small fine. At first comparatively few were transported, and it was not until after 1660 that the practice became at all common. From that time onward – indeed from the very beginning – transportation was more often than not decreed as a less severe sentence than what might otherwise be inflicted. Given the large number of capital offences for which people could be convicted, the chance to start a new life in the colonies was far preferable to the hangman's rope. Up to 1718 the majority of those deported seem to have been destined for the West Indian sugar plantations, but the pattern completely changed thereafter, when Maryland and Virginia became the almost invariable landing places. The act of 1717 'for the further preventing robbery, burglary and other felonies, and for the more effective transportation of felons' set a pattern for the rest of the colonial period. Official encouragement was given for the dumping of offenders on the colonies, and with it went the keeping of judicial records giving particulars of names, indictments and sentences. Consignments of convicts with a certified list of their names were put on board ships by Treasury Clerks who had to keep records for account-

ing purposes. Many of these, having survived, provide prime genealogical source material.

Southern and northern fringes

The Trustees of Georgia, who founded that colony in 1732, were a
group of philanthropists, the best known of whom was James Ogle-
thorpe. They sought permission to establish a colony in America to be
an asylum for debtors. Although the Crown distrusted proprietary colonies in the eighteenth century, permission was granted partly because
the proposed colony would be a buffer between South Carolina and the
Spanish in Florida. The coastal region of Georgia is suitable only for the
plantation system of agriculture, which requires, as in Virginia, much
labour. Because of a shortage of labour, Georgia developed slowly. At
the expiry of the original proprietary charters, Georgia became a royal
colony.

North of Massachusetts, Maine and Nova Scotia were also English
projects. Maine had originally been granted to Sir Ferdinando Gorges
in the early seventeenth century, and it continued part of the Massachusetts Bay colony until after the American Revolution. Nova Scotia
was useful to England as an outpost against the French in Canada.
While economically rather like the original thirteen colonies, Nova Scotia was never part of their potential value as an advanced military base.
Newfoundland, however, was only used as a fishing base and was
never successfully populated before the United States won
independence.

During the first half-century of colonization, due in large measure to
a variety of hazards, not the least of which was the inefficiency and
dishonesty of some merchants, planters, mariners and, indeed, the
government, there were a large number of disputes which ended in
litigation in the English courts. Ships would be sent out leaky; grants
of land were imprecise; charters were given to rival adventurers for
territories whose boundaries were ill-defined; people died intestate and
without known heirs; a whole host of matters over which the litigious
English could indulge in lengthy argument and dispute. Until the
mid-seventeenth century the more weighty of these cases were heard
in the Chancery and Admiralty Courts in London, and their records,
especially the depositions of witnesses, remain among the most valuable
of genealogical and historical sources.

After the Restoration in 1660, colonial courts were usually able to
handle all but the most complex cases, and the number of colonial cases
heard in England declined. At the same time, however, there were still

many in which colonial residents were required to swear affidavits or to give sworn testimony in cases heard by English judges at home.

We have considered so far only English emigration to the colonies of North America. People were moved to emigrate by discontent: poverty drove some; others left home because they found their economic ambitions frustrated by their permanently landless status. These considerations certainly influenced many Scots, Irish and Welsh.

Scots and Irish

During the seventeenth century and especially after the Restoration, many Scots emigrated or were exiled to America. The emigrants fell naturally into a number of fairly distinct categories. Between the restoration and the Union of 1707, the English government barred Scots as they barred other 'foreigners' from trade with the English colonies. Thus Scots could not emigrate as indentured servants.* Ships taking over Scots servants required a special warrant from the English Privy Council, but enough were issued to allow a good many Scots into the colonies. At least 26 warrants were issued between 1665 and 1685 for conveying Scots servants to English settlements in America.

Before the Union, it was not uncommon for Scots judges to sentence criminals or vagrants to transportation to the English colonies. Many of these were petty malefactors or homeless paupers. At various times in the seventeenth century, military and political prisoners were sent from Scotland to the colonies. Of 4,000 able-bodied prisoners taken at the battle of Dunbar, at least 1,250 were ordered to America, but the arrival of only 150 is recorded. After the battle of Worcester in 1651, 1,610 prisoners were granted as servants to people who wanted them for Virginia; of these at least 150 were sent to Virginia and 272 to Massachusetts.

In 1621 the Scottish Privy Council at the desire of James I and VI made a grant of Nova Scotia (including what is now New Brunswick) to Sir William Alexander of Menstrie, later Earl of Stirling. Sir William sent out a few settlers, but they did not stay long owing to Charles I's agreement with the French to abandon colonization in what they regarded as their sphere of influence in Canada.

The Scottish settlements in Ulster eventually produced what can almost be called a new ethnic group – the Scottish-Irish. By 1672 it is estimated that there were about 100,000 Scots in Ulster. Round the end of the century, the economic policy of the English Parliament brought

* *Colonists from Scotland 1707–1783* by I. C. C. Graham, 1956.

ruin to the Ulster wool-growing and cloth-manufacturing industries. This began a great movement to America, most of the emigrants going as indentured servants. By 1776 perhaps as many as 150,000 had settled there. It must, however, be noted that only about one-third as many Scots emigrated directly from Scotland to America in the same period.

The Scottish-Irish settlements in America were distinguished from those of the Scots from Scotland geographically and in other ways. The Ulster immigrants began to settle along the Eno and the Haw rivers in Western North Carolina in about 1783. They had come south from Pennsylvania with Germans, Englishmen and Welshmen, when they filled a great tract of land around the central Appalachians. They were cut off from the sea by the intervening country and by the settlements in Cape Fear which were fully occupied by the Highland Scots. The history of direct Scottish migration to America, however, differs from the history of Ulster migrants. The two differed not only in overall scale, but in the incidence of their peak period. The Ulster migration went through two intensive and protracted phases, the first roughly between 1710 and 1730, and the second from 1765 to 1775. The Scottish migration was fairly gradual until about 1768, when it gathered momentum and continued to grow in scale down to the Revolution. The nineteenth century saw the largest migration of Irishmen following the disastrous famines which occurred in mid-century. The majority of these came from the south of Ireland.

Welshmen

Wales, a small country about the size of Massachusetts, sent some 100,000 emigrants to America.* The records of indentured servants sent from Bristol to America, New England and the West Indies between 1654 and 1685, contain the names of many hundreds of Welsh people, most of whom came from the counties bordering the northern shore of the Bristol channel. In the eighteenth and nineteenth centuries Welshmen played an important role in the development of the American coal, steel and slate industries.

It was the legendary Prince Madoc ap Owain who in about 1170 was supposed to have led an expedition from Wales to found a new nation in the West across the ocean. This legend gave rise in the late eighteenth century to the myth of Welsh-speaking Indian tribes – a story which has, alas, been proved without foundation. Madoc's voyage, however, was put forward in 1584 by Sir George Peckham to justify the claim of

* *Emigration from Wales* by E. G. Hartman, 1967.

143

Queen Elizabeth, herself the grand-daughter of the Welshman Henry Tudor (Henry VII) to the eastern seaboard of America, over that of Spain.

The name 'Welsh' comes from the Anglo-Saxon word for 'foreign'. The Welsh call themselves Cymry (comrade), their land Cymru and their language Cymraeg. The Welsh language is similar to the Breton spoken in Brittany, Highland Scots Gaelic and Irish Gaelic, and developed from the Celtic language spoken by the natives found by Julius Caesar when he invaded Britain in 54 BC.

If we disregard the legend of Madoc we cannot ignore the tradition of orally transmitted legends including lengthy pedigrees which were handed down from medieval times to the present day. However, the first Welshman to play an active part in American colonization was not Prince Madoc but Sir William Vaughan, a large Carmarthenshire land-owner, who received a patent in 1616 for a settlement in Newfoundland. After twenty years of struggle against the hostile conditions of that island, the vast majority of those that survived returned to their native land.

Among the many non-conformist Welshmen, the most famous was John Myles, father of the Welsh Baptist movement, as well as of the Welsh Baptist sect in America, who was born in a Welsh-speaking area of Herefordshire. He founded the first Baptist church in Wales in 1649 near Swansea, which flourished during the Cromwellian Common-wealth but which, on the Restoration of Charles II in 1660, became the object of severe persecution. Myles and a number of his followers emigrated in 1663 to Rehoboth, Massachusetts. Here, however, they soon came into conflict with the local religious authorities, whereupon they moved to Kelly's Bridge in Barrington Township. Later they moved their church to its present site about 10 miles from Providence, Rhode Island. Myles remained Pastor of the Swanzey (as they spelt it) church until his death in 1683.

Welsh Quaker settlements followed in Pennsylvania, for Penn himself claimed Welsh descent. What became known as the 'Welsh Barony' was established on the west bank of the Schuykill River to the north-west of Philadelphia. Between 1682 and 1700 the Welsh were the most numerous body of emigrants to Pennsylvania.

During the greater part of the eighteenth century, emigration was confined to isolated individuals, but after 1795 a stream of Welshmen and their families began leaving Wales in a migration that continued for almost a century. Bad economic conditions at home were the main factors influencing this movement. The bulk of emigrants were those primarily interested in agriculture, but there were many skilled labourers and craftsmen. The majority seem to have favoured Pennsylvania, but from 1801 many went to Ohio and further west, and to upper New York State.

21

German migration to America

Richard O'Connor, the author of *The German Americans* (1968) has said that it is not 'the menacing Prussian eagle but the Wandervogel that is the national bird'. The Germans have been a race of migrants since the dawn of recorded European history, and nowhere has this instinct had greater effect than in North America. From colonial times to the First World War there has been a steady flow of German emigrants to America, until today it is estimated that one-sixth of the entire American nation has some fraction of German ancestry.

Amongst the earliest settlers at Jamestown there were at least three and probably more Germans recruited by Captain John Smith, along with some Poles, to assist the work-shy English gentlemen, who imagined that they were leaving England for some earthly Utopia where hard work would be even less essential than upon their estates at home. It was three Germans who were ordered to build a house for the Indian Chief Powhatan, the purpose of which was to lure that crafty potentate into the power of the English settlers. Being no fool, or perhaps being warned by the Germans, far from occupying the house that had been built for him, he moved away to another part of the country taking the Germans with him.

The first German of prominence in America was Peter Minuit (or Minnewit), who arrived in New Amsterdam in 1626 to be director of the Dutch colony of New Netherlands. It was he who bought the island of Manhattan from the Indians for 60 guilders. He subsequently joined the Swedes and helped to found their settlement of Fort Christina near present-day Wilmington, Delaware.

The first sizeable German settlement was established by such pietist sects as the Quakers, Mennonites and Schwenkfelden, all of which were outside existing German laws which recognized only the Roman Catholic and Lutheran religions, regarding the others as atheists. Their migration to America was encouraged by William Penn, who made two visits to Germany to recruit persecuted religious sectaries for settlement in Pennsylvania. Penn's German agent was Franz Pastorius of Frankfurt-am-Main. He organized the despatch of thirteen Mennonite families from Krefield in the Rhineland in the ship *Concord* in 1683, which became known as the German *Mayflower*. They were settled on a 43,000 acre tract soon to be called Germanstown, where they were joined by other settlers from south Germany. There they began raising flax and making linen. The majority were artisans, craftsmen and farmers, unlike John Smith's labouring contingent at Jamestown. Within a few years, Germanstown became a prosperous centre for the manufacture of paper and cloth. This group came to be known as the 'Pennsylvania Dutch', the English confusing the German word for themselves (Deutsch) with the English word for a Hollander.

When word reached Germany of the success of the Germanstown colony and its offshoots in Pennsylvania and elsewhere, thousands began migrating to New Amsterdam, particularly after the turn of the eighteenth century. Of all European countries at that time, Germany had the greatest surplus of population. Conditions there, especially in the Palatine, Württemberg and Baden, both political and economic, were bad as a result of a succession of wars, religious persecution, and the tyranny of petty German princelings. In 1709 following the war of the Spanish Succession, it was rumoured that Queen Anne of England was willing to provide free transport for all Germans who wanted to emigrate to America. No fewer than 13,000 penniless Germans made their way to England, where they lived in the streets of London and Liverpool until they could be disposed of, some going to Ireland and others to America.

After the horrors of almost a century of continuous wars in which more than 75 per cent of the population of some German states was killed off, it is small wonder that the migration agents were hailed as saviours, and that every rumour was quickly seized upon by a desperate population. In 1709 the English government shipped several hundred 'Redemptioners', as they were called, and gave them land at Newburgh, New York, in return for their labour in manufacturing naval stores.

There was a tendency among these early settlers to keep themselves to themselves. Like other settlers in the eighteenth century, they pushed inland, leaving the coast to those who had settled there in the previous century. In New York state they founded a line of settlements up the Hudson and Mohawk rivers, where they established particularly (and exceptionally) close relations with the Mohawk Indians. The northern parts of New Jersey were also thickly settled by German immigrants who had first arrived in 1707.

In Virginia the earliest German settlement of consequence was at Germanna in Orange County, where twelve families of ironworkers

147

settled in 1714. Subsequently eighty families from Württemberg settled in Madison County, and in both the Carolinas Germans appeared in force from 1710 onwards. A sizeable colony of silkworkers, for instance, established itself at Purysburg in Beaufort County, South Carolina, under the leadership of John Peter Pury from Neufchâtel. In the colonization of Georgia, the Crown sought to give preference to Scottish Highlanders and Germans from the neighbourhood of Salzburg, which resulted in the founding in 1751 of the German colony of New Ebenezer, twenty five miles from Savannah. In New England the principal German settlement was Waldoborough in Maine. It was named after Samuel Waldo, a Pomeranian soldier, who migrated to Boston but who returned in 1783 to recruit 40 families from Saxony and Brunswick to settle on his land.

During the Revolutionary War, the Germans were solidly for independence from Britain, not so much because they were anti-British as because they were anti-royalist. They also had a vested economic interest in the success of the revolution. By the time the colonies revolted, German migrants had settled on much of the best farming land in the colonies; furthermore, they had acquired considerable military experience during the French and Indian wars, and were thus able to make an important contribution to the Revolutionary Army. The British Army sent by George III to fight the colonists had likewise been recruited in Germany, principally in his Hanoverian kingdom. It is small wonder that so many unwilling 'Hessians' deserted at the first opportunity to join their American compatriots. Following the irruption of Napoleon into Germany after 1800, German migration to America increased to a torrent. With it came the dream of a New Germany in America.

Like Italy, however, Germany was no more than a geographical expression, consisting as she did of a plethora of disunited states. The war with Napoleon made the Germans conscious of their 'Germanity', particularly among intellectuals. It was people of this sort which formed the second wave of migration, the first having been composed mainly of dispossessed persons and other uneducated people. Among this new type of emigrant was Gottfried Duder, who went to America in 1826, lived on a Missouri farm for three years and returned to Germany to describe his experiences. The message he conveyed of life in middle-America spread like wildfire, until the idea of America became a kind of fever – the political Utopia of young Germany. By 1830 the young German leaders could see no hope of constitutional or democratic reforms at home. Their aspirations were tinged with nationalism, and there were many who longed to found a new state, preferably with German customs and laws, within the broad bounds of North America. Groups of such emigrants set up German-speaking enclaves in various

American states, though few physical traces remain intact today. Time has wiped out the distinctive features of the German migration to the Missouri valley and large sections of North and Central Mississippi and southern Illinois. Individually the people who colonized these areas put down deep roots. They settled on the prairies and the higher healthier ground; but though they may have been intellectually exclusive, they did not settle in empty and undeveloped country remote from other settlements; rather they chose regions already partly settled, and their hope of establishing an exclusively German state in America vanished because it was impractical.

Germans began settling in Texas even while it was a Mexican province, many of them hoping to establish their New Germany there. But that dream also faded, though thousands of Germans have contributed their own distinctive elements to the Texan character. Most of them came between 1836 and 1845, many of them sent by a syndicate founded in 1842 by several Hessian noblemen led by Prinz Karl von Solms-Braunfels. This venture was encouraged by the British government which wanted to prevent the annexation of Texas by the United States, and thus favoured the establishment of a German colony there. However, only enough people went to Texas to build a few scattered settlements. By 1857 there were about 35,000 Germans in Texas – one-sixth of the total population.

The failure to establish German Republics in Texas and Missouri did not prevent a further attempt in Wisconsin, whither thousands of Germans began moving in the 1830s and 1840s. Wisconsin is usually regarded as the most Germanic state in the Union, but the German-American contingent has never exercised political supremacy there. In the twenty years between 1830 and 1850, some 40,000 south Germans, many of them Catholics, migrated to Wisconsin. The early foundation of a diocese of Milwaukee encouraged many Catholics to migrate from the Rhineland, Bavaria and other south German states. This tended to concentrate the German population around Milwaukee, but the steady stream of migrants from Italy, Poland and Scandinavia effectively ended all hope of a New German Republic on American soil.

In old Germany, Jews were treated as non-persons. They were not persecuted as the Catholics and Protestants persecuted each other, but were penned up in ghettos and deprived of civil liberties. Their treatment varied from state to state; some were harsh, others tolerant. In Frankfurt, for example, Jews were subjected to gross restrictions from which they took the first opportunity to escape to America. Before the Civil War there was little overt anti-Semitism in America. As Cleveland Amory wrote in *Who Killed Souley?*: 'No families in America have more genuine claims to aristocracy than the Jews', and named the Sephardic families of Baruch, and Cardazo. He also mentioned a number of German Jewish families, most of whom dominated the banking world, and whom he terms 'the Jewish Grand Dukes'. Probably the most striking example of social and financial success was August Belmont, but this may be attributed to his devotion to assimilation. By deserting the synagogue for the church, he was untypical of thousands of other Jews who came later, but the fact that these early Jews attempted to hide their Jewishness must be borne in mind by the genealogist of today.

Jews were established in North America before 1800, and there was a Sephardic Congregation in Philadelphia as early as 1740. In June 1841 President Tyler pleaded for more emigration to America, and this resulted in substantial numbers of Jews emigrating from eastern and central Europe – often making their way down the Rhine to the port of Antwerp. Here they were required by the authorities to register and to spend at least three days before embarking. This piece of bureaucracy is of extreme value to modern genealogists, for it is often the only clue remaining as to the ultimate place of origin of many Ashkenazi emigrants. This was followed by another influx later in the century, by which time South Africa had also opened its doors to Jewish refugees from Europe.

Records of Jews emigrating from England can often be found in the records of the Jewish communities and from the Collyer Ferguson pedigrees housed in the Jewish Library in London. Naturalization and Denization papers for themselves or members of their families are sometimes to be traced in the Public Record Office. The Mocatta Library (University of London) has a complete set of the *Jewish Chronicle* from 1844, in which much valuable information is to be found.

22

Dutch settlements in America

Just as the English had ignored the Pope's division of the New World between Spain and Portugal, so the Dutch ignored England's claim to all lands between Florida and Newfoundland. Although the Netherlands based its claim on the activities of the Greenland Company in 1598, there was no Dutch exploration in North America until 1609. In that year the Amsterdam Chamber of Commerce of the Dutch East India Company employed Henry Hudson, an Englishman, to sail to the Arctic to discover a route via the north-east to China. Finding his passage blocked by ice in the region of the Russian Island of Novaya Zemlya, he turned about and sailed across the Atlantic to the as yet unnamed Delaware Bay. Sailing north he arrived at Manhattan in September 1609. On the basis of this voyage the Dutch laid claim to all the American territory between Cape Cod and Delaware Bay. Dutch merchants maintained their country's interest in this part of America for more than a decade after Hudson's voyage, but it was not until about 1630 that any really permanent settlements were made.

The inhabitants of the Dutch colonies were by no means all Netherlanders, nor were they contented under Dutch rule. The population consisted of four main elements: first, the townspeople (of many nationalities) of New Amsterdam, which was the centre of Dutch shipping; second, there were fur traders at three of the chief trading stations, Fort Orange (now Albany), Fort Nassau (now Trenton) and Fort Good Hope (now Hartford, Connecticut); third, there were the wealthy Dutch landlords living on great estates along the banks of the Hudson River; and finally there was a group of English 'squatters' from Connecticut at Westchester on Long Island.

The population of Manhattan, the chief centre of population, increased from about 300 in 1609 to 1,500 in 1664, when it was taken by the English. At that time, the total population of New Netherlands was less than 5,000 while that of New England had risen to nearly five times that number. New Netherlands never developed a tradition of self-government like the English-speaking colonies, but continued largely to function as a commercial enterprise directed from Holland. The Englishmen were naturally discontented with Dutch rule, and even the Dutch themselves disliked it. The Dutch West India Company, under whom the colonies were administered, was more interested in dividends and paid more attention to its West Indies and South American colonies than to New Netherlands. Peter Stuyvesant, the most efficient of a not very efficient line of governors, ruled from 1647 to 1664. He tried to enforce uniform obedience to the Dutch Reformed Church and persecuted the Lutherans, Quakers and Baptists who had settled in the colony.

The men who prompted English mercantile policies objected to the Dutch dominance of the American carrying trade and to Dutch incursions in the African slave trade. American planters, on the other hand, were very friendly with the Dutch, who gave them lower freight rates than the English, and greatly assisted them in the cultivation of sugar and tobacco. So long as the Dutch maintained their foothold on Manhattan and along the Hudson River, there was no hope that the colonies would contribute to the growth of English mercantile power.

The English government, therefore, launched a propaganda war against Holland in 1664 to justify its seizure of New Amsterdam, and a fleet was sent in August that year to take it. Stuyvesant could get no help from Holland or from the inhabitants of the colonies themselves, and was consequently forced to surrender without firing a shot.

23

Scandinavian migration to America

During its brief existence, New Netherlands was harassed not only by the Indians and the English, but also by the Swedes.* In 1638 an expedition of two ships sent out by the Swedish West India Company moved up the Delaware River and established a settlement at Christiana Creek. The Swedish government was no more enthusiastic in support of this settlement than the Dutch were of theirs. In 1642, after sending a further handful of colonists, most of whom were Finns regarded as undesirable citizens because of their tendency towards petty lawbreaking, the Swedish government assumed direct control over the colony which had till then, like its Dutch neighbours, been largely a private enterprise. But Sweden had been impoverished by war and distracted by European politics, and could give little support to the tiny colony, which had totally failed to grow. From a total population of 300 in June 1644 less than 100 were alive ten years later. After years of neglect, the colony offered no resistance to the Dutch of New Netherlands who annexed it in 1655 to put an end to competition in the fur trade.

It was not until 200 years later that a substantial number of emigrants left Sweden to settle in North America. Gustaf Unonius of Uppsala, leader of the Pine Lake colony near Milwaukee, came to America in 1841. Initially his settlement consisted of military men, merchants and students. Among these early emigrants were Baron Thott, Lieutenant van Schneidau and a Norrköping merchant named Wadman. This colony was not successful, and after a relatively short time was disbanded. Unonius became a pastor of the Episcopal church and finally returned to Sweden. The second colony from Lund University settled at Koshkonong Lake, 40 miles from Madison, Wisconsin. It was led by Thure Ludvig Kumlien.

These early settlers were intellectuals and adventurers. Unonius

* *The Background of Swedish Emigration to the United States* by J. S. Lundberg, 1930.

wrote articles and letters which gained wide distribution and inspired many to emigrate, among them Daniel Larson from Hanrida in Småland. In company with about fifty people he left for America in 1844. During the following year Peter Cassel from Kisa in Östergötland led a party to America. New groups from the region around Kisa joined these, coming in 1846 and 1847, and by 1850 as many as 300 people had emigrated from Östergötland and northern Småland. Several religious groups left between 1846 and 1854, the most prominent of which were the Erik Jansonists who went in several groups.

Increasingly large groups went to Chicago, and in 1847 about forty families arrived there. This number rose in 1849 to about 400 people, in 1850 to about 500, and by 1852 to 1,000 people annually. Also in 1849 about 140 people came from northern Sweden, led by Pastor L. P. Esbjörn. The following year a sect known as the Luthläsare emigrated from Gävle in northern Sweden.

S. M. Swensson after visiting Texas in 1838 returned there ten years later with fifty farm-hands to start a Swedish colony in that state. Group migration such as this prevailed until 1860 or thereabouts, but after this time the tendency was towards individual emigration.

Many early Swedish emigrants were Baptists. By 1875 Baptist emigration was considerably stronger relatively speaking than total emigration, and by 1900 about 10,000 had emigrated.

Like the Germans, many Swedes in America tended to settle close together when they first emigrated. People from the same district usually settled in the same locality in the new country; those from the same village sometimes planned their community on the Swedish pattern at home. The majority of emigrants, however, had only a limited knowledge of Sweden as a whole or of Swedish culture and history. Their home province was thus better known and understood than the country at large. This strength of local feeling is shown by its survival even into the second generation. The settlers were largely old friends, relatives and acquaintances, so that a feeling of continuity with the old social patterns persisted in America. For the genealogist this is a factor which must be borne in mind and which is of great assistance when looking for Swedish ancestors.

Finland was part of the Kingdom of Sweden for about 600 years.* When Sweden became a centralized state in the seventeenth century, Finland was seen as a group of provinces extending alongside the provinces of Sweden. The language and culture of Finland was Swedish: the educated classes, whether of Finnish, Swedish or foreign stock, all eventually adopted Swedish as their mother tongue. Nevertheless the

* *The Finns in North America*, edited by R. J. Jalkanen, 1969.

Finnish language and culture persisted, despite a certain amount of friction between the two races. By the middle of the eighteenth century the balance of power in northern Europe had changed, and in 1721 south-eastern Finland and the Baltic states passed from Swedish to Russian rule. From 1742 Russia offered Finland the status of an autonomous protectorate within the empire. In 1808 all Finland was formally annexed by Czar Alexander I. Many high officials entered Russian service, but the Army, both officers and rank and file, and the whole peasant population, remained loyal to Sweden. In the negotiations which followed the treaties of Tilsit and Erfurt, Finland became, to quote Alexander I, 'a nation among nations'. The old title of 'The Grand Duchy of Finland' was revived and took on a new meaning. Finland never became a province of Russia, therefore, for in 1809 Sweden ceded the eastern half of her kingdom to Russia.

Finland was granted a measure of autonomy by the Czars in their capacity of Grand Dukes of Finland. Their government made its own decisions on less important matters, but submitted its views on more important ones to the Czar for approval. There was also a small enlisted army and a customs frontier with Russia, and Finnish citizens enjoyed rights not enjoyed by Russians. In 1811 Alexander I returned the territory in the south-east of the country to Finland, which had been ceded to Russia under the treaties of 1721 and 1743. Throughout this period Finland was able to retain her Scandinavian social system and customs. Finland remained part of Russia until 1918.

The majority of Finns who emigrated to America in the mid nineteenth century came from the central part of the country bordering the Gulf of Bothnia. A considerable number also emigrated from Northern Satakunta and Northern Tarrastland, the regions of Rauma and Åland. In 1800 Finland had a population of about 900,000; a century later it stood at 3 million. The country as a whole experienced a rapid increase in population, but the average growth was far surpassed by that of newly pioneered areas such as Bothnia and Northern Satakunta. However, the mere increase in population was not the sole factor which led to emigration, since Finnish cities and the general economic life of the country offered the excess rural population other ways of earning a living. In certain areas emigration became a fashion: in others, not. The political situation also played its part. Under a decree of 1878, three years' compulsory military service seemed excessive to many young Finns, who preferred to emigrate rather than submit to it. The repression instituted by Czar Nicholas II was another cause of inducing men and women to seek a more liberal home in America.

Finnish interest in America began to flourish about the time of the California gold rush. Finnish seamen began deserting their ships when they docked in American harbours. In the 1860s emigrant recruiters began travelling in Finland and in the following decade the steamship companies issued a stream of propaganda designed to attract would-be emigrants. In 1874 one such company spread literature from Sweden depicting Canada as an earthly paradise, and during the next decade many Finns emigrated there helping to build the trans-continental railroad. United States agents sent by the railroad companies were especially active in the 1880s and the flow of Finns to America soon became a flood: more than 350,000 out of the 1900 population of about 3 million left the country in search of better conditions on the other side of the Atlantic.

However, Finns had gone to America long before the nineteenth century. During the sixteenth century and seventeenth centuries Sweden had encouraged Finnish settlers to develop Värmland in West Central Sweden. It is estimated that 40,000 Finns crossed the Gulf of Bothnia to take up their abode in this hitherto uninhabited region of Sweden. When the Swedes founded their colony of New Sweden on the Delaware in 1638, a number of Värmland Finns took part in the venture. Before the Dutch captured New Sweden in 1655, it is estimated that 500 Finns arrived in Delaware. They were soon assimilated by their neighbours, however, a century later it was impossible to find any Finnish-speaking families in the area, though certain Finnish customs remained.

During the first half of the nineteenth century, when Alaska still belonged to Russia, a number of Finns moved there as fishermen and whalers. Two Finns actually served as governors of Russian Alaska. After the United States bought Alaska in 1867, some of the Finns returned home, but others moved to the United States or Canada. When gold was found there in 1880, the Finns started to move there again, and during the first decades of this century Finns, together with Norwegians, were the largest foreign-born group in Alaska.

Between 1825 and 1918 about 760,000 Norwegians migrated to America.* This movement originated in the rural hinterland of Norway, where land was scarce and difficult to cultivate, and where life was hard. Many Norwegian peasants had become discontented with the system under which they were living, by the formalism of the established church and the aloofness of the clergy. Many were alarmed by the rapid increase in the country's population, which nearly trebled between 1800 and 1900. Bad harvests and the none-too-distant threat of starvation were powerful factors influencing Norwegian peasants to leave their country. The main stream of migrants began in 1836, and

* *A Voice of Protest* by Jon Wefald, 1971.

during the following four years 1200 Norwegians arrived in America. About 17,000 more came in the 1840s, 36,000 in the 1850s, and roughly 700,000 between 1860 and the outbreak of the First World War. By 1920 there were approximately 2 million Norwegians in America, some of whom had been there for five generations.

The majority preferred the western Middle West, especially the states of Wisconsin, Minnesota, Iowa and the Dakotas. By 1900 nearly half of all first-generation Norwegians in America owned or managed farms, and nearly two-thirds of the second generation did so too. Being overwhelmingly a rural movement, it is not surprising to find that the people from one community or district at home would often sail on the same ship and settle in America as a unit. For example, Norwegians who came from Gudbrandsdal developed the Coon Prairie settlement in Wisconsin; those from Numedal settled at Jefferson Prairie, Wisconsin; people from Sogn went to Goodhue County, Minnesota; and Stavanger settlers chose the Stone City area of Iowa.

When building their new communities these emigrants retained much of their native ethic and customs, maintaining a lack of social stratification which distinguished them from their English neighbours.

24

Frenchmen in America

On 13 April 1593 Henri de Navarre, King of France signed the Edict of Nantes, which granted liberty of conscience to all Frenchmen. It restored to the Huguenots their full civil rights and gave them their freedom to worship unmolested.* After the death of Henri IV the old persecution began to be reasserted, until in 1685 Louis XIV revoked the Edict and ordered the destruction of Huguenot churches, forbidding the gathering of Protestants to worship together. Both before 1598 and after 1685, French Huguenots sought refuge in Switzerland, Germany, Holland and England, where they were welcomed as industrious and intelligent people. The majority who escaped were noblemen, gentry, merchants and manufacturers, bankers and skilled artisans, but few peasants.

The first serious attempt to found a French colony in North America was made in 1562, under the leadership of Jean Ribault who sailed from Le Havre to Florida. Like Raleigh's expedition to Roanoke twenty years later, it survived less than two years, and it was not until forty years later around the turn of the century, when Pierre de Monts, a Huguenot gentleman from Saintonge received a Royal Commission to settle in what is now Nova Scotia, New Brunswick and Canada, that French settlements in North America began in earnest. The new colony was to give freedom of religion to all-comers, and Calvinism and Catholicism were to exist side by side. A hundred and twenty people, Protestant and Catholic, of high and low birth, sailed from Le Havre in March 1604 and landed at what is now Annapolis Harbor in the Bay of Fundy. De Monts named it Port Royal, but it had to be abandoned in 1607 largely on account of commercial pressures brought against him at home. Undismayed, de Monts, together with Samuel de Champlain, set sail in 1608, but this time they made their way to the St Lawrence, where in the summer of that year they landed on the site of Quebec

* *The French Blood in America* by Lucian J. Fosdyck, 1906.

and established a trading post. De Monts now took with him the rivals who had formerly broken his trading monopoly, and also engaged the active support of many merchants of La Rochelle. Champlain, who was a Catholic, succeeded de Monts as Governor of French North America, but with the death of Henri IV it was only a matter of time before religious liberty was abandoned and Jesuit missionaries installed in the new colony. The formation of the Company of New France in which no Huguenots held office, under the patronage of Cardinal Richelieu, made sure that New France would remain within the Catholic fold. When in 1628 Charles I of England renewed the grant given earlier by his father James I to Sir William Alexander to trade and settle in Nova Scotia and Canada, he appointed as the Admiral in charge of his expedition David Kirke who, with his brothers, were the sons of a French Huguenot mother and natives of Dieppe. Other Frenchmen included Jacques Michel, an ardent Calvinist, who had been in the service of Guillaume de Caen when that staunch Huguenot leader had been head of the former Canada Company led by de Monts. David Kirke captured Quebec in 1629. Peace had been signed between England and France three months before, but during the three years which followed while negotiations for its return to France dragged on, Lewis Kirke was in command. The Kirkes were the sons of Gervase Kirke who came from Derby, but whose distant forbears were Scottish. Gervase had lived and married in France, and Lewis Kirke's policy was to induce French and English families to remain in Quebec and to give them religious liberty. This example, alas, was not followed by the Jesuits sent out by Richelieu, whom Kirke had permitted to say mass undisturbed. It is, however, significant that it was a Huguenot, Emery de Caen, who was made Agent of France to receive back her American province. In May 1633 Champlain was reappointed governor, and from that time forward Canada was closed to Huguenots as colonists.

After the fall of La Rochelle, the Baron de Sauce, one of its defenders under the Duc de Rohan, took refuge in England. In 1629 he asked permission to establish a colony of Huguenots in Virginia 'to cultivate vines and to make silk and salt there'. The request was received favourably and he was granted Letters of Denization for himself and his son, so that he might return to France in safety to get his family and property. Careful preparations were made, and in due course the expedition sailed for Virginia, settling in Nansemond County on 200,000 acres then known as Southampton Hundred. No records of this colony have survived, and its fate is a matter of conjecture. Due to its unhealthy situation, it is probable that the immigrants succumbed to malaria, though undoubtedly some survived, for Huguenot names are found in the early Norfolk County records. Among the leading families of Virginia many of these names (either obvious or in disguise) can be found, the best known being Battaille, Durand, De la Mundaye, de Bar, Dabney (D'Aubigné), Jourdan, Martiau, Noel, Plouvier, Ravenell, Rigault, Sully, Vicomte, Vasker, Fantleroy (Faunt le Roi).

In the last decade of the seventeenth century, at least one thousand French Protestants came to America, not less than 700 of whom went to Virginia. In 1700, four fleets sailed from Gravesend and the settlers picked on a site 20 miles above Richmond, where they were given 10,000 acres which had formerly belonged to the Manikin Indians, after whom they named their settlement Manikintown.

This is not the place to write the history of the Huguenots: but many settlers in New England and Virginia during the seventeenth century were of French Huguenot descent. Their fathers and grandfathers had gone from France either to England or Holland, and from thence to America. Many anglicized their names, but diligent research by the Huguenot Society of London has identified them by their correct French ones. Certain confusion arises, however, from the double migration of many Huguenot families, first to England, Holland or Germany, and then to America. Historians of the city of Maine have failed to notice that the founders of Dresden, the early settlement on the Kennebec, were French and not German. They were Huguenots who had first fled to Germany after the revocation of the Edict of Nantes, and then migrated in company with a few German families in 1752 to America. They had originated in the eastern provinces of France closest to Germany, and of the 46 emigrants who left Frankfurt in 1752, 28 were of French origin and 5 only of German. Another example of double migration can be found among the settlers of New Rochelle in Westchester County, New York. In 1689 some Huguenots for New York were joined by others from the West Indies where they had hastily sought refuge after the Revocation. However, the majority came from England and were Rochellois who had left their city 4 years before and fled to the Ile de Rhé and from there to England, where they found an English ship to take them to America.

Prior to the grant to William Penn in 1681 of the region now known as Pennsylvania, there were many French refugees amongst its inhabitants. Some of their names took on a Dutch or Swedish flavour, thus adding to the difficulties of genealogists, but the majority of them lost their French identity because they did not come direct but through Germany or Holland, where most of them had long resided, and where many of them had been born. The names Kieffer and de Witte do not immediately suggest the original French names of Tonnellier and Le Blanc, and the famous 'German' Peter Minnewit was in reality Pierre

Minuit, which he found an easier name for the English to pronounce so reverted to an approximation of the French original.

The majority of the French settlers in the Delaware region came over at the time of the first general influx from the Palatine between 1654 and 1664. Among the records of Christ Episcopal Church in Philadelphia there are many Huguenot names dating from as early as 1709.

More than a century after the failure of Coligny's plans to establish a French colony in South Carolina mentioned above, William Sayle an Englishman established the first permanent settlement there near the site of Port Royal in 1670. The earliest settlers were a mixed lot. From England there came both Royalists and Republicans; a group of Dutch settlers came down from New Amsterdam after the English had turned it into New York; and in 1679 Charles II sent a group of French refugees there. Their religious leader was the Rev. Elias Prioleau who brought a considerable part of his congregation from France. He was the grandson of Antonio Prioli who had been Doge of Venice in 1618. In addition to these Huguenots who came direct from France, a considerable number of refugees had gone first to New York and New England, but after a short residence there opted for the warmer climate of Carolina. A considerable group came from Acadia (the region on the borders of Maine and New Brunswick) when, after Nova Scotia had finally surrendered to England, the French settlers there were dispersed among the other English colonies as a precautionary measure. About fifteen hundred of them were sent to Charleston in South Carolina. In 1764 another colony of Huguenots came from France by way of Plymouth in England to a settlement which they named New Bordeaux after the capital of the province from which most of them came. It was they who introduced the manufacture of silk into South Carolina.

Louisiana was opened up by French missionaries bent on establishing a New France to contain the English on the eastern seaboard. The actual occupation of Louisiana did not begin until the end of the seventeenth century, when Pierre Le Moyne d'Iberville established a settlement at Biloxi on the shore of the Gulf of Mexico.* There were in addition to this, and at New Orleans, two other centres of French settlement: one in the vicinity of present-day St Louis and the other at the junction of Lake Erie and Lake Huron. Additional posts were established during the eighteenth century, but they were primarily military establishments or trading posts rather than permanent colonies.

Relatively few people were involved in the first occupation of the Gulf coast. There were about 12 Canadians, some 10 artisans, a few

---

* *A History of French Louisiana* by Marcel Giraud, translated by Joseph C. Lambert, 1974.

cabin boys and some freebooters, the total amounting to not more than eighty men. The wives and children of the married men of the garrison were to be authorized to come to Louisiana if the men requested it. Emigrants were to be recruited from the poorer classes, and a number of poor families from the region of Avranches in Normandy had expressed a wish to emigrate, but d'Iberville's plans were largely thwarted by the Minister in France, who did not favour large settlements. Consequently nothing was done. The outbreak of the war of the Spanish Succession in 1702 further retarded colonization: five years later the population was still predominantly Canadian. By 1717 the population had still failed to increase, so that in that year it was decided to institute forced migration, not dissimilar from the transportation of convicts adopted by the English. Condemnation to the galleys was commuted by transportation for life in Louisiana, where after three years they were released but forbidden to return to France.

Shortly after assuming power as Regent of France on the accession of Louis XV in 1715, Philippe duc d'Orleans sponsored John Law of Lauriston, one of the most colourful figures in American history, to build up Louisiana as a viable colony.* Law was responsible for recommending the formation of the Compagnie de l'Occident (Company of the West) which was chartered in 1717 for twenty-five years. During this time it enjoyed a total monopoly of trade in Louisiana. It undertook to send out 6,000 white settlers and 3,000 slaves within ten years. The Company established a town on the Mississippi; and in 1718, 300 concessionaires with land grants, among them Bernard de La Harpe and Le Page du Pratz emigrated, followed in 1719 by 100 more from France, but it quickly became clear that voluntary emigration alone could not meet Louisiana's needs. It was therefore decided to draw upon criminals of all degrees and ages, women as well as men, and to deport them to Louisiana. Between 1717 and 1721, the population thus increased from about 400 to 8,000, including negro slaves. This policy provoked protest from leaders of the colony and within six months the Regent had forbidden the deportation of any more criminals to Louisiana, but even before this, John Law had begun to look elsewhere for families to settle on his own large concession near the mouth of the Arkansas River. Agents were sent to Germany, where peasants from the Palatine, Alsace Lorraine, Baden, Württemberg, Mainz and Trier flocked to enlist as emigrants. About 6,000 Germans reached the ports of embarkation for the Mississippi, of which only about 2,000 actually reached the colony, and the bulk of which Law sent to his own settlements on the Arkansas. For genealogists, this migration of Germans to French-speaking America

* *Ten Flags in the Wind* by Charles I. Dufour, 1967.

has set some interesting problems. Names such as Buchwalter became Bouchevaldre; Katzenberger became Casbergue; Schön became Chaigne; Himmel became Hymel; Edelmaier, Delmaire; Vogel, Fauquel; Kleinpeter, Clampetre; and Kissinger, Quisingre. Possibly the most startling change was the transformation of Johann Zweig into Jean La Branche, from whom descends one of the most prominent Louisiana families today.

From the arrival of the Germans, of whom about 1,500 survived, dates the beginning of stability for Louisiana, but the foundation of New Orleans in 1721 must also be reckoned as a significant milestone in the development of the colony.

After Louisiana was ceded to Spain in 1762, it took two years before the fact was made known to the settlers. The news was greeted with consternation. In 1765 Charles III of Spain appointed Antonio de Ulloa governor, but he was greeted coldly by the populace, and in 1768 he was faced with an uprising. On 28 October of that year, a band of Acadians, French settlers who had come to Louisiana from Nova Scotia, and 300 German settlers entered New Orleans, but were evicted by a large Spanish force the following August. During the Spanish occupation 1,600 Acadians were imported from France in 1785, after they had gone there following their expulsion by the English from Nova Scotia in 1755. The Acadians remained the only element in Louisiana which preserves the French language. They settled around the towns of Lafayette, New Iberia, Abbeville, Houma, Thibodaux, Opelousas, St Martinville, Beaux Bridge, Lutcher and Donaldsonville.

On 5 November 1762 France by a secret treaty ceded to Spain the 'Island' of New Orleans and of all Louisiana west of the Mississippi.* Spanish ownership continued until 1801, when again by secret treaty the territory was ceded back to France. The transfer was slow, and a military expedition planned in 1802 never sailed. On 30 April 1803 Louisiana was sold to the United States and the final transfer of the whole territory of Louisiana took effect on 10 March 1804. The thirty eight years' sovereignty of Spain over part of the Mississippi valley is a fact which is sometimes forgotten when considering this part of the United States, which was for so long part of the French colonial empire.

The French from their northern base in Canada made the first moves into the middle west and down the Mississippi valley. The Jolliet-Marquette expedition of 1673 from the north, and La Salle's expedition in 1682 to the delta, paved the way for French colonization of middle America at the expense of Spain.

---

* *The Spanish in the Mississippi Valley 1762–1804*, edited by J. F. McDermott, 1974.

25

Spanish-speaking groups in the United States

According to the US census of 1950, there were 1,861,400 Spanish-speaking Americans, who form a minority in many ways unique in America.* The Spanish Americans or Hispanos who live in the high-lands of New Mexico and South Colorado constitute a cultural island of colonial Spain which has developed in geographical isolation from the rest of the country. The Indian Mexicans and Malay Filipinos have different racial and cultural backgrounds, and will not be considered here; likewise the Puerto Ricans, among whom a negro element exists. The genealogical problems of these groups fall outside the scope of this book, and we shall consider only those Spanish-speaking Americans of European ancestry. These are broadly speaking the Mexicans of south-ern Texas and Minnesota and those Spanish political refugees who have settled in the United States during the present century.

More than three hundred years ago Spanish soldiers reached the north-western outpost of Spain's empire, New Mexico. They married women of the native Indian population, and their children not only spoke Spanish, but developed a culture which was a mixture of Spanish and Indian tradition. Since that time, the descendants of these colonists have retained to a remarkable degree the culture of eighteenth century Spain. These communities were annexed to the United States after the Mexican war of 1846. They call themselves 'Hispanos' (short for Hispano-Americanos) to distinguish themselves from 'Anglos', or Anglo-Americanos. They reserve the term 'Mexicanos' for those who live in or who have emigrated from Mexico. This pattern is found in southern California and in Colorado where both Hispanos and Anglos feel that they rank above the recently emigrated Mexicans. Little inter-marriage has taken place between Hispanos and Mexicans, less between Hispanos and Anglos, and in the last hundred years surprisingly little between Hispanos and Indians. More than half of the population of the state of New Mexico is Hispano.

* *Spanish-speaking Groups in the U.S.* by John H. Burma, 1954–74.

26

Italians in America

No records of Italian emigration to America were kept until 1825.* Emigration prior to 1856 was negligible, not more than a few hundreds being admitted each year. Between 1870 and 1875 there was a small increase, but the trickle resumed until 1882 when it jumped to 30,000. From that time it increased more or less regularly until 1907, when 285,731 emigrants arrived; there was then a fall-off to between 120,000 and 190,000 during the next five years, when again emigration rose to over 280,000 a year in 1913 and 1914. During the First World War it fell rapidly, as was to be expected, but in the decade 1906–16 more than two million Italians emigrated to the United States.

The first all-Italian Parliament was convened in 1861.† Prior to that period the country had been dominated by the Habsburgs in the north, the papacy in central Italy and the Bourbons in Naples and Sicily. Scattered between these three power blocks were smaller states, each of them independent and with their own sovereigns. By 1870 Venice and Rome had become part of the new Kingdom of Italy which now for the first time took on the aspect of a modern unitary state. The Italians have had a class system which has placed the northerner over the southerner, and given prominence to Tuscans while relegating Sicilians to the lowest ranks. Even in America, many Sicilians were ostracized by other Italians. But the true differences were of course economic, and the true heart of the 'Southern problem' was the central government's denial of its existence. Following unification, the new national government put most of its effort into developing the economic growth of the industrial north, while leaving the south to fend for itself.

The start of Italian migration to America was soon after the establishment of Jamestown in 1607. As early as 1610, the Virginia Company imported European wine growers, and by 1622 had sent for a small

* *Italian Colonies in America (Sons of Italy)* by Antonio Maugana, 1917.
† *The Italian Migration* by Luciano J. Lorizzo and S. Mondello, 1971.

group of Venetians in an attempt to establish glass works and a silk industry. In 1648 Maryland passed a law to encourage French, Dutch and Italian emigrants. The Toleration Act of 1649 ensured religious freedom to Catholics, and it was not long before the clergy included a number of Italian Jesuits. Later, Italian Protestants and Jews settled peacefully in Georgia, the Carolinas and New York. After the British took control of Florida in 1763, more than a hundred Italians from Leghorn were attracted to the ill-fated colony of New Smyrna, but by 1778 it had collapsed and the surviving Italian and Greek settlers moved to St Augustine. During the next three-quarters of a century and more, Italian priests were active missionaries in America, mainly in the south and along the Mississippi.

Political oppression in Europe caused many Italian intellectuals to seek refuge in America, the best known of whom was Filippo Mazzei, a friend of Thomas Jefferson. Hundreds of political exiles driven from Italy in the period immediately preceding the unification of the country followed Mazzei's example, probably the best known of whom was Mozart's librettist, Lorenzo da Ponte.

Prior to the migration explosion of the 1870s, Italian merchants were to be found throughout the country, especially in Chicago, where the Genoese formed a large group. In California, Italians worked mostly in the mines, agriculture and as fishermen and as general traders. In New York, Italian artisans made a mark for themselves as interior decorators, cabinet makers, painters, stone cutters, and musical instrument makers; and of course Italians played a most important part in the artistic and musical life of the country.

Those Italians who came to America before 1880 were mostly from the north. There were comparatively few of them, so they were overwhelmingly outnumbered by south Italians and Sicilians who came between 1880 and the early 1920s. The early north Italian colony, made up as it was largely of skilled artists, intellectuals and merchants, was overshadowed by the mass migration of south Italians, who provided a pool of unskilled labour for America's rapidly expanding industry. The American census of 1850 records only 3,645 Italians in the United States; ten years later this figure had reached almost 10,000, and by 1880 it was 44,230. These Italian migrants were located from Maine to the Pacific, all over the Missouri and Mississippi valleys, Nevada, California, Oregon and elsewhere.

The agricultural problems of southern Italy are age-old and deep-seated. Between 1870 and 1900 the population greatly outstripped the increase in gross national product, and produced a marked decline in real incomes. There was not only a glut of labour, but also a shortage of food, which gave every inducement to leave. The state of Italian agriculture became more precarious with the flood of American and Russian grain into Italy, and the emergence of fruit production in Florida and California, so that thousands of growers in Calabria, Basilicata and Sicily were ruined in the 1880s and 1890s. The wine growers of Apulia, Calabria and Sicily suffered likewise. High taxation and low wages in southern Italy at this time and malnutrition made thousands vulnerable to diseases such as malaria, pellagra and gastro-intestinal disturbances, and such cities as there were had nothing to offer them. Prior to 1895 Italian emigrants had preferred South America, especially Brazil and the Argentine, but the Brazilian economy was going through a difficult period and the wages offered by Brazilian employers were not much greater than those offered at home. The United States therefore became a haven for hundreds of thousands of peasants, whose passage was organized on a massive scale by the agents of the steamship companies which we have already observed operating in Scandinavia. Many of these were unscrupulous speculators, trafficking in human misery, but despite these abuses, sophisticated Italians as well as humble peasants persisted in regarding the United States as a country which offered the opportunity to make a fresh start in life. Over 3 million emigrated in the first fourteen years of this century. The movement was accelerated by chain migration, a process whereby Italians in America acted as personal labour agents and informed their friends and relatives when and where jobs were available. Apart from the years of the two world wars the process has continued, and the average migration between 1945 and 1970 steadied to between 11,000 and 25,000 per year.

27

Polish migration
to America

Poles have played an important part in the building of America.* They
went in their greatest numbers in the years between 1880 and 1910, but
many had gone earlier. Accounts of Polish emigration usually begin
with John of Kolno, a town in north central Poland, who was a seafarer
in the service of the king of Denmark, and who is said to have piloted
a fleet of Danish ships to Labrador and then sailed down to the mouth
of the Delaware River in 1476. There is another legend which says that
Sir Walter Raleigh employed Polish pitch burners on his Roanoke expedition in 1584/5. It is an established fact, however, that Captain
Christopher Newport took several Poles in the *Mary & Margaret* to
Jamestown in 1608. They were Michael Lowicki, Zbigniew Stefanski, a
glass blower, Jan Mata, a soap boiler, Jan Bogdan of Kolomyja, a
ship-builder, Stanislaw Sadowski, and Karol Zrenica. They were followed by more than sixty others. Captain John Smith in his *True Travels*
expressed great respect for the Poles in early Virginia, and recognized
them as good soldiers against hostile Indians. Without the hard work
and skill of these early Polish pioneers, it is no exaggeration to say that
the infant colony might well have failed to survive. So vital were they
to its economy, that in spite of the wishes of the Virginia Company
they were given the same rights as Englishmen at the Council of 30
June 1619, after they had threatened to go on strike if they were not.
Close social and economic relations between Poland and Sweden during
the seventeenth century, ensured that there were a number of Poles in
the colony of New Sweden. The organizer of the South Company for
Swedish Colonization in America, William Usselinx, toured Poland in
1627 to raise funds for the project. When the Swedes founded Fort
Christina in 1641 they sent over a number of Poles with their other
settlers.

During the sixteenth and seventeenth centuries, Poland conducted a

* *America's Polish Heritage* by Joseph A. Wytrwal, 1961.

busy trade with Holland, and Amsterdam became the home of a group of Polish Protestants. In 1659 Governor Stuyvesant, to prevent the English disrupting the Dutch beaver trade in America, tried to induce the Dutch West India Company to send him twenty-five or thirty families from Poland. This is but one of several instances of joint Dutch/ Polish colonial enterprise. Among the early Polish settlers to reside in New Amsterdam was Daniel Litscko. There is a record of the baptism of his daugher Anna there in 1647. He died in 1661 after playing an important part in the life of the Dutch colony. Anna married Colonel William Peartree who was Mayor of New York from 1703 to 1707. Another prominent Pole in North America was Dr Alexander Karol Kurezewski, known in Dutch records by the name of Curtius, who was appointed a teacher in 1659 to give lessons in Polish and Russian. He was also a Doctor of Medicine, and is known to American history as Alexander Curtiss. This tendency to translate difficult Polish names into more easily understood English or Dutch is a cause of great difficulty for genealogists, and something that has complicated the task of ethnic historians from the earliest times well into the eighteenth century.

In 1662 an exiled Polish nobleman called Olbracht Zaborowski, who claimed descent from King Jan Sobieski, settled in New Amsterdam, and later obtained a large tract of land in New Jersey. He married a Dutch woman, and was one of the founders of the Lutheran church at Hackensack in New York, where he died in 1711. He left five sons, who intermarried with the most prominent colonial families, and his son John changed his name to Zabriskie. During the Revolutionary War, John Zabriskie remained loyal to the British Crown, and thereby lost his estate. His descendants, however, have played a prominent part in the life of New Jersey down to the present century.

Poles settled in the Delaware valley as early as 1650, and there was a thin trickle of Polish immigrants into Pennsylvania and Virginia throughout the next hundred years. The pioneering successes of Poles in the seventeenth and eighteenth centuries stimulated Paul Mostowski, an eighteenth century Polish statesman, to formulate plans for a Polish colony in the southern part of North America to be called New Poland. Unfortunately the partition of Poland between Prussia, Russia and Austria meant not only the end of this venture, but also the end of independent Poland.

The American struggle for independence inspired many Poles to join the fight for freedom. The events of 1776 and the subsequent years coincided with events in Poland which favoured emigration to America. Men of great distinction, soldiers, noblemen, artists and teachers, made a substantial contribution to American life. Chief of these were Kosciusko and Pulaski, who played an important part in the training of

American soldiers to fight the British. Between 1794 and 1830 Poland enjoyed a measure of independence in the kingdom set up in 1815 following the end of the Napoleonic Wars, though in reality this formed part of the Russian empire. Patriotic elements revolted in 1830 and 1863, but the collapse of these insurrections resulted in wholesale migration of the military and intellectual élite to Western Europe, and of a considerable contingent of soldiers and members of the lower nobility to the United States. In 1835 the 'Polish National Committee in the United States' was formed, which persuaded Congress to grant a large tract of land in Illinois to Polish refugees. For a number of reasons these settlements did not survive, perhaps because the majority were men who married among the local citizenry.

Although Polish immigrants have made an impressive mark on American life, it was in Texas that the first considerable Polish settlement was founded. In 1854, 800 men and women under the leadership of Father Leopold Moczygemba carrying ploughs, bedding, kitchen utensils and a large cross from their old parish church, landed at Galveston and made their way inland to found the settlement of Pann Maria in honour of the Blessed Virgin Mary. By 1906 the Polish population of Texas was between 16,000 and 17,000. Wisconsin was another goal for emigrant Poles. In 1858 a Polish family from East Prussia came to Portage County and founded a settlement called Polonia which grew to be a prosperous rural community.

Up to 1870 Polish emigration was, however, essentially sporadic, and linked closely with political conditions at home. But the quality and intellectual abilities of those early settlers was out of all proportion to their numbers. With hopes of Polish independence ended by the defeat of France by Prussia in 1870, thousands of Polish aristocrats, political exiles and peasants made their way to America. In 1870 there were some 50,000 Poles and ten Polish parishes in America: by 1889 there were close on 800,000 Poles in the United States, 132 churches and 122 schools. The peak was reached during the years 1912–18, when the number each year reached as high as 174,000, and by 1920 there were approximately 3 million Americans of Polish parentage.

28

Croat and Slovene migration to America

The Croats are a Slav people, whose homeland is situated within the modern state of Yugoslavia south of the Drava and Danube rivers.* There are approximately 4½ million Croats in Yugoslavia out of a total population of 22 million. A little less than one quarter (i.e. about 1 million) are Muslims, the rest nominally Roman Catholic. They form part of a much larger grouping of Slav peoples consisting of thirty-nine nationality groups. This complexity of groups was reduced by the US Immigration Department to eight, which in numerical importance are as follows:

1 Polish
2 Slovak
3 Croat and Slovenian
4 Ruthenian (properly Ukrainian)
5 Bohemian and Moravian
6 Bulgarian, Serbian and Montenegrin
7 Russian
8 Dalmatian, Bosnian and Herzogovinian

This is an extremely arbitrary classification and takes little or no account of mutual antagonisms and wide differences of history, culture and political background.

By the end of the fifteenth-century, Croatia was hopelessly divided, and the political centre of the country had shifted to the region of Zagreb, which is today's capital of Croatia. During the sixteenth century, the country was fought over by the Christian west and the Muslim east. The Adriatic coast of Croatia became in time part of the Venetian Republic after 1420, while inland Zagreb came under the influence of Austro-Hungary. In the south, the ancient city of Dubrovnik (known also as Ragusa) developed an enterprising seafaring tradition, and as

* *Croatian Immigration in America* by George J. Prpic. Philosophical Library, New York, 1965.

early as 1491 Dubrovnik traders in alliance with or in the service of Spain were trading with America. In 1520, the Konkendjević brothers sailed for America where they stayed for thirty years, and in 1537 Bazilije Baziljević sailed from Seville to Peru. Men of Dubrovnik also traded with England, and the name 'Ragusa' gave the English language the word 'Argosy', synonymous with the richest kind of galleon.

Most of the early Croat emigrants were from the Adriatic regions of Istria, Dalmatia and Dubrovnik. In 1526 the Turks defeated the Hungarians and Croats, and soon after the greater part of the country passed under Turkish rule. In 1680 Ivan Ratkaj the Croat Jesuit missionary, left Europe and became the first known emigrant to America from continental Croatia. His missionary life was largely spent in Mexico, and he was followed by other Croatian missionaries to Spanish America, including California and Colorado.

Several American sources assert that around 1715 some 1,200 Croat and Slovenian Protestants who had been living in Prussia came to Georgia where they settled at a spot where a creek which they named Ebenezer flows into the Savannah River. There they undertook silkworm culture, and for 150 years continued to thrive until the Civil War destroyed their economy and forced them to abandon their colony. Only a cemetery with Croat and Slovenian names on the headstones remains as a monument to these early settlers. There is, however, no historical evidence that any Croat or Slovene immigrant ever lived at Ebenezer. Writers who have mentioned these alleged Croat Protestants have never quoted a reliable source. It is, however, authoritatively proved that Ragusan ships sailed in the early eighteenth century for Cuba and San Domingo and that they went on from there to Philadelphia and New York.

After the Congress of Vienna in 1815, Croatia became part of the Austrian Empire. Since then many Croats who formed a large part of the crews of the Austro-Hungarian naval and merchant vessels were sailing regularly to America. The height of prosperity for the Adriatic shipbuilding industry was reached in the 1870s, when sailing vessels of up to 2,000 tons were built at Dubrovnik and Pelješac. Many of these ships reached New Orleans, Philadelphia and other major American ports, and many of the seamen aboard them decided to remain. Some based themselves principally in New Orleans, but others moved up the Mississippi and there are traces of Croat settlements in Alabama before the Civil War. There are small Croat colonies also in the Mississippi delta, where the colonists supported themselves with fishing and the gathering of oysters. These pioneers devised special vessels to catch oysters and their enterprises prospered. By 1849 there were quite a large number of Croat businessmen in New Orleans, and by 1860 there were many more, such as sail-makers, jewellers, restaurant keepers, in addition to oyster and shellfish sellers and fruiterers. In 1838 Father Josip Kundek sailed to New York to join a mission at Vincennes, Indiana. His activities were limited to the southern part of the diocese which included the whole of Indiana and part of Illinois, including Chicago. In 1839 he founded a new town called Ferdinand, and in 1843 another settlement called Celestine. To begin with, most of his settlers were German Catholics, but in 1851 he returned to his native Croatia to recruit other missionaries. Meanwhile, Mateo Asnerich, a native of the Island of Brać in Dalmatia, found his way in 1849 to San Francisco. By 1852 he had become a gold miner and one of the first Croat settlers in the Santa Clara valley. He was one of the first to join the gold rush, for after 1849 California became the home of many hundreds of Croat emigrants and San Francisco became their largest settlement. After 1870 migration from Croatia in common with migration from Europe generally, greatly increased. For lack of reliable statistics, it could be assumed that about 10 per cent of all emigrants from Austria before 1880 were Croats. Following the discovery of silver in Nevada, many migrated there as well as to Idaho and Montana. Croats were also among the pioneers of the state of Washington, as well as in Alaska.

Whereas most of the old Croat emigrants were from the Adriatic coastal region, a small number came from inland Croatia. However, during the later period, a much greater number came from Croatia proper and Slavonia. Thus early emigrants from inland Croatia came mainly from the region around Delnice, Ogulin, Gospić, Karlovac, and Zagreb. Between 1850 and 1865 these areas sent miners to Pennsylvania and other industrial centres. From 1870 to 1880, the number of emigrants leaving Croatia, Dalmatia and Bosnia-Herzegovina rose to about 1,000 per year. The high tide of Croat emigration was reached during the years 1900 to 1914. During this period more than 160,000 left the country, though inadequate statistics make it appear that the figure was almost certainly much higher than this.

29

Greek migration to America

Emigration to the United States from Greece took place chiefly in the late nineteenth and early twentieth centuries.* The emigrants came from a country of peasants and poverty, and their coming was part of what some observers have seen as a national renaissance. During the late 1890s, Greece was making economic advances, and Athens and the Piraeus were booming. But by 1899 this had changed: drought, crop failures, and a decline in the value of the currency brought a temporary recession, but after a few years the economy revived. This revival was partly due to the foundation of the Greek merchant fleet, which nearly trebled in size between 1896 and 1904. The completion of the Corinth Canal in 1893 was another landmark in Greek economic expansion. But there was another side to the coin. Modern Greece began as a nation with a poor neglected agricultural population. Centuries of Turkish misrule had resulted in millions of untilled acres. The new national government did less than it might to improve the lot of the peasantry, and mounting discontent produced political disturbances in 1906. The Balkan wars of 1912–13 increased the number of refugees and landless people. Agriculture, however, as an occupation was held in low regard in Greece, so that the tendency was for the more ambitious to enter the professions. As late as 1928, despite the inroads of urbanization, commerce and manufacturing, the rural class comprised 67 per cent of the total population. Greeks had been enthusiastic for America since the time of their War of Independence in the 1820s. At the time of the Spanish-American war, rumours had circulated in Greece that volunteers were needed for the American army and navy and the United States Consulate in Athens was besieged by thousands of would-be volunteers, especially from Crete. The Consul expressed his gratitude, but had to say that the rumours were false and that he had no authority to accept volunteers.

* *Greeks in the United States* by Theodore Saloutos, 1964.

There were, however, three main phases of Greek emigration to America. The first arose out of the activities of American missionaries in the 1820s and 1830s, but was comparatively small. The second revolved around the representatives of Greek-owned commercial firms established in various cities in the country during the mid-nineteenth century and the third had its origins among the Spartans of the late 1870s and 1880s, who came to be known as the Greek Pilgrim Fathers.

The missionaries who went from America to Greece and other near-eastern countries in the early years of the last century were mainly Congregationalists, trying to recruit young boys to go to the United States to be educated. When their studies were complete they were supposed to return home and to contribute to the moral regeneration of their country.

After 1850, Greek firms such as that of the Ralli Brothers, were established in New York, New Orleans, Savannah and other American cities. A number of these were interested in the cotton trade, and their founders and managers became prominent American citizens. For all practical purposes, the pace of emigration was set by the Greeks of the Peloponnese, the Islands, the mainland, and the Turkish-dominated areas of western coastal Turkey, who came during the late nineteenth and early twentieth centuries.

Heavy emigration from Sparta began during the 1870s, and reached a peak between 1890 and 1910, when an estimated three-quarters of the male population between the ages of 18 and 35 left for America. In 1882 about seventy left the area of Tsintsinon, from which a number had emigrated in 1877, most of whom were married men aged 25 or more. After 1890, Greeks began departing from all parts of the country. Emigration from Arcadia began in earnest between 1892 and 1894, and increased steadily until it exceeded that from the Peloponnese. It affected the provinces of Argolidos and Corinthos, Achaea and Elidos, Messinia, Attica and Boetia, Phthiotidos and Phokidos, Aetolia and Akarnanios. Emigrants left from the region around Larissa, Trikkala and Artis; from the islands of the Cyclades, the Eastern Aegean, the Dodecanese, Crete and Zakynthos.

The exodus of the 1890s was precipitated by the decline in the price of currants, the principal export crop, as a result of a drop in demand. A series of natural disasters increased the flow, so did an inefficient government, military service and the archaic dowry system. Greeks emigrating from the Ottoman empire before 1912 usually left for political rather than economic reasons. Greek immigrants gained the reputation of sending more money home per head than those of other nationalities. Many likewise returned to spend the years of their retirement in the land of their birth; a custom which continues today.

30
The settlement of Canada

We have considered the French contribution to the life of North America elsewhere, and have necessarily touched on the early history of Canada. There was sporadic French emigration during the middle years of the seventeenth century, but virtually none after 1675.* The population of 1750 represented several generations of native-born French, whose outlook and attitude differed from those at home. Indeed, there was considerable friction and resentment on the part of Canadians against the tepid support they received from France in their attempts to develop Canada as a French-speaking colony in the face of English expansion. The principal centres of settlement by the time Canada fell to the English at the end of the eighteenth century were three: Acadia, which covered more or less the same area as Nova Scotia; New France, the area to the north-west of the St Lawrence between Quebec and Lake Ontario, and the lands immediately to the south of Lake Erie. The struggle for Canada lasted rather more than seventy years, ending with the Treaty of Paris whereby France abandoned all her possessions on the mainland of North America. Canada was ceded to the British and Spain was given Louisiana. The acquisition of Canada presented problems to the British government, whose initial attempt to assimilate its new possession into the empire was by establishing a uniform system on the model of the older colonies.

After Acadia had been taken, it was proposed to annex it to Massachusetts. This idea was abandoned when Nova Scotia, as it now once more was called, became a separate province ultimately designed to be self-governing on the model of Virginia. It was, however, some thirty years before efforts were made (about mid-century) to promote immigration. Discharged soldiers and distressed artisans from England were sent, but so too were French and German Protestants. The most efficient settlers, however, were New Englanders whose influx was speeded up

* *Canada – A Political and Social History* by Edgar McMinnis, 1947, 1949, 1969.

as Acadians, unwilling to become British subjects, moved on to Louisiana, then still French. A large migration of New Englanders began in 1760; they settled round the Bay of Fundy, while a number of displaced Scottish Highlanders sought lands at Cape Breton and Prince Edward Island as well as on the mainland.

Following the Independence of the United States, Canada became the only British possession on the American mainland. By 1791, six provinces had come into being: Lower Canada, the most populous and the longest settled, was overwhelmingly French in population; Upper Canada and New Brunswick had only just been created; the settlement of Prince Edward Island (formerly St John Island) had barely begun; Newfoundland and Nova Scotia were older British possessions, but their populations were only 15,000 and 40,000 respectively. The British population of Canada differed radically from that of the thirteen colonies which had seceded. Many loyalists had fled from the thirteen colonies to avoid persecution at the hands of American radicals, which meant that they were not only staunchly royalist but also very conservative.

At first there was little emigration from Europe or Britain to Canada, and comparatively few settlers arrived before 1814, though there were many who spilled over into the region of the St Lawrence from the expanding former colonies in the northern United States. By 1814 the French character of this region had been changed by the influx of some 200,000 English-speaking Americans. By 1851 the whole of the north bank of the St Lawrence, Lakes Ontario and Erie and the eastern shore of Lake Huron were settled, as well as a substantial area to the south of the St Lawrence around the towns of Sorel, Richmond and Sherbrooke. Between these two dates, by 1825, 2,000 Irish immigrants had settled in the Peterborough area north of Lake Ontario.* Near Kitchener, further west, German families from Pennsylvania established efficient farms and a flourishing community. Today the area still shows evidence of their own culture. In 1827 John Galt, a Scotsman, as agent for the Canada Company, bought 1,100,000 acres known as the Huron Tract fronting the lake and extending sixteen miles inland, and established a number of settlements with people from Britain.

Among the early settlers in Manitoba were a group of Russian Mennonites who had left their native land to avoid persecution. They settled in country that resembled the southern Russian steppes they had left, and soon gained the respect of earlier settlers by their honesty and business acumen. They were followed by a group of Icelanders, who had escaped the eruption of Mount Hecla in 1873 which had ruined their farmlands. They settled first in the Muskoka district of Ontario,

* *Canada: Colony to Centennial* by D. C. Willows and Stewart Richmond, 1970.

but this proved an unsatisfactory site and in 1875 they moved to an area west of Lake Winnipeg. After these early pioneers came Poles, Germans, Ukrainians, Hungarians, Jews and Doukhobors, another Russian religious group whose home was in the Caucasus. It is estimated that between 1832 and 1902, 2¼ million Scandinavians left for North America. Until 1870, only a few settled in Canada, though after 1873 a number of families settled near Minnedosa in Manitoba. Another Swedish settlement, New Stockholm, Saskatchewan, was founded in 1886. The earliest Norwegian colony in western Canada was founded in Alberta in 1893 and appropriately named New Norway. In the following year a second settlement was founded by people from Bardo, Norway. After the British Isles, Germany was the most important source of emigrants to Canada from the mid-nineteenth century up to 1914. By 1931 it was estimated there were about 250,000 people of German and Dutch descent in western Canada.

Of all the earlier pioneers in the Canadian west, the Ukrainians were the most difficult to integrate. The Ukrainian peasant in the late 1800s was little better off than a medieval serf. Two provinces of the Ukraine, Galicia and Bukovina, supplied most of the emigrants. An estimated 200,000 settled in Canada between 1896 and 1914. They went to the north-east of Edmonton near Star at first, but other Ukrainian settlements were established in Manitoba and Alberta near Vegreville. Often entire villages emigrated, bringing with them their customs, language and way of life, thus presenting an exclusive front to the surrounding population of mixed settlers.

Among other early settlers in western Canada were the Jews. During the 1870s and 1880s, Polish Jews underwent great privation in Europe. The first group of refugees arrived in 1882 and settled in Saskatchewan, but as they were not country people they soon drifted to the towns and the settlement was abandoned. Later, in 1899, groups of Russian Jews arrived and also settled in Saskatchewan, but they proved successful farmers, until by 1938 15 per cent of the Jewish population of Saskatchewan lived on the land.

In 1888, twenty Hungarian families settled near Winnipeg, to be followed by other groups, who settled in Alberta and Saskatchewan. The Doukhobors had the reputation of being among the best farmers of Russia. They were devoutly religious, and lived God-fearing and peaceful lives. Between January and July 1899 about 7,500 arrived in Winnipeg, and others followed until the total was nearly 9,000. They settled near Yorkton and Rosthern in Saskatchewan, and maintained a highly strict and circumscribed way of life, which on occasions brought them into conflict with the law.

31

The settlement of Australia and New Zealand

In 1606, the year that the London Virginia Company was fitting out the expedition which successfully established a permanent English settlement on the North American continent, Willem Jansz, a Dutch sea captain, made landfall on the west coast of Australia in the ship *Duyfken* on his voyage to Java. Unlike America, the European settlement of Australia was delayed for more than 180 years after its discovery. Abel Tasman, in 1642, discovered Tasmania and New Zealand, but both his voyage and Jansz's only touched the barren western coast of mainland Australia, yielding nothing to either adventurer. The English sent out an expedition under Dampier in 1699 to try to discover the continent's eastern coast, but instead he discovered the islands of New Britain and others to the south-east of New Guinea.

The South Sea Company, founded in 1711, was established to exploit the supposed riches to be found in the islands to the south of the East Indies; its collapse in 1720 brought its activities to an abrupt end, but the Company had, at least, stimulated interest in Pacific exploration. In 1768 Captain James Cook was put in command of an expedition to Tahiti, whose main purpose was to observe the astronomical phenomenon of the transit of Venus across the face of the sun, but whose lasting achievement was the thorough exploration of the east coast of Australia. This famous voyage completed, more or less, the discovery of the continent's coastline and thus established its vast extent.

However, there was no compelling reason in the eighteenth century to found settlements in regions as remote as Australia, especially since there remained the vast, empty spaces of central North America as yet unsettled by white men. Although the early European pioneers in North America had had their troubles with the Indians, these were never as fierce or hostile as the Australian Aborigines or New Zealand Maoris, with whom most European expeditions had failed to establish any worthwhile contacts. Settlement, therefore, did not attract any group of private investors, as had happened in the seventeenth century. For its part, the British government was far more concerned with the struggle it was waging against the French in North America. This led first to the taxation of the American colonies, and it was only when this resulted in revolution and ultimately to independence, that it began to turn its attention to Australasia.

Coincidentally, the 1750s and 1760s were a period of rapid industrialization leading to increased population as well as to increased unemployment and crime. With the Declaration of Independence in 1776, the North American colonies were no longer a dumping ground for undesirables. Australia, on the other hand, could be. Increased pressure on English prisons as well as the need to find a place for dispossessed loyalists from North America both combined to make Australia an attractive place for government-sponsored settlement. The foundation of the Botany Bay penal settlement, it was hoped, would lead to self-sufficiency within three years: no thought of founding any greater colonial enterprise entered the government's head. The First Fleet of convicts in 1787 was a journey without hope. Because the original convicts lacked agricultural and other skills so vital for the successful establishment of a thriving settlement, it rapidly became necessary to send out freemen trained in the various crafts without which success could never be achieved. The government despatched the first free settlers in 1793. Nine years later, during the beginnings of the war with France, there was an increase in the rate of emigration designed partly to strengthen the infant settlements against French attempts to seize them. As it turned out, this was merely a scare, for Napoleon never had any designs on Australia.

For twenty of the colony's first twenty-seven years England was always at war; all available shipping, therefore, was needed to patrol the seas nearer home. This meant not only that Australia's isolation remained, but also the invalidation of the theory that convicts could return home after completing their sentences; in practice there were no ships to take them. The ten years between 1814 and 1824 saw an increase in the transportation of criminals as well as of free emigrants. Up to this time, as earlier in Virginia, no entirely satisfactory economy had been developed by the infant colony. It was not until 1802 that the first Merino sheep were introduced, but thereafter the development of sheep farming grew steadily. In the course of twenty years or so this led to Australia becoming attractive to free farmers as well as to businessmen with capital to invest.

The year 1838 saw a change of emphasis in government policy towards Australian settlement from the transport of convicts to the encouragement of family emigration. This change of policy had a levelling effect on the sex ratio between men and women, for up to that time men had outnumbered women many times over. Convict transportation finally came to an end in 1840, to be replaced by assisted free migration. By mid-century, gold had been discovered, which greatly augmented the flow of migrants. Between 1830 and 1850 almost half of all assisted immigrants were of Irish origin: England and Wales provided 40 per cent and Scotland 12 per cent. In 1846 the Family Colonization Loan Society was founded by Mrs Caroline Chisholm. This society chartered ships and brought pressure to bear on the government to give free passage to wives and children of men who had gone earlier.

Between 1790 and 1850 the Jewish population of England rose from about 12,000 to 35,000 inhabitants. Thus, by degrees, from among the enormous criminal population of Georgian and early Victorian London, a Jewish element soon became noticeable, and so on most convict ships which carried Britons to Australia there were Jews who shared their fate.

Among the 751 convicts transported in the First Fleet at least eight, and possibly fourteen, can be identified as Jews. Esther Abrahams, Henry Abrams, Daniel Daniells, John Harris, Frances Hart, David Jacobs, Amelia Levy and Joseph Levy were certainly Jewish; Sarah Burdo, Aaron Davis, Sarah Davis, John Jacobs, Thomas Josephs and Joseph Tuso may have been. Joseph Levy is typical of the kind of petty criminal who was transported to Australia. His crime was the theft of a copper kettle worth eight shillings in May 1784 from its hob in a London street. He was caught as he ran away with the kettle in his hand and sentenced to seven years' transportation. He died in April 1788 and became the first Jew to be buried in Australia. The lives of these First Fleet convicts can be traced through English and Australian records, which show that all of them were transported for crimes which nowadays would be regarded as paltry. Not all, however, suffered the fate of Joseph Levy. Esther Abrahams, for example, was convicted of shoplifting and sentenced to seven years transportation. She, too, sailed aboard the *Lady Penrhyn* for New South Wales in April 1787 with the First Fleet. In the same ship sailed Lt. George Johnston, who on 26 January 1788 became the first European to set foot at Sydney Cove. On the voyage Esther had become Johnston's mistress, and subsequently bore him several children. Twenty-five years later, after Johnston had risen to a position of prominence and responsibility in the young colony, she became his wife. In this bizarre, haphazard way Australia became the only community of European people in which Jews were present from the moment of its establishment. Through the documents of Australian history it is possible to trace stories of people torn from the confines of London's Jewish East End ghetto and forced to create a new life in this totally alien world. The transportaton of Jewish men often caused the migration of whole families, drawn by ties of kinship or friendship. Of the 145,000 Britons transported to Australia between 1788 and 1852, at least 1,000 were Jewish. Most of these were men or boys born within the London community that numbered 30,000 at most.

Abel Janszoon Tasman was born in 1603 in the province of Groningen, Holland, and in 1633 went to the East Indies in a merchantman.* He became skipper of a yacht, trading and fighting smugglers and natives and doing a certain amount of charting and surveying. In 1636 he returned to the Netherlands, but two years later sailed to the East again and there spent the rest of his life. His discovery of New Zealand in 1642 made little impact on Europe, and left it isolated and unvisited for another century or more. The first systematic settlement of New Zealand dates from the beginning of the last century. The first sheep were brought to the Bay of Islands in 1814 and they came from Sydney, Australia, but it was not until 1840, when Auckland had been well-established, that British settlement of the northern shores by farmers was begun. The first regular emigrants to Auckland and the north were Scotsmen from the Clyde. They were mostly Lowlanders from Ayrshire and Galloway, but twelve years later came the first Highlanders in what became known as the Gaelic migration from Nova Scotia.

It is well known that Scottish Highland evictions, the Irish potato famine and English labour conditions were prodigious influences in the migratory movements of the middle of the last century, but it would be incorrect to say that New Zealand was populated by people who were starving in their mother countries. The proportion of early immigrants born in the industrial towns of England is very small. It needed tougher men to break in a raw new country. Many early settlers were men and women of education and culture, and the majority of those who settled on the land in the first four decades of New Zealand's history as a British country were of yeoman stock and agricultural workers.

The Highland settlement of Waipu consisted of crofters who had been driven from their homes in Ross-shire, Sutherland and other parts of the highlands, and who had gone first to Cape Breton in Nova Scotia. The Reverend Norman McLeod, the pastor of this little community, had a son who found his way to Australia, and the accounts he wrote of that country were so attractive by contrast to the hard land of Nova Scotia that the Highlanders, pastor and all, were seized with a desire to migrate once more.

They built a ship called the *Highland Lassie*, and another called the *Margaret*, loaded them with their goods and set sail for Adelaide in south Australia. When they arrived there they discovered that condi-

* *New Zealand Centennial Surveys*, vols. 2 and 4, 1940.

tions were not as bright as they had been painted, so they got in touch with the then Governor of New Zealand who persuaded them to settle in North Auckland. And so in 1854 these much-travelled Scots at last found a place to settle. Other Nova Scotians followed, numbering 876 people in all, but while the Highland feeling is still strong in this part of New Zealand, the Gaelic language has died out.

Among the earliest settlers were people of several European races, though the majority of New Zealanders are predominantly Anglo-Celtic. There were some Danes and Norwegians, who founded the towns of Dannevicke and Norsewood; there was a colony of Bohemian (Czech) settlers at Puhoi, north of Auckland, which was founded by 83 men from the town of Staab in Bohemia, then part of the Austro-Hungarian empire. This settlement was founded in 1863. The chief migration of Irish to New Zealand took place between 1875 and 1878, consisting mainly of two groups of settlers from Northern Ireland brought out by George Vesey Stewart, of County Tyrone.

32

Genealogical sources in Australia and New Zealand

Australia

Australia is, by European standards, a young country but its records contain a wealth of material which is of great significance for the genealogist. How can the individual compiling the history of his family in Australia use that material to the best advantage? The answer to this question, like the answer to most questions about genealogical research, is not a simple one. The key to it is an understanding of Australia's history and development as a group of separate states which, though eventually formed into a commonwealth, retained control over their own archives.

As all Australian children know, Captain Cook landed at Botany Bay in New South Wales in April 1770 and claimed the territory for the British crown. However, it was not until August 1786 that the British government decided that the new colony should succeed the recently independent United States as the place to which convicts sentenced to transportation should be sent. Arthur Phillip, a retired naval officer living on half pay, was appointed Captain-General and Governor in Chief of New South Wales and on 13 May 1787 he set sail from England with 750 convicts, certain civil and military officers and a contingent of marines. In January 1788 the First Fleet arrived in Botany Bay. Later in the same month, Botany Bay being found unsatisfactory, all the settlers moved to Sydney Cove where on the 26 January the British flag was unfurled and the history of European settlement in Australia began.

Australians tended for many years to speak little of convict ancestors but recently a considerable amount of interest in genealogy has been shown by descendants of persons sentenced to transportation. Evidence of this interest is provided by the existence of the Fellowship of First Fleeters, an organization which encourages individuals of convict ancestry to find out about their forebears. It is important that anyone wishing to trace ancestors in Australia should realize that, in the case of early emigrants, it is frequently easier to obtain information about those who were convicts or assisted immigrants than it is about those who were free settlers. The reason, in the case of convicts, is that records exist of the date and place of the trial in each case and from them can normally be discovered the age and place of birth of the convict. Where a convict received an absolute or conditional pardon the records also give the place of birth together with the name of the ship in which the individual arrived, the name of the master of the ship, the year of arrival in the colony, the occupation of the convict, the place and date of his conviction, his sentence, the year of his birth, a physical description and the date of the conditional pardon. Tickets of leave and certificates of freedom for convicts give similar information. These records are to be found in the Archives Office of New South Wales, which also holds Indents (Records) of Convict Ships 1788–1842, lists of convicts 1788–1820 and lists of convicts, free men and officials for the year 1826. Transportation of convicts to New South Wales ceased in 1849, to Tasmania in 1853 and to Western Australia in 1868, but there are various records later than 1870 relating to each of these states.

Many immigrants to Australia were provided with assistance to go there by the government, religious bodies and business men. For certain periods the records of assisted immigrants are very extensive and give the age, birthplace or place of residence prior to embarkation, the father's full name, occupation and place of residence, the mother's name and maiden surname, her father's occupation, often the maiden surname of her mother, and the education and occupation of the immigrant. In 1835 the Bounty System was introduced whereby the immigrant's passage was paid provided he or she produced testimonials of good character. These certificates of character usually have baptismal certificates attached to them.

Free settlers began to arrive in Australia at an early date. From 1856, when registration of births, marriages and deaths began in New South Wales, there is frequently no problem in discovering their origins because the information given on certificates is very extensive. New South Wales death certificates give the name, sex, age and occupation of the deceased, the date and place of death and burial, the name and occupation of the deceased's father, the Christian name and maiden surname of the deceased's mother, the deceased's birthplace and the number of years the deceased had been in the Australian Colonies or States, indicating which, the name of the deceased's spouse, the date and place of the marriage and the deceased's age at the time, the names of the deceased's children, their ages and whether living or dead. Various other details, of less interest normally to the genealogist, also appear on New South Wales death certificates. Marriage certificates in

New South Wales are also helpful to genealogists. They give the date and place of the marriage, the names, occupations and places of residence of the parties, their condition, their birthplace and age, the name and occupation of the father and the name and maiden surname of the mother. New South Wales birth certificates, from the beginning of registration in 1856, give the date and place of birth, the name and sex of the child, the name, occupation, age and birthplace of the father, the date and place of the marriage, the name, maiden surname, age and birthplace of the mother and the names and ages of other living children and the sexes of deceased children. Before 1856 copies of church records are in the custody of the Registrar-General in Sydney. They give the name of the child, the names of the parents, their abode, the occupation of the father and the date and place of birth and baptism.

Details, similar to those given on New South Wales certificates appear on certificates of birth, marriage and death in Victoria, where registration began in 1853. Before Victoria became a separate state in 1851 it was known as the Port Phillip District of the Colony of New South Wales. Most of the Victoria church records prior to 1853 are in the custody of the Government Statist in Melbourne.

In Queensland registration of births, marriages and deaths began in 1856, although the area remained part of New South Wales until 1859. Certificates are obtainable from the Registrar-General in Brisbane. Various church records dating back, for baptisms and burials, to 1829 and for marriage to 1839 are also held by the Registrar-General.

Births, marriages and deaths in Western Australia have been registered since 1841 and the details given are similar to those for New South Wales, Victoria and Queensland. The records are held by the Registrar-General in Perth.

The two other Australian States, Tasmania and South Australia, provide problems for the genealogist, largely because of the paucity of information provided by their certificates. Tasmania, originally settled in 1803 and known as Van Diemen's Land, became a separate Colony in 1825 and evolved into the State of Tasmania in 1856. Registration of births, marriages and deaths began in 1838 and is under the control of the Registrar-General in Hobart. Certain earlier church records, back to the year of settlement, are also held by the Registrar-General. The Tasmania death certificates do not give any informatioin about the parents of the deceased, or his date and place of birth. Likewise, birth and marriage certificates do not contain a great deal of detail.

In South Australia registration of births, marriages and deaths dates from 1842. The records are held by the Principal Registrar in Adelaide, who also has certain church records from the foundation of South Australia as a province for free settlers in 1836. Copies of these earlier records from 1836 to 1842 are also held by the South Australian Archives. The only genealogical information on South Australian birth certificates from 1842 to 1856 is the date of birth, the name and sex of the child, the name and surname of the father and the maiden surname of the mother. In 1856 the address of the parents was added. From 1908 onwards South Australian birth certificates also give the age and birthplace of the father, the age, maiden name and birthplace of the mother, the year of marriage, the number of previous issue, living or deceased, and the occupation of the father. South Australian marriage certificates from 1842 to 1856 give the date and place of the marriage and the names, ages, occupations and descriptions of the parties. From 1856 to 1868 the fathers of both parties are given – their names only, no occupations. In 1907 were added the place and country of birth of these parties. Death certificates in South Australia up to 1907 simply recorded the date of death, the name of the deceased, his or her age and occupation and the cause of death, although from 1856 to 1874 the place of the death and the usual residence of the deceased were added. In 1907 death certificates became more informative, giving, in addition, the birthplace of the deceased, the length of residence in the Commonwealth, the age at marriage or re-marriage and details of issue, living or deceased. Northern Territory formed part of South Australia until 1911. The Registrar-General in Darwin has records from 1870.

It is important, at this point, to emphasize that in no part of Australia is the public permitted to make searches for certificates. They can only be obtained by personal or postal application to the relevant Registrar – in Melbourne, the Government Statist. The fees payable vary from state to state and according to the urgency or otherwise of the enquiry.

Genealogists familiar with census records in England, Scotland and Wales, will be disappointed if they try to locate similar archives in Australia. The personal details given in Australia census records since the early nineteenth century have never been made available to the public. Instead, they are destroyed some years after they have been taken, when the statistical information they contain has been extracted. The census material of most interest to the genealogist interested in Australian records is that contained in the New South Wales Census of 1828. This lists the name, age, year of birth and religious affiliation of every person in the Colony, whether a convict or free settler, together with the name of the ship and the year of arrival of the individual concerned, his occupation, place of residence, amount of land and stock, and, where the individual is a convict, his sentence. There were earlier New South Wales Musters in 1806, 1811, 1814 and 1825, and a Convict Muster in 1837. In Tasmania Census and Muster records have survived for 1842 and 1846.

Wills and Administrations, another useful source of information, are kept on a state basis at the probate office in each capital city. The Society of Australian Genealogists has, on microfilm, all the New South Wales wills and administrations up to 1900.

A great deal of work has been done by Australian genealogists on the copying of tombstone inscriptions. The Society of Australian Genealogists has many volumes, some printed, others in manuscript, showing information from that source. The Genealogical Society of Victoria has a card index of monumental inscriptions, which is steadily increasing in size as the tombstones in more cemeteries are transcribed.

Another useful source of information for genealogists is directories. The Mitchell Library in Sydney, which is the special portion, concerned with Australasia, of the State Library of New South Wales, has a fine collection of Directories of Sydney. An excellent set of Melbourne Directories is to be found in the La Trobe Library in that city.

Newspapers in Australia contain announcements and obituaries which can be of great assistance in compiling the history of a family. The periods they cover vary, of course, from one area to another. The library of the state concerned should always be consulted in order to discover what newspaper files exist. A useful index to Birth, Marriage and Funeral Notices in the *Sydney Herald* (*Sydney Morning Herald* from 1842) is being published by two Australian genealogists, Malcolm Sainty and Keith Johnson. So far volumes I (1831–42), II (1842–7), III (1848–51) and IV (1851–3) have appeared.

A number of histories of Australian families have been published. In some cases they are works dealing with several families; in others they relate to one family only. An example of the former kind of family history is P. S. Mowle: *A Genealogical History of Pioneer Families of Australia* (Sydney, 1948). Among instances of the latter sort of family history may be cited the numerous works on South Australian families listed in A. G. Peake: *Sources for South Australian Family History* (Adelaide, 1977), a particularly useful publication as it lists source material in South Australia, which can provide assistance when information on certificates is scarce.

The various genealogical societies in Australia produce their own journals which print source material and articles of interest to genealogists. The journal of the Society of Australian Genealogists in Sydney is named *Descent*. That of the Genealogical Society of Victoria is called *Ancestor*. In Victoria there has also existed since 1973 the Australian Institute of Genealogical Studies whose magazine is *The Genealogist*. It was the Instittue which organized the very successful First Australasian Congress on Genealogy and Heraldry held in Melbourne in 1977. The Heraldry & Genealogy Society of Canberra produces *The Ancestral*

Searcher. The South Australian Genealogy and Heraldry Society publishes *The South Australian Genealogist*. The senior genealogical society in Australia is the Society of Australian Genealogists, founded in 1932. Its library possesses a fine collection of Australian and overseas genealogical material, including many specialized collections. Nancy Gray, one of its members, has produced a helpful guide *Compiling Your Family History*. The Genealogical Society of Victoria also produces a useful booklet *Ancestors for Australians*.

Addresses

New South Wales: The Registrar of Births, Deaths & Marriages,
Prince Albert Road,
Sydney, N.S.W. 2000.

The Archives Office of N.S.W.,
CAGA Centre,
8 – 18 Bent Street, Sydney,
N.S.W. 2000.

The Mitchell Library,
State Library of N.S.W.,
Macquarie Street,
Sydney, N.S.W. 2000.

The Society of Australian Genealogists,
Richmond Villa, 120 Kent Street,
Observatory Hill,
Sydney, N.S.W. 2000.

The Fellowship of First Fleeters,
Box 4441,
G.P.O. Sydney, N.S.W. 2100.

The 1788–1820 Association,
G.P.O. Box 1212,
Assembly Hall, Margaret Street,
Sydney, N.S.W. 2001.

Victoria: The Government Statist,
295 Queen Street,
Melbourne, Victoria 3000.

The Public Record Office,
328 Swanston Street,
Melbourne, Victoria 3000.

The La Trobe Library,
State Library of Victoria,
304–328 Swanston Street,
Melbourne, Victoria 3000.

The Genealogical Society of Victoria,
Room 4, 1st Floor,
Block Arcade, 98 Elizabeth Street,
Melbourne, Victoria 3000.

The Australian Institute of Genealogical Studies,
P.O. Box 89,
Hampton, Victoria, 3188.

Queensland: The Registrar-General,
Old Treasury Building,
Brisbane, Queensland 4000.

The Queensland State Archivist,
162 Annerley Road,
Dutton Park,
Queensland 4102.

Western Australia: The Registrar-General,
Oakleigh Building,
22 St. George's Terrace,
Perth, W.A. 6000.

The J. S. Battye Library,
State Library of Western Australia,
Perth, W.A. 6000.

South Australia: The Principal Registrar,
G.P.O. Box 1351 H,
Adelaide,
S.A. 5001.

The South Australian Genealogy & Heraldry
Society,
P.O. Box 13,
Marden, S.A. 5070.

Tasmania: The Registrar-General,
Box 129,
North Hobart,
Tas. 7002.

The Tasmanian Archives,
State Library of Tasmania,
91 Murray Street,
Hobart, Tas. 6000.

Australian Capital   Australian Archives,
Territory: P.O. Box 358,
Kingston, A.C.T.

The Heraldry Genealogy Society of Camberra,
c/o G. Thorn,
48 Derwent Street,
Lyons, A.C.T. 2606.

New Zealand

Registration

Registration of European births and deaths was first required in New
Zealand by legislation in 1848. Marriage records date from 1854. Before
this time births, deaths and marriages were recorded in the parish
registers held by churches. Copies of many registers are held in the
registrar general's office. Registration of Maori births and deaths did
not become compulsory until 1913. Some early registrations were made
in the European system, but not a great many. On the other hand,
registration from 1913 could not be effectively enforced in the early
stages, and it is now being found that a great many births, deaths and
marriages were not registered as they should have been. In 1955 the
separate Maori and European marriage laws and recording system were
amalgamated. The amalgamation of births and deaths registration was
instituted in 1962.

In the early days the particulars required for registration were far fewer than they became as the recording system developed. The births and deaths registration Act of 1848 required the following to be registered: *Births*: date and place of birth; child's name and sex; parents' names; occupation of father; maiden name of mother. From 1875 further information was included in the birth registers: date and place of marriage of parents; the age and birthplace of each parent. From 1912, birth entries further included the sex and ages of previous living issue of the marriage, and the number and sex of previous deceased issue. It will be noted that the names of the previous children are not provided for.

Deaths: from 1848 the entries for deaths showed date of death; full name; sex; age; occupation; cause of death. After 1875 the following information was added: full name of the parents of the deceased; the father's occupation; the mother's maiden name; the place of birth of the deceased; the length of time deceased had lived in New Zealand. If the deceased had been married, there was included the following: place of marriage; age of deceased at the time of marriage; name of the person to whom married; sex and age of surviving children; place and date of burial. From 1912, the age of the surviving wife is added. It should be noted that the names of the children are not shown.

Marriages: under the Marriage act of 1854 the only particulars recorded were the date and place of marriage; the full names, ages and conjugal state of the bride and bridgroom; the occupation of the bridegroom. Positive identification is not possible if the name of only one of the parties is known. By the Act of 1880 were added birthplace and usual place of residence of each party; full names of the parents of each party; the occupation of the father in each case; maiden surnames of the mothers.

Maori registration

For the duration of the separate system of Maori registration, the particulars required for registration were different from those for Europeans. This system applied to persons of half or more Maori blood for the period 1913–61 for births and deaths, and 1911–54 for marriages. The particulars recorded are: *Births*: name and place of birth; first names of child and sex; full names and residence of parents; tribe and degree of Maori blood for each parent. *Deaths*: date and place of death; full name and residence and tribe of deceased; sex and age; name of husband or wife; number and sex of living children; causes of death; names of parents of deceased and their places of residence, tribe and degree of Maori blood. *Marriages*: particulars of marriage are similar to those for Europeans, except that the details of the parents of the bride and bridegroom are restricted to the names only.

New Zealand records are not open for search except by members of the official registry office staff. The forms of the various certificates are governed by the principle of privacy and are prescribed by statutory regulations. Certificates do not give all the particulars shown in this entry. A certified copy of a birth entry does not give particulars of the marriage of the parents. Applications for *bona fide* research are considered sympathetically, however.

Normally a marriage certificate does not show the particulars of the parents, but there is a form of marriage certificate available to include the particulars of the parents of the parties to the marriage. This can be supplied on request. In most genealogical research cases it is probable that the actual certificate will not be required. Items of information will be given from any entry for a fee of 50 cents if the year of the event is known plus or minus one year. The amount of information given is limited to three items from any one entry. When some information is already known, then any other three items from a birth, death or marriage registration may be requested; for example the maiden surname of the mother, the place of birth of the father, the age of the mother, the time of birth of the child, etc. If information beyond the three items is required, or causes of death asked for, these will only be given in a certified copy of the entry for a fee of NZ$2. If the year of the event is not known, a search fee is payable: ten years for NZ$1, from ten years and up to twenty years, NZ$2, over twenty years NZ$5. There is no further charge for quoting the three items if a search fee is paid. The certificate fee, however, is payable in addition to search fees. Where a search is unsuccessful the search fee is retained and the certificate fee refunded. The period to be covered by any search must be clearly stated in years by the applicant, e.g. 1900–9. It is important that the year of the event is given, the surname of the person concerned and the Christian names. Information such as names of the parents is sometimes required to assist in distinguishing between persons of similar names, and those who perhaps unexpectedly prove to be registered under the mother's maiden surname. If the year is not known to the applicant, the procedure under extended searches is necessary.

Searches can be expensive, particularly when Christian names cannot be given. This is because every register entry under a given surname indicated by the index books for the years involved has to be inspected to ascertain the names of the parents for identification. This could run into a formidable list in the case of the more common surnames, and could mean that twenty, thirty or forty registers must be inspected. For any particular search, the more the range of the search can be limited, the more promptly the service can be given. Unfortunately, with the lesser detail given in Maori registers over the period of the separate

193

registration system, searching is very much more complicated. The difficulty is increased by the lack of continuity in the earlier stages of what could be called a family surname. It was the custom for a son perhaps to take for a surname what we would call the father's first name, i.e. a patronymic. Thus one generation's registrations could be in a different family name from the preceding one, or the succeeding one. Added to this is the complication of the very common use of aliases and unofficial adoptions from an early age with consequent change of name. All of which tend to lead to the original name of the registration becoming lost. Sometimes registrations were made in the name of adoptive parents, and in earlier years unfortunately no registration was made at all.

National Archives

The Archives Act 1957 established a National Archives to provide for the custody and preservation of public archives of New Zealand. No public archives as defined in the Act can be destroyed, without the approval of the chief archivist who has powers of inspection and of direction in respect of the keeping of public records. Government records of permanent value are deposited with the National Archives, and considerable original research is done in the National Archives by scholars and students, officials and the public. The National Archives has a Record Centre in Lower Hutt and one in Auckland. These provide storage for semi-current government records as well as public archives. Some public archives of regional interest are deposited with certain non-government repositories approved by the Ministry of Internal Affairs, such as the Hocken Library in Dunedin, the Canterbury Museum in Christchurch, the Hawke's Bay Art Society Gallery and Museum in Napier, the Auckland Institute and Museum, the New Plymouth Public Library, and the Marlborough Historical Society Museum in Blenheim. National Archives and the Alexander Turnbull Library are to join in establishing a War History Documentary Centre to preserve documentary material about New Zealand's part in the Second World War. The National Archives publish an annual summary of work, including a list of new accessions to its holdings.

Addresses

Library, Statistics Department,
Private Bag,
Wellington.

Public Trust Office,
P.O. Box 5024,
Lambton Quay, Wellington.

Registrar-General Births,
Deaths and Marriages,
Departmental Building,
P.O. Box 8023,
Lambton Quay,
Wellington.

The New Zealand Society of Genealogists,
P.O. Box 8795,
Auckland.

The Armorial and Genealogical Institute of New Zealand,
P.O. Box 13301,
Armagh,
Christchurch.

33

South Africa

History

Europeans have lived in South Africa for more than 400 years.* If the arrival of the Portuguese is taken as a starting point, European Africa has a history as long as that of Latin-America; if, on the other hand, one takes the Dutch occupation of Table Bay as the beginning, South Africa has a history almost as long as that of the United States. For the purpose of this book, however, the European occupation of the regions of the continent south of the Zambesi is what concerns us, and particularly those settlers of European stock who have developed the country during the past three centuries. These are made up of Afrikaners descended in the main from Dutch, Belgian, West German and French ancestors; people of various British stocks; a considerable number of Jews principally from central and eastern Europe; Germans in South West Africa (Namibia), and Portuguese in Mozambique Province.

The annexation of Portugal by Spain at the end of the sixteenth century opened the way to attacks on Portuguese traders and settlements by the enemies of the king of Spain, the chief of which were the Dutch who had long had an interest in far-Eastern trade. When Philip II closed Lisbon to Dutch merchants in 1581, he forced them to go to the Far East themselves. In 1595, Cornelis Houtman sailed round the Cape to Java, and three years later a score of Dutch ships made the voyage to India. In 1602 the Dutch East India Company received its Charter from Prince Maurice of Nassau. The states general nominally claimed sovereignty over the prospective possessions of the Company East of the Cape and West of the Straits of Magellan, and it took over 20 per cent of the loot of Spanish and Portuguese shipping and Customs dues on certain classes of goods. Only Dutchmen were allowed to hold shares, but small subscribers were encouraged. The Company acted

* *History of South Africa* by Eric A. Walker, Longmans, 1957.

196

with speed and vigour. In 1604 it captured Bantam, the Moluccas and Java, seized Amboyna and half Timor, and made a series of unsuccessful attempts to capture Mozambique.

More than 150 years passed after its discovery before a permanent European settlement was established at the Cape of Good Hope. The Portuguese had avoided it because it seemed to offer them no economic advantages. The Hottentots who inhabited the region had a reputation for savagery which discouraged settlers, and in any case the Portuguese who occupied St Helena and Mozambique had no real need for a staging post in between. The course of vessels from northern Europe to India took them south-west to the coast of Brazil, and from there south-east to the Cape of Good Hope, at which latitude they sailed eastwards towards the coast of Australia, then north-eastwards to the East Indies. The homeward voyage lay south of Madagascar to the Cape once more, and home by way of St Helena.

In 1615 Sir Thomas Roe put into Table Bay with four ships on which were some Japanese returning to their own country, and eight convicts whose lives had been spared on condition they went exploring. These men were set ashore at Table Bay. One was killed outright by the Hottentots, four others were drowned when their raft capsized, and the survivors were rescued and taken home to England. In 1620 Andrew Shilling and Humphrey Fitz Herbert of the English East India Company took possession of the Bay in the name of James I, but he declined the gift. It was not until 1647, when the Dutch East Indiaman *Haarlem* was wrecked and the crew remained there a year, that the Dutch government began seriously to consider the possibility of founding a permanent settlement. This task was entrusted to Johan van Riebeeck who, with three ships and a company of men, women and children founded the colony of the Cape of Good Hope in April 1652.

Generally speaking, the Dutch East India Company was against colonization. That was not its aim; hence, only a small settlement of nine free burghers, all of them married men of Dutch or German birth, was established in the Lisbeeck valley in 1657. They were bound to stay for twenty years, to take turns in manning the fortifications, and to grow no crops that might compete with the Company's monopolistic trade. With about 5,000 visitors per year en route to or from the East Indies, this meagre group of settlers soon ran short of labour to grow such crops as were needed to support themselves and to re-victual passing ships. Van Riebeeck tried to meet the demands for labour by importing slaves from Java, Madagascar and Angola. Between the departure in 1662 of van Riebeeck and the arrival of Simon van der Stel seventeen years later, the colony was very small. There had been 46 free adults and 14 children in 1660; in 1672 there were 64 freemen, who with the garrison gave a total of 370 all told. By this time, due to mixed marriages of Europeans with Hottentots, Indians and Asians, the Cape Coloured population had begun to emerge.

The last two decades of the seventeenth century and the first two of the eighteenth are the most important in the early history of South Africa. The Dutch East India Company made a deliberate effort to transform its refreshment station at the Cape into a genuine colony. This period of assisted emigration saw the arrival of the majority of the ancestors of the Afrikaans-speaking inhabitants of South Africa. The Company sent out Dutch and German settlers, but not enough to expand it as quickly as they would have liked. Furthermore, there was difficulty in finding enough volunteers of the right kind. The solution was found among the French-speaking Walloons of the United Provinces, who had fled there from the Spanish terror at the close of the previous century. These refugees were now being joined by Huguenots, some of whom left France for Brandenburg, others for England and America, yet others for the Free Netherlands, especially after the Revocation of the Edict of Nantes in 1685. In the Netherlands these numbers became something of an embarrassment, and the chance was taken to send out skilled artisans to the young South African colony. Huguenots and some Piedmontese who were prepared to take the Oath of Allegiance were given a free passage to the Cape, to be repaid in kind as opportunity offered. They had to undertake to stay there for five years at least. The Piedmontese refused to sail in the end, but the French began to arrive in 1688, and they were treated as if they had been freeborn Dutchmen. They were never very numerous – no more than 200 souls all told – but their influence was out of all proportion to their numbers. They were nearly all young and married.

By 1740 there were at the Cape about 4,000 free burghers – men, women and children – and 1,500 Company servants and soldiers with their families. In 1778 there were 9,867 burghers, 1,122 servants and 454 soldiers. The church registers show that 1,526 men and 449 women arrived between 1652 and 1795, and left descendants as follows:

	Dutch	French	Germans	Various
Men	494	74	806	152
Women	322	72	48	7

The preponderance of Dutch women, the youthful vigour of the French and the comparative age and exhaustion of many of the Germans has been remarked by G. M. Theal. H. T. Colenbrander in his *Afkomst der Boeren* reckons a higher proportion of German blood in the Afrikaner people than Theal does, but he counts as German all those who came from German Swiss Cantons and part of Germany along the Dutch border, whereas Theal notes that many of these Germans were descended from sixteenth-century Dutch refugees and counts as Dutch all who were members of the Dutch Reformed Church.

The first British occupation of the Cape lasted from 1795 to 1803. At that time, there were some 16,000 Europeans, 17,000 slaves and an unknown number of Hottentots and Bushmen. This period was followed by the brief rule of the Batavian Republic (1603–06) before the second British occupation which lasted from 1806 to 1823. During this period the flow of missionaries began, at first confined to the Moravian Brethren and the London Missionary Society, later swelled by German, Dutch, Danish and French missionaries and followed in 1820 by groups of Irish, English and Scottish settlers.

In common with the United States, Canada, Australia and New Zealand, South Africa took its share of immigrants during the late nineteenth century and early twentieth, the reasons being the same as those which prompted migration to these other countries.

The Union of South Africa was formed in 1910 by the union of the Colonies of the Cape of Good Hope, Transvaal, Natal and the Orange Free State. It became a Republic outside the British Commonwealth in 1961. Genealogical research in South Africa is comparatively easy due to the small population of the country before 1820, when there were only 43,000 European settlers, 9,000 of whom lived in or near Cape Town. The three northern provinces were not opened up until the Great Trek of 1838.

General registration

The first uniform law for the registration of births, marriages and deaths for the whole of South Africa was the Births, Marriages and Deaths Registration Act no. 17 of 1923. Before 1921 each republic/colony/province had its own legislation regarding the registration of births, marriages and deaths. Although South West Africa is governed by its own laws, provision was made for any amendments or regulations relating to the South African Births, Marriages and Deaths Registration Act, also to be brought into force in the territory (Proclamation no. 38 of 1923).

In Cape Colony the registration of births and deaths was made compulsory by the Act no. 7 of 1894. Provision, however, was made during 1880 for the voluntary registration of births. Matrimonial courts were established as early as 1804. The registration of marriages was governed by the Marriage Order in Council of 1838 as amended by Act no. 16 of

1860. The Board of Orphan Masters requested Church authorities in 1711 to submit the names of persons whose funerals they conducted. The earliest remaining registers date back to 1758. The office of the Master of the Supreme Court came into being during 1834.

The registration of births, marriages and deaths was first controlled by the Natal colonial government in terms of Ordinance no. 17 of 1846. Law no. 16 of 1867 of the Natal parliament made provision for the registration of births and deaths. The registration of marriages in Natal was governed by the Marriage Order in Council of 1838 as applied to Natal by Ordinance no. 17 of 1846.

In the Orange Free State the registration of births was made compulsory by Proclamation no. 15 of 1902. The first enactment in the O.F.S. for the voluntary registration of births was contained in Ordinance no. 1 of 1879. Ordinance no. 1 of 1859 laid down that the church or magistrate who performed a marriage had to send a copy of the certificate to the government. Ordinance no. 4 of 1871 made it incumbent on the nearest relative to forward a signed death notice to the Master's Office together with the will, if available.

The earliest registration of births and deaths in the Transvaal was governed by Proclamation no. 27 of 1900 and by Ordinance no. 19 of 1906. The registration of marriages of Europeans was laid down by Law no. 3 of 1871, whereas the registration of non-European marriages was made compulsory by Law no. 3 of 1897.

The civil registration of births, marriages and deaths commenced in South West Africa during January 1893. Proclamation no. 38 of 1923 which provided the territory with an identical Births, Marriages and Deaths Act to that of South Africa, repealed the Protectorate Act of 10 September 1900 and the Ordinance of the Imperial German Chancellor of the 27 March 1908 relating to the registration of births, marriages and deaths.

There is no inventory to show the exact whereabouts in the Republic of genealogical documents. Researchers of the Human Sciences Research Council's Institute for Historical Research, Private Bag X41, Pretoria 0001, are at present engaged, however, in investigating the possibility of compiling such an inventory.

All the indexes on the birth, marriage and death registers in South Africa and South West Africa, from the earliest dates, are in the keeping of the Registrar of Births, Marriages and Deaths, Department of the Interior, Private Bag X114, Pretoria 0001. The Transvaal and Central Archives Depots have the following registers in their custody:
Birth registers Cape Colony 1842–96 (Europeans and Blacks)
       Natal Colony 1904–8 (Blacks)
Marriage registers Cape Colony 1820–99

Natal 1868–99

Transvaal 1861–99

Orange Free State 1872–99

The following death registers are in the keeping of the Intermediate Archives Depot: Cape Colony (1895–1954), Transvaal (1888–1954), Natal (1863–1954), Orange Free State (1916–54), South West Africa (1893–1954), and South Africa (1955–63).

The other existing birth, marriage and death registers are, however, in the custody of the Registrar of Births, Marriages and Deaths.

Articles on the most important genealogical sources in the holdings of the government archives depots at Cape Town, Pietermaritzburg, Bloemfontein, Pretoria and Windhoek appear in the Genealogical Society's bilingual quarterly journal *Familia*. This society, which was established on 18 June 1964, has rendered valuable assistance in respect of the opening up of genealogical sources. The society also undertakes particular research tasks on behalf of the general public at a fixed fee.

The addresses of the various government archives depots and the Genealogical Society are given below.

Cape Province

Church records of births, deaths and marriages together with wills provide the main source of data. Before 1838 marriages were recorded in Church registers after which they are to be found either in Church registers or in the office of the registrar of marriages. An Ordinance of 1838 compelled marriage officers to send up to the registrar a duplicate of the register entry. In 1676 the Dutch established a matrimonial court which examined all those contemplating matrimony. They were required to give their names, place of birth, religion, occupation and marital status. These details were registered and if the court was satisfied there was no legal impediment, a certificate was issued so that the banns could be published on three consecutive Sundays. Regrettably the records of this court only exist for the years 1793–1827, when the court was abolished.

Baptisms are recorded in church registers, but it was not until 1895 that the registration of births was made compulsory throughout Cape Colony. There was a form of registration by an Ordinance of 1825 which placed this under the responsibility of the superintendent of police in Cape Town. In 1828 a law compelled the heads of families to report births and deaths to this official. Before this time deaths were registered with the board of orphan masters established by the Dutch in 1673. The board's chief duties were the administration of the estates of people dying intestate, or who had not specifically excluded the orphan masters in their wills from the administration of their estates, or had specially appointed them as executors; the administration of the property of minors or of unknown heirs; the registration of wills and the keeping of a death register. It was the duty of the church to report the burial of all deceased persons to the board, but this was frequently omitted. The first death register of the records of the board of orphan masters begins in 1758 and subsequent registers continue to 1833 when the board was abolished. Its functions were then taken over by the master of the supreme court, who ordered that all deaths had to be reported in prescribed form and lodged at the master's office in Cape Town. Among the requirements were the names of the deceased's parents, marital status, date and place of death, names of children (if any) and whether there was any property in the estate. It was not until 1895 that death registration with the registrar of deaths became compulsory. This was in addition to filing a death notice with the master.

During the seventeenth and eighteenth centuries the Nederduitsch Gereformeerde Kerk (Dutch Reformed Church) was the only officially recognized Church denomination in South Africa and practically all the whites in the Cape belonged to it. The earliest baptismal, marriage and death registers in the keeping of the Dutch Reformed Church Archives (Queen Victoria Street, Cape Town 8001) date from *c*. 1665. Photocopies of the original registers are in the keeping of the Transvaal Archives Depot.

In 1778 freedom of public religious worship was granted to the Lutherans at the Cape. The original baptismal and marriage registers (1780–1864) of the Evangelical Lutheran Church are kept in the vault of the church building in Cape Town. Microfilms of the registers are in custody of the Human Sciences Research Council's section for genealogy. In South West Africa the early registers of the different congregations are housed with the office of the Evangelical Lutheran Church, Windhoek 9100.

Wills were registered with the orphan chamber from 1689 and so continued until its abolition in 1833, after which time they were registered with the master of the supreme court. Indexes of these wills exist, as well as details of inventories and liquidation accounts.

In South Africa the custody of estates is grouped on a provincial basis. Estates in the Cape Archives Depot cover the period 1686–1916, whereas the remainder are in the charge of the master of the supreme court. Natal estates up to the mid-1850s are housed in the Natal Archives Depot. Estates thereafter are to be found at the office of the master of the supreme court. Free State estates from 1852 onwards are kept by the master of the supreme court. Insolvent estates, however, for the period 1854–1917 are housed in the Free State Archives Depot. Transvaal estates 1873–*c*. 1940 are in the keeping of the Transvaal Archives and Intermediate Depots, but the remainder are to be found at the office of the master of the supreme court. In South West Africa the wills from 1893–1915 are located in the Archives Depot of the Territory, and from 1915 onwards are kept by the master of the supreme court.

Land records

When crown land was granted, a title deed was given to the grantee and a duplicate filed at the deeds office. Deeds of transfer were similarly filed. Registration and transfer of land began in 1685 and the office records are complete to date. Marriage contracts and donations *inter vivos* over the value of £500 are also registered there. South African land registration is considered to be among the best in the world.

Legal records

The records of the superior and inferior courts contain much valuable information not unlike that contained in the proceedings of the English courts described elsewhere. The higher court from 1652 to 1827 was known as the Court of Justice, at which date it was superseded by the Supreme Court. The secretary of the Court of Justice, now known as the registrar, acts in the role of notary public.

Cape archives and other genealogical sources

1 Cape archives

Orphan Chamber 1673–1833
1 Death registers 1758–1833
2 Wills 1689–1833
3 Inventories 1673–1834
4 Liquidation accounts 1709–1835
Court of Justice
1 Civil and criminal cases 1652–1827
2 Documents passed before the secretary 1652–1827
3 Original wills passed before the secretary
Colonial Office
1 Memorials from 1806
2 Permissions to remain in the colony 1806–40

2 Masters of the Supreme Court

1 Death Notices from 1834
2 Wills from 1834
3 Inventories and liquidation accounts from 1834

3 Deeds Office

1 All title deeds and deeds of transfer relating to landed property from the seventeenth century.
2 Marriage contracts and donations *inter vivos*.

4 Churches

1 Marriages
2 Baptisms

5 Registrar of Births, Marriages and Deaths

1 Marriages from 1838 (Transvaal 1869, OFS 1872, Natal 1880)
2 Births and deaths from 1891 (Transvaal 1901, OFS 1902, Natal 1868)
Note: The Office of the Registrar is c/o Population Register Building, Scholman and van der Walt Streets, Pretoria; the relevant documents for the Cape were transferred at the time of the Union in 1910.

6 The South African Public Library, Cape Town

1 Newspaper files from 1800.

Natal

Parish Registers

The Natal Archives has no parish registers, and believes that these are to be found with the ministers of individual parishes.

Probate Records

Deceased estate files up to and including 1943 are deposited in the Natal Archives Depot, after which they are kept in the office of the Master of the Supreme Court, Pietermaritzburg.

Legal Records

The Supreme Court Records for Natal up to and including the year 1945 are housed in the Natal Archives Depot.

Censuses

There are no individual returns from the state of Natal, only statistical material of no interest to genealogists.

General Registration

Particulars of general registration are held by the Department of the Interior in Pretoria.

Immigration Records

Assisted immigration records for the period 1845–1910 only are to be found in the Natal Archives Depot.

The Human Sciences Research Council's Institute for Historical Research established a section for Genealogy in 1971 at the request of the Suid-Afrikaanse Akademie vir Wetenskap en Kuns (South African Academy for Arts and Science), and with the approval of the Minister of National Education. The genealogy section not only provides the public with valuable information as to where genealogical sources are to be found, but is also at present compiling a manual which would indicate how genealogical research should be undertaken in South Africa.

A list of the publications which are most often consulted by genealogical researchers in South Africa is given below.

Archives depots and other addresses

Archives Depot of the Territory, Private Bag 13250, Windhoek 9100.
Cape Archives Depot, Private Bag X9025, Cape Town 8000.
Central Archives Depot, Private Bag X236, Pretoria 0001.
Free State Archives Depot, Private Bag X20504, Bloemfontein 9300.
Intermediate Archives Depot, Private Bag X236, Pretoria 0001.
Natal Archives Depot, Private Bag X9012, Pietermaritzburg.
Transvaal Archives Depot, Private Bag X236, Pretoria 0001.
The Genealogical Society, 15 Queens Road, Tamboerskloof, Cape
  Town 8001.
The Master of the Supreme Court, Private Bag X0584, Bloemfontein.
The Master of the Supreme Court, Private Bag X9018, Cape Town
  8001.
The Master of the Supreme Court, Private Bag 1010, Grahamstown
  6140.

The Master of the Supreme Court, Private Bag X5015, Kimberley 8300.
The Master of the Supreme Court, Private Bag 9010, Pietermaritzburg
 3200.
The Master of the Supreme Court, Private Bag X60, Pretoria 0001.
The Master of the Supreme Court, Private Bag 13190, Windhoek 9100.
The President, Human Sciences Research Council, Private Bag X41,
 Pretoria 0001.
Censuses, Orphan Records and General Registration: Department of
 the Interior, Private Bag X114, Pretoria 0001.
Department of Immigration, P.O. Box 2072, Pretoria 0001.

Appendix 1

Heraldry and genealogical research

The roles of the family historian and of the detective have much in common; both must be able to spot and make use of every available clue. In essence much of heraldry is really no more than pictorial genealogy, vitally concerned with identification and inheritance, yet there is probably more nonsense and misunderstanding associated with heraldry than with most subjects. Heraldry can be an extremely valuable aid to the researcher, whose role it is firstly to identify an individual or his immediate connections and then to weave him or her into the appropriate place in the tapestry of the family. For family history is a tapestry and not only should it be colourful in itself, but it is also the product of the interaction of many different coloured strands.

This is not the place to dwell in any detail on the origins of heraldry other than to say that they can be traced back for eight centuries or more and that they were all bound up in the need for personal identification, both on the medieval battlefield and by means of seals which were all-important in that illiterate age. Inevitably, the emblems adopted for shield and seal, if not the shield and seal themselves, were handed down from father to son over the generations and thus became an integral part of each family's history, and all the more so when associated with heroism or success. But heraldry would be absolutely meaningless without the inheritance factor. Later on in the 'Age of Chivalry' jousting became fashionable and such tournaments provided a perfect setting for heraldic display in all its splendour.

For personal use, the olden-day seal or mark was the equivalent of an individual's signature today; nevertheless, while seals are seldom used personally nowadays, they are still much in evidence in companies and other corporate bodies. The signet ring bearing arms or crest is a relic of the ancient seal and is still used by individuals.

On the battlefield, heraldry was as vital and relevant to medieval warfare as aircraft markings were in the Second World War or other electronic identification aids will be in the next World War. For without some outward means of identification, a knight in armour, like an aeroplane or a warship today, was no more than a faceless grey mass.

Indeed, the colour and pageantry of heraldry helps to prevent our lives from becoming equally grey and drab. For whether or not we appreciate it, an abundance of heraldry is evident all round us in most European countries as well as in the British Commonwealth and many remaining colonies. It exists in our towns and villages; on corporations, institutes, associations, banks and companies; on all kinds of public and commercial vehicles; on and in buildings, schools, universities, colleges, offices, houses and churches; on tombstones, hatchments and memorials; on letterheads, newspapers, cheques, old school ties and on the shirts and badges of football teams and clubs; on flags, road signs and inn signs; on furniture, panelling, portraits, bookplates and on signet rings; on wine labels and food packaging as well as on much of the coinage of the realm; it also appears on medals and insignia, on jewellery, clan regalia, company seals, on regimental badges and buttons and ships' badges, and it even has been carved out of chalk on the hillside at Fovant in Wiltshire. It comes painted, sculptured, printed, drawn or carved on wood, metal, stone, leather, silver, plasterwork, mosaics and in stained glass windows.

So heraldry is very much alive. Without it, we would have, no doubt, to resort to trendy logos and cyphers. These would become dated and outmoded in no time, while sacrificing in part the aura of continuity and respectability that heraldry somehow imparts. But despite the 'glitter' of heraldry, it provides a fitting reminder of our past, linking it securely with the present – and that surely is what civilization is all about. Of course, like anything historical, it alludes to our forefathers – but it is they who, in general terms, are the target of our researches. There is, therefore, much information readily available, if only the researcher has the eyes to see it.

The early heralds attempted, on behalf of their sovereigns, to introduce some order into the process of assuming, granting and registering arms and settling the squabbles that arose therefrom. Their position and authority was strengthened by the introduction of laws or customs, and in some countries heraldry is actually upheld by force of law. In many countries, such as Scotland and Spain, heraldry is governed by statute law, whereas in other countries, such as England, it is international law (based more on the precepts of armorial Roman law and the old civilian's law than common law) that prevails. Prior to 1592 Scotland had a Common Law jurisdiction in armorial matters. The legal position of a confirmation or grant of arms must first have been granted or have been recognized by, or on behalf of, an appropriate sovereign, and its transmission or destination (usually in the paternal line) follows that set out in the original patent or confirmation, just like most hereditary peerages. In Scotland, only the eldest son inherits his father's arms, but all younger sons have the right to matriculate a differenced version of their paternal arms. Elsewhere than in Great Britain non-noble arms have often been assumed without any authority and thus have no legal protection.

Most people associate heraldry exclusively with the nobility, and in European countries this is largely true, despite the considerable number of non-noble arms. However, in practice its ramifications are much wider, for not only have many noble families fallen on hard times (especially resulting from the law of primogeniture and from crippling taxation) and therefore may have sunk in the social scale, but many a *nouveau riche* has wanted to cement the dynasty he has founded by acquiring for himself and his descendants a suitable coat of arms and the certificate of nobility which often accompanies it. Yet, in only a few generations, the ink will have faded and the parchment yellowed and his descendants will walk on an equal footing with the oldest families in the land, secure in the knowledge and pride of their forefathers' achievements.

Thus, over the centuries, society in general has become sufficiently flexible to allow such social fluidity both upwards and downwards, thereby at least ensuring that heraldry is widely disseminated. This is particularly true in Scotland where the concept of the clan is strong. There have, of course, been certain notable exceptions, where some countries have paid the price of revolution for adopting too rigid a nobiliary structure, yet ironically it was France which was one of the few countries whose burgesses and peasants were not only allowed, but actively encouraged, to bear 'roturier' arms (i.e. without helm or crest), if only to swell its exchequer by the tax levies on armorial bearings.

Moreover, it is clear that today heraldry has never had a greater or wider appeal. For instance, in the Lyon Office in Edinburgh, 64 volumes of the Public Register of Arms span 308 years since 1672 (an average of over 1 volume per 5 years), yet half of these volumes cover only the 40 years 1939–80 (an average of nearly 1 volume per year). The same general trend has also been experienced by the College of Arms. Perhaps this reflects the increasingly impersonal and statistical world in which we live, where more and more often the individual is reduced to no more than a computer digit. No wonder he may wish to assert his individuality pictorially by canting (punning) arms, family arms, or some other appropriate arms surmounted by a helmet and/or a coronet, or a clerical hat befitting his degree.

It is only to be expected that heraldic practice, like everything else,

has differed to some extent from one country to another. Nevertheless, it is true to say that heraldry falls into five broad categories:
(a) Familial
(b) Individual
(c) Territorial
(d) Augmentations and additaments
(e) Corporate
I shall therefore deal with each category in turn, relating it principally to heraldry as practised in the British Isles.

Familial heraldry

It is really familial heraldry that is practised throughout Europe in one form or another, although Scotland and to a lesser extent Spain are notable exceptions. Familial heraldry, for our present purposes, pertains to a family (as distinct from an individual) whereby all male descendants of the original grantee bear the same family arms undifferenced save perhaps for a temporary mark of cadency (i.e. a difference to show a son's position in his family). But such a system is really only practical where there is a multiplicity of different surnames. Unfortunately, straightforward though the system may be, its rules seem to be honoured much more in the breach than in the observance, largely, I suspect, from the mistaken idea that there is a coat of arms for every surname, and that the arms are there for the taking. Furthermore, in England the laws governing the bearing of arms and indeed the Earl Marshal's Court (The Court of Chivalry) that attempts to enforce them, have few teeth and many gaps, which makes it difficult for the College of Arms to ensure that the law bites in practice.

The College of Arms is responsible for all aspects of English and Welsh heraldry and for much of Irish and Commonwealth heraldry too. It is an independent and semi-private body of kings of arms, heralds and pursuivants, responsible to the sovereign via the Earl Marshal. Garter Principal King of Arms is in overall charge; Clarenceux is responsible for all of England south of the River Trent and for Wales, and Norroy and Ulster is responsible for England north of the Trent and for Ireland. The College is in a privileged position in that its officers have exclusive access to the old medieval rolls of arms, many priceless manuscripts and details of all grants and confirmations of arms and the registration of pedigrees which date from its foundation in 1484 and are housed at the College in the City of London. All approaches to the College must be made via one of its officers of arms.

The College and its officers still grant and confirm arms and bring pedigrees up to date, but unfortunately its high fees act as a severe deterrent. Nevertheless, even though the publications of many English arms have appeared in *Papworth's Armorial, Fairbairn's Book of Crests,* or in *Burke's General Armoury,* etc., researchers would be wise not to attach too much importance to familial heraldry unless they take some positive steps to prove or disprove any particular case. There has been, and still is, much unlawful use of personal arms, both in Britain and America, which can be most misleading to the genealogist. Moreover, the position is aggravated by many heraldic bureaux which have sprung up in recent years and now offer to sell heraldic plaques or paintings of the arms appropriate to any surname, even though they may disclaim any proper connection between the two. Not only is this confusing for the researcher but it also flouts the spirit of the law, which was designed to protect the arms of those rightly entitled to them. In most cases it will usually be best and necessary to approach the appropriate authority for confirmation of the arms; if the right to arms can be properly established, then often so should much of the genealogy.

The English practice of marshalling arms helps to make familial heraldry rather more meaningful to the researcher. For the arms of an heraldic heiress (which has nothing to do with her fortune but alludes solely to the fact that, having no brothers, she is heiress to her father's arms) can be borne as quarterings by her descendants. Thus, if an heraldic heiress marries an armiger, their children will bear a quartered shield with the paternal arms in the first and fourth quarters and the maternal arms in the second and third quarters. The result of all this is that in any family there is likely to be a number of different *cumulatio armorum* for different branches, and this can help the researcher to narrow down the field. Quarterings, therefore, assume a greater importance than in Scotland, but they can make English heraldry rather cluttered and unwieldy. Taken to an extreme the arms of Lloyd include 228 quarterings!

In much the same way, if a wife's (paternal) arms are impaled or displayed *accollée* with those of her husband, this too will aid identification, as will any augmentation of arms, or the impalement of certain official arms or any insignia denoting decorations or membership of an order of chivalry. This aspect is discussed further under Augmentation and Additaments. (An impaled shield is when it is split vertically with the husband's arms on the left and the wife's on the right. *Accollée* is where the arms of both spouses are on separate shields side by side.)

Certain temporary differences are sometimes employed to show a person's position in the family, but more often than not, these can be more of a hindrance than a help, for few people seem to know when, where, and in what circumstances, to assume or discard them.

The Chief Herald of Ireland in Dublin administers Irish heraldry in very much the same way as the College, although over the years most old Irish records have been destroyed.

On the continent, there is very little control or sanction over the use of heraldry. The position in France has already been discussed in Chapter 2. Spain, Ireland, Scotland and England are the only countries to have a proper and positive heraldic administration, although there are certain national heraldic and nobiliary associations (whose names and addresses are given on p. 220 et seq.) and these help to bridge the gap and provide information for the researcher. Germany tends to use different crests to identify one branch of a family from another, rather than differencing by quarterings; she also makes use of territorial quarterings, of which more later. Nowadays subject to a few specific embargoes, there is little or nothing to stop citizens of most European countries (except England, Holland, Scotland and Spain) from assuming or discarding whatever arms they choose. However, without the discipline imposed by law or custom and the hereditary factor, this sort of heraldry seems meaningless and of no use whatsoever to the researcher. But this is not to say that in the past there may not have been a proper heraldic administration, the records and vestiges of which may have been taken over by the various associations to which I have already referred.

It is perhaps surprising that in most European countries, noble heraldry, which in general set such store by the *seize quartiers* – proof of sixteen great-great-grandparental quarterings – should now be so disorganized and confused, but perhaps this is the price for having become too rarefied.

Individual heraldry

As the name implies, individual heraldry as practised in Scotland and Spain means that an individual is assigned a unique coat of arms. These allude to factors such as his position within his family, ownership of any fiefs, baronies or other titles, or, as happens particularly in Spain and Portugal, his four grandparental quarterings can be marshalled together. By its very nature, individual heraldry is therefore of most aid to the researcher.

Nowhere is the system of individual heraldry better demonstrated than in Scotland, a country notorious for its heraldic and genealogical awareness as evidence by the clan system. The high proportion of its nobility to the total population in 1707, the relatively small population and the comparatively few surnames (which would make the familial system of heraldry quite unworkable), its feudal system of land tenure, coupled with the precision of the Scottish temperament has encouraged everybody not only to know of each other, but also to know their relative place vis-à-vis their chief or laird. Perhaps this feeling was further encouraged by the massive emigration that took so many Scots away from their native land, aggravated no doubt by the law of primogeniture. But the family bonds that now span the oceans would seem to be every bit as strong as they used to be, as vividly illustrated by the number of foreign clansmen at the International Gathering of the Clans in Scotland in 1977, and the many clan societies which flourish overseas.

In sharp contrast to English and most continental practices, statute law (and in particular the 1592 and 1672 Acts) governs heraldry in Scotland, and the Lord Lyon King of Arms as the Judge of the Lyon Court, sits in judgment. However, he is armed with sufficient powers of imprisonment, fining, erasure and horning to command rather greater respect and obedience than in other countries. Besides his role as a judge, Lord Lyon is also a minister of the crown and responsible direct to the Sovereign for all Scottish heraldic and genealogical matters as well as for all matters relating to clans, their chiefs, tartans, badges and designations, etc. The records of his court, and particularly those dating from 1672, which contain the Public Register of all Arms and Bearings of Scotland (64 volumes) and the Public Register of All Genealogies and Birthbrieves (4 volumes) form part of the Public Records of Scotland and can be inspected by the public on payment of a nominal fee. Indeed, all the Lyon Office fees, including those for grants and matriculations, go to swell the national coffers; moreover, the fees amount only to about one-quarter of those charged by the College of Arms.

The upshot of all this is that individual heraldry thrives in Scotland. Only the grantee or his representer (often, but by no means always, his heir male) is entitled to undifferenced or basic arms. All younger brothers and their descendants have only the right to petition the Lord Lyon for a differenced version of their basic arms which are then matriculated (costing about £140), and this then forms the basis for the arms of that line. This system enables cadets to update their pedigrees and thus becomes invaluable for the researcher. The main differences employed to distinguish arms are as follows:

(a) the bordure – of different metals and tinctures or combinations of them, with a variety of different edges – invected, engrailed, embattled, etc.

(b) alteration of the tinctures or of the number of charges borne;

(c) substitution of one of the charges for another, perhaps for one in the petitioner's maternal coat, or perhaps in allusion to his occupation or achievements;

(d) the addition of a quartering either of an heiress, or territorial, or as an augmentation, or even occasionally as a quartering of 'affection' (which almost invariably involves a blood descent as well as the acquisition of an old family fief);

(e) the inclusion of a canton.

Great emphasis in Scotland is placed on the bearing of the undifferenced arms, as a representer of the grantee, rather than acquiring a multiplicity of quarterings as in England.

What more can the researcher ask? He can establish with certainty whether or not a person is armiger; if so, he can ascertain his pedigree and position in the family. The Scottish system encourages families to rematriculate and bring their pedigrees up to date; even the early matriculations, now 300 years old, though scanty in genealogical detail, usually give some pointer to guide the researcher. With the recent publication by the Lyon Office of *An Ordinary of Arms 1902–73*, and Balfour Paul's *Ordinary of Arms 1672–1902*, all Scottish Arms from 1672 can now be easily identified.

On the other hand, it is unfortunate that most of the supporting papers have been lost or destroyed over the centuries, which means that, while the Lord Lyon's judgment may be recorded, there is often no record of his *obiter dicta* let alone the pleadings or evidence, and over the years there have indeed been a number of surprising and controversial decisions which one now can only accept, however strange they may seem. Some such judgments have been overruled in later years, but understandably Lords Lyon are reluctant to reverse the decision of a predecessor without exceptional reason. As an aside, the fact that, within the United Kingdom there are two different systems of heraldry operating under the aegis of the same Sovereign can make life confusing. It can also lead to squabbles over jurisdiction between the College of Arms and the Lyon Office, aggravated, no doubt, by the different systems and levels of remuneration.

The College claims armorial jurisdiction over all those of English, or Welsh, Irish and Commonwealth domicile or descent, whereas the Lord Lyon claims jurisdiction over all those of Scottish domicile and of Scottish descent, irrespective of their domicile or residence. The trouble can arise because of the large number of Scottish emigrants domiciled in countries which were part of the British Empire. Sometimes it has led to one man having to have two coats of arms, one for England and one for Scotland, as has happened to Sir Hugh Wontner, a former Lord Mayor of the City of London. But this does seem unnecessarily complicated within one small island. It also blurs the demarcation lines for the researcher.

The position has been exacerbated by the recent appointment of a New Zealand Herald Extraordinary who appears to come within the aegis of the College of Arms and through which he will no doubt channel his business, regardless of the petitioner's paternal descent. It is to be hoped that with the recent changes of leadership at the College of Arms, a concerted effort to diffuse the armoury will be made.

As can be seen, these squabbles over jurisdiction do confuse the issue for citizens of Commonwealth countries, in particular Australia, Canada and New Zealand. If and when these problems of jurisdiction between the College of Arms and the Lyon Office can be settled once for all, it is to be hoped that each will refer to the other cases that rightly belong to them. There is ample business for both, prompted perhaps by such successful television series as *Roots*.

Spain is now the only other major country to have an active heraldic administration. It is still much concerned with the rather exclusive and much intermarried Spanish nobility and aspirants to the old military orders of chivalry. The office of the Cronista Rey de Armas brings pedigrees up to date and confirms arms, often in the form of the 'four quarterings' (the minimum proof of hidalgo or Spanish nobility), which virtually ensures statistically that the *cumulatio armorum* is unique to all but those of the full blood. But of course in the next generation the arms of those brothers' children would be differenced by the inclusion of their respective mothers' quarterings. Needless to say, this form of individual heraldry can be a godsend for the researcher providing that he is able to identify the various coats of arms. The Cronista Rey de Armas in Madrid also claims jurisdiction over all the former Spanish Empire which, it is claimed, included no less than ten states of the United States of America. I understand that many grants of arms are now made to citizens of those states or countries on the grounds of births or domicile, irrespective of ethnic race. For the researcher, it can be confusing if a Californian of Irish descent is granted arms by the Spanish armorial authorities!

The question of recognition of such Spanish grants of arms by the College of Arms and the Court of the Lord Lyon is now under active consideration, although the Chief Herald of Ireland has long recognized them. Nevertheless, it must be said that as the United States has no armorial jurisdiction of its own, if it were not for such Spanish grants of arms, only those Americans of English, Scottish, Irish or Spanish descent could properly and legally bear arms today. These Spanish grants do therefore fulfil a need for other American citizens of other descents in that it permits them to bear non-noble arms legally and properly. Moreover, these grants of arms are in many ways very similar to the honorary grants of arms made by the College of Arms to those Americans of English ancestry or the posthumous grants of arms that have been granted by the Lords Lyon to the Scottish ancestors of the petitioner. In all these cases proper control is being exercised by the appropriate authorities and the grantee is assured of his right to those arms. The position is only likely to change in the unlikely event of the Government of the United States establishing an armorial jurisdiction of its own.

Territorial heraldry

This affects both familial and individual heraldry in countries such as Germany, France and Scotland. In such cases, historically, a particular coat of arms became associated with, if not inseparable from, a barony or fief, thereby entitling its owner (whether by inheritance or purchase) to marshal the territorial arms with his own family arms. However, confusion can arise (as with Scottish designations or continental titles which operate in much the same way) when, after three or so generations, the territorial quartering vests with the family irrespective of ownership of the barony or fief, and so forms part of their achievement. But this does not prevent any later owner from petitioning to bear the quartering alluding to his newly acquired barony in exactly the same way.

It is perhaps worth mentioning that many a royal coat of arms includes the arms of the lands governed, sometimes marshalled with sovereign's family coat. Indeed, the British royal coat of arms consists of the coats of arms of England, Scotland and Ireland – the three kingdoms over which the Queen rules. (Wales is, of course, only a Principality.)

Augmentations and additaments

In effect, augmentations and additaments personalize family arms for the recipient, whether the origin of his arms is familial or individual. An augmentation is when the sovereign grants a special heraldic additament in the form of a special charge or quartering or inescutcheon (a mini-shield placed in the centre of the family arms) as a tribute for some service rendered. In this way the recipient is in exactly the same position as a grantee and the augmentation will pass to his descendants in the normal way. Examples of this include the first Duke of Marlborough (with his inescutcheon of the arms of France superimposed on St George's Cross), the Duke of Wellington (with his inescutcheon of the Union Jack), and Admiral Lord Nelson (with a special chief including the sea, a disabled ship, a ruined shore battery and a palm tree), to name but three.

In exactly the same way baronet's badges (a canton containing the Red Hand of Ulster), or the award of decorations, but not campaign medals, and/or membership of the orders of chivalry usually enable the recipient to display these upon, around or below his shield as appropriate. In some orders of chivalry, the cross of the order can be borne as a chief, or even as a quartering. The same principle holds true for the holders of certain offices (e.g. Kings of Arms, archbishops or bishops) who are permitted to impale their personal arms with the arms of their seal of office, for so long as they hold it.

Certain hereditary offices entitle the holder to place batons or other devices behind their shields, and the Lord Chief Justice, Sergeants at Arms, Kings of Arms and Heralds may encircle their shield with the silver-gilt collar of SS, with or without badges, as appropriate. In England and Scotland grants of supporters are limited to certain persons, thereby aiding identification.

Whilst all these additaments are for life or for the duration of their office, they help to personalize familial heraldry and aid identification of an individual. A well-known example of this in England is Sir Winston Churchill, who bore the arms of the Dukes of Marlborough (without supporters) distinguished only by the collar of the Order of the Garter. It was fortunate, therefore, that the then Duke of Marlborough was not also a Knight of the Garter. On the continent especially, the style and use of helmet and/or coronet and/or supporters is important for identification although no common system is in force throughout Europe.

Corporate heraldry

This includes all arms of countries, sovereign states, counties, towns, boroughs, companies, corporate bodies, associations, institutes, dioceses, monasteries and official offices, etc. Understandably, corporate heraldy is likely to be of less use to the genealogist than the other categories. But it should not be completely ignored because many a corporate shield will include charges from the arms of its founder or local magnate which could in turn provide a valuable lead for the local family historian.

One cannot hope in the space available to do justice to European heraldry, to say nothing of Oriental heraldry. One can only scratch at the surface. However, it will be apparent that heraldry is another system of communication, albeit a colourful and expressive one. If one can but understand the language, there is much information to be gleaned. The list that follows attempts to give some of the principal textbooks, reference books, armorials, associations and authorities for the many different countries, so as to enable the researcher, like the good detective, to leave no stone unturned.

Appendix 2
Chief sources
of information

	Text books	Armorials and other heraldic reference books and repositories	Nobiliary and heraldic authorities and associations
General	*Treatise on Heraldry – British and Foreign* (Woodward and Burnett) 1892 *International Heraldry* (L. G. Pine) 1970 *The Nature of Arms* (R. Gayre of Gayre and Nigg) 1961 *Heraldry of the World* (Von. Volborth – ed. Chesshyre) 1975.	*Armorial Général* (J. B. Reistrap) *Manuel de Blason* (G. L. Galbreath) *Dictionnaire des Figures Heraldiques* (T. de Renesse) 1895 *The Armorial Who's Who* (ed. Gayre of Gayre and Nigg) 1975 *Armorial Universel* (Koller and Schillings) 1951	
United Kingdom		*Burke's General Armoury* 1894 *General Armoury 2* (ed. C. R. Humphery-Smith) 1973 *Armorial Families* (A. C. Fox-Davies) 1929 *Ordinary of British Armorials* (Papworth) *Fairbairn's Crests of Families of Great Britain and Ireland* 1905	
England and Wales	*Boutell's Heraldry* (ed. J. P. Brooke-Little) *An Heraldic Alphabet* (J. P. Brooke-Little) 1972 *The Complete Guide to Heraldry* (A.C. Fox-Davies) 1920	(See United Kingdom)	The College of Arms, Queen Victoria Street, London EC4

Scotland	*Scots Heraldry* (Sir T. Innes of Learney) 1956 *System of Heraldry* (Alexander Nisbet) 1816 *Science of Herauldrie* (Sir G. Mackenzie of Rosehaugh) 1680 *Manual of Heraldry* (Sir F. J. Grant) 1924	*Scottish Arms* (R. R. Stoddart) 1878 *Heraldic M. S. S.* (Sir D. Lindsay of The Mount) 1878 *An Ordinary of Arms in the Lyon Register* (Sir J. Balfour-Paul) 1903 *An Ordinary of Arms 1902-1973* (The Lyon Office) 1977	Court of the Lord Lyon, H. M. New Register House, Edinburgh 1
Ireland	(See England and Wales)	(See United Kingdom)	The Chief Herald of Ireland, Genealogical Office, Dublin Castle, Dublin Ulster King of Arms, The College of Arms, Queen Victoria Street, London EC4
Austria		*Österreichische Wappenrolle*	Heraldisch-Genealogische, Gesellschaft, Adler, Vienna II, Haarhof 4A
Belgium	*Legislation Heraldique de la Belgique* 1595–1895 (Averdt and de Ridden) *Jurisprudence de Conseil Heraldique* 1844–95	*Armorial Général de la Noblesse Belge* (Ryckman de Betz) *Armorial Général de Belgique* (Koller and Relin)	Conseil Heraldique, Brussels, Belgium
Denmark		*Lexicon Over Adeliza Familier i Danmark Norge og Hertugdommerne* 1782–1813 *Danmarks Adels Aarbog*	Heraldic Counsellor of Danish State, Copenhagen, Denmark Societas Heraldica Sphragistica Danica, Copenhagen, Danmark

France	*Grand Armorial de France* (Soc. de Grand Armorial) *Armorial Générale France* (H. Jougla de Morenau) 1934 *Nobiliare Universel de France* (M. de St. Allain) *Histoire de la Noblesse de Provence* (J. A. Pithou Cunt) 1750 *Le Sang de Louis XIV* (Père Anselme)	L'Association d'Entraide de la Noblesse Française, 9 rue Richepance, 75008 Paris La Société du Grand Armorial de France, 179 Boulevard Haussmann, Paris Société d'Héraldique et Sigillographie, 113 rue de Courcelles, Paris 75017
Germany	*Deutsche Wappenrolle* *Kenfenheuer* *Genealogischen Handbuch*	Der Herold, Verein fur Heraldic Genealogie und Verwandte, Wissenschaften, 62 Wiesbaden, Dieselstrasse 24
Italy	**Enciclopedia Italiana 1929-37** – *Araldico* (C. Manaresi) *Dizionnario Storico Blazonico delle Famiglie Nobile* *Nobiliario e Blasonario del Regno d'Italia* (Mannucci) *Libro d'Oro de la Nobiltà Italiana Italiane Estinte et Fiorenti* (Crollalonza) 1886.	National Heraldic Council of the Italian Nobility, Rome The Heraldic Office of H.M. King Umberto II
Netherlands	*Nederlands Adelsboek*	Supreme Court of Nobility, 7lb Zeestraat, The Hague Konin Klijk, Nederlandsch Genootschap, Voor Geslacht en Wapenkunde, 5 Bleijenburg, The Hague Nederlandse Genealogische, Vereniaging, P.O. Box 976, Amsterdam Central Bureau Voor Genealogie, 18 Nassaulaan, The Hague

Norway	*Norscke Slektsvapen* (Cappelen and Heyerdahl)	University of Oslo Library, Universitets biblioteket i Oslo, Dramensveien, 42B, Oslo
	Lexicon Ober Adelize Families i Danmark Norge of Hertugdommenne 1782–1813	
Poland	*Armorial de la Noblesse Polonaise Librée* (S. Konarski)	Historic Records Archive, Archiwum, Gownyn, Akt Dawnych, Warsaw, Ul Dluga 7
Portugal	*Manual de Héraldica Portuguesa* (A. de Mattos) 1941	Director Arquiva Naccional da Torre do Tonbo, Lisbon
	Armaria Portuguesa (A. Braamcamp Freire) 1917	Conseillio de Nobreza, Praca Luis de Cammas, 46, 2 Lisbon
	Resenha das Familiar Titulam e Grandee do Portugal	Instituto Porgugueso de Heraldica Largo do Carmo, Lisbon
South Africa		The Registrar, State Heraldic Bureau, Pretoria, S. Africa
Spain	*Tratato de Heraldica y Blason* (J. Ascensio y Torro) 1929	Cronista Rey de Armas, Ministry of Justice, Madrid
	Encyclopadia Heraldica y Genealogica Hispano-Americana (Alberto and Arturo Garcia Oaraffa)	
	Armeria y Nobiliario de los Reinios Espanoles (Int. Institute)	
	Diccionario Nobiliario (Julia Atienza)	
Switzerland		State Archives of Solothurn, Switzerland
USA		The American College of Arms, Heralds Mews on Longdock, Harbourmaster Buildings, Baltimore, Maryland 21202 USA

Index

The Author

Noel Currer-Briggs has been a professional genealogist for twenty-five years, specialising in families emigrating from Britain to the colonies and the United States, with special reference to Virginia and New England before 1670. He is a consultant to Debrett Ancestry Research, a Fellow of the Genealogists' Society, and a founder member and former Chairman of the Association of Genealogists and Record Agents. He lectures and broadcasts on genealogy, and has written a number of books on the subject.